The Far East

U.S.S.R.

SAKH

Lake Baikal

MONGOLIA

Ulan Bator

Harbin

Urumchi

Mukden

Huang Ho

Peiping

KOREA

C H I N A

Yin-ch'uan

Seoul

Lan-chou

Tokyo

JAPAN

Nanking

Lhasa

Yangtze

Wu-han

Shanghai

Brahmaputra

NEPAL

BHU

Chungking

Mekong

K'un-ming

Taipei

PAK

TAIWAN

BURMA

Hanoi

Canton

Macao

HONG
KONG

LAOS

PACIFIC

Rangoon

Vientiane

THAILAND

Bangkok

VIETNAM

Manila

PHILIPPINES

CAMBODIA

Phnom
Penh

Saigon

OCEAN

CEYLON

MALAYSIA

BRUNEI

Kuala Lumpur

MALAYSIA

SUMATRA

Singapore

BORNEO

I N D I A N

CELEBES

TER
OF
PAP
AND
GUIN

Djakarta

I N D O N E S I A

O C E A N

JAVA

PORT
TIMOR

AUSTRALIA

The Responsibilities

of

World Power

by
U. S. Senator Gale W. McGee

THE NATIONAL PRESS INC.
128 C STREET, N.E.
WASHINGTON, D.C. 20002

Library of Congress Catalog Card No. 68-19118

Printed in the United States of America

TABLE OF CONTENTS

"Those who cannot remember the past are condemned to repeat it."

—George Santayana
The Life of Reason

The historian Carl Becker used to remind his students that "Facts do not speak for themselves. They have to be spoken for." One becomes especially mindful of that statement in the midst of the events accompanying our policy crises in Vietnam. Nor is the task of sorting out facts made any simpler in this computerized age of reason.

It would be safe to predict that the average layman has been saturated by more "facts" in regard to the war in Vietnam than have been assembled or even asserted in any other interval of modern history. Visually, orally, and in print, information and speculation have gushed out of Saigon and its satellite reportorial posts like a veritable tidal wave. As a result of it, the man-in-the-street is supposed to be better informed about the events of our time. In fact, he has been nearly drowned by their sheer mass and emotion. At the very least, the people in our own country have become so immersed in the minutia of daily events that it has become no longer possible to view the conflict in the perspective of the times.

To return to historian Becker, if facts have to be "spoken for," who speaks for them, which facts are more relevant than others, and how they are related one to the other determine the kind of assessment contemporaries make. In the interest of dignity, the composite result might be called judgment.

That the judgments of men could be so diverse and become so extreme perhaps reflect the emotions generated by proximity to the events as well as the harshness of living in a world without law. For the idealists, the extremes of dissenters reflect the eternal clash between the dreams of what should be with the reality of what is;

the hopes of where we someday may be and the pragmatism of the here and now.

From the interminable dialogues on Vietnam have emerged elements of constructive gain such as the greater awareness of the general public about the facts of international life. But with it also has come a fallout with serious implications.

One is the journalistic obsession of stereotyping positions with such names as doves and hawks. As a result, the efforts in the ranks of both groups to stand on moderate ground, to pursue a policy of restrained responsibility, have often been obscured by the harsher profiles suggested in the use of dove and hawk.

A second negative consequence has been the strained effort to categorize those who support American policy as conservatives and those who oppose it as liberals. This does violence to the positions and the integrity of outstanding personalities in both groups.

The author, for example, has strong voting credentials as a liberal; yet he consistently supports American policy in Asia. In his view this is not a contradiction of terms. One complements the other.

A third negative consequence falling out from the bitterness of dissent has been the tendency to judge in absolutes. One side in the debates is totally right; the other side, totally wrong. The chance that there may be something right in *both* positions receives little acknowledgment. Particularly in the academic community where the principles of tolerance and dissent are totally paramount values, the intolerance and one-sidedness of a point of view have become striking characteristics of the protesters.

Out of it all, hopefully, we will as a people and a nation acquire a deeper sense of the complexities of our changing international problems. In the process we may learn to live more gracefully in a time when issues no longer fall into convenient rights and wrongs or truths and falsehoods. The measure of our ability as a nation to come to terms with questions and crises that are neither black nor white but shades of gray will record in direct proportion our sophistication in rising to the responsibilities of world leadership.

This short volume, then, becomes one man's interpretation of the events around us. It seeks not to record history any more than it would pretend to inspire a crusade. With full acknowledgment of the limitations of contemporary biases, with an inhibiting sense of the shortcomings of human judgment, this monograph is an effort to select the meaningful facts of our time, as seen by the author, and fit them into the context of current history.

If there is a cause or crusade detectable in the book, it is the fear of a returning isolationism or national provincialism that could place in jeopardy the chances for meaningful peace in our time. The understandable frustrations of undeclared war, the exuberant impatience of a nation of people who have come to expect instant miracles, the compassionate feelings of a citizenry that believes in love over hate—all call into question the requirements of *real* politics. Yet, in truth, the test of our international maturity will be met in proportion to the sense of direction which these attributes can give when integrated with the responsible grasp of the realities with which we must cope.

In sum, the world is round. The United States of America is an integral part of it. And the best protection on it and from it is to remain involved with it.

CHAPTER I

Good News From Foggy Bottom

Well over a billion words have already been written about the struggle in Vietnam, several million still pictures (and several million feet of motion picture film) have been taken. The average citizen has long since been swamped by the "overkill" of information and news about the war. Yet, of those billions of words and millions of pictures, perhaps a handful will survive as history. Those which do survive will record the deeper implications of today's crisis in the Far East. That crisis—currently Vietnam—must be set in the wake of the critical events which have occurred since World War II. Those events need to be restored to the context of history.

It seems in order, therefore, to attempt to reduce the violence and the emotions of the present to the few pages of a history book which they will one day fill and to suggest some of the more significant elements of current change at stake in them. What follows is an attempt to recast the dimensions and the frustrations of the present in the perspective of our time.

It all hinges on understanding what World War II did to the world in general and to the United States in particular. As a consequence of that great conflict, the American government, as one of the two most powerful victors to emerge from the war, has suddenly been cast in the role of restructuring the balance of power. What this has meant to the individual American has been an adjustment, the magnitude of which would be difficult to exaggerate.

1

The individual who would take a moment to reflect on where he, as an American, is today would have to pinch himself were he to reflect on the simple proposition, "From whence have I come?" For his country, in 1968, stands as a giant in the minds of millions of people around the globe. To them, the United States is man's best hope for bringing about freedom and a better world. Remembering that scarcely a generation ago the United States was isolated and isolationist, it is all the more essential to draw the sharp contrast between then and now.

At the turn of this Century the foreign policy of the United States was little more than a collection of memos and an inadvertent series of declarations, articulated in haphazard pronouncements, with no particular sense of direction and with no conscious objective in mind. The State Department had just survived a proposal that it be abolished. Foreign policy, moreover, was made by half a dozen persons who read the cables. Few others comprehended what it was all about, and 99 percent of the American people couldn't have cared less.

A State Department composed mostly of clerks and secretaries in 1900 exploded into a State Department of some sixteen thousand in less than fifty years. To put it more dramatically, in 1939 the State Department had 3,466 employees; ten years later there were 13,618. The impact of our country's emergence as a great power forced quick adjustments to be made in the nation's capital.

The more obvious and material of these changes was the move of the Department of State from the old gingerbread State-War-Navy Building, next to the White House, to new quarters nearer the banks of the Potomac River—an area of Washington commonly referred to as "Foggy Bottom." The Washington press quickly affixed this appellation to the Department of State.

What has emanated from that new, massive concentration of policy in the more than twenty years since has altered the course of the history of the world and changed the lives of millions of our own people. On balance, the changes have been for the better. Thus, this is the "Good News from Foggy Bottom."

Some of us from the academic world need look back no further than the 1930's to recall the professional judgments of the problem of public opinion in making policy. We often suggested that it was only necessary to persuade the elite, which meant the upper 20 percent of the population. Because the man-in-the-street was supposed to be lethargic and indifferent to matters of foreign policy, it was believed he would be content to follow the guidelines preordained by the collective wisdom of the top one-fifth of our people—the professional politicians, the college graduates, the international travelers.

But by the end of World War II, this was no longer true. What happened to the United States and to the problems confronting the policy-makers as a result of the war is a measure of the viability of the American people in rising to new needs. Consider the harsh world which confronted us upon the cessation of hostilities in 1945. Our never-never world of imagined isolationism lay shattered around us. For more than a century the United States had enjoyed immunity from the strife of Europe—enforced partially by the width of the Atlantic Ocean, and partially by the insignificance in world politics of this new Republic. In those "good old days" the United States had enjoyed the luxury of "choosing-up sides" in the wars of the Old World. We had been able to determine which side represented the best interests of our country. But no more. World War II forced us to become one of the two sides.

Likewise, in our earlier geographic isolation we had enjoyed the luxury of being encircled by friendly nations which insulated us from the frontiers of strife. In time of war in Europe, those "buffer states" had held the line while we prolonged committing ourselves. But no more. Because of World War II we found we were suddenly on the front line, not only in Europe but in Asia as well.

At such a time, one could be forgiven for reflecting upon the private thoughts of a world figure of an earlier day, Otto von Bismarck. In the New Imperial Germany of the 19th Century, it will be recalled, Bismarck bent all of his energies toward the goals of national power and international greatness. His every move was calculated to usher his beloved Fatherland on to the stage of world politics. It disturbed him that those "immature, cocky Americans" across the sea should be stumbling into greatness. And when—in the last years of the century—the United States did emerge as a global power (albeit unintentionally), Bismarck was provoked to observe that, "there seems to be a Divine Providence that watches over drunks, little children, and the United States of America." Luck indeed had played a fortuitous role in the emergence of the new America.

But by 1945, having come forth from two world wars on the winning side, the United States could no longer trust to "Divine Providence" or luck to protect its future.

The American of 1945 found his private world suddenly overturned; the protective custody of the British Fleet and the land armies of the French shattered beyond repair. The kind of world it was and the kind it might become represented the opposite poles between which the United States sought to find a new course into the future. Two extremes seemed to be at war with each other to contradict principles and to obscure laudable objectives. Whether the people of the United States would be able to rise to the demands of the times as well as to blend the realities of power politics with the dreams of idealism constituted the great test to be run in the years following the war.

Understandably, the men from the New World set sail in their ships of idealism first. To their war-time allies, including the Soviets, they offered economic assistance and development. To the vanquished, they offered not only the hand of assistance in rebuilding, but the heart of forgiveness. The combination of these two trusts among the victors and the vanquished alike was distilled in the Marshall Plan. It represented the first time in the history of man that a victorious power had been so magnanimous toward those it had defeated in battle. Carrying its idealism still further, the United States offered to share with the Soviet Union (the other major power to survive the war) its then private monopoly on atomic capability.

With vigor both the people and their leaders in the United States placed great hope in the new United Nations. And as if all of this was not enough testimony to the altruism of the Americans, they proceeded quickly to dismantle the most awesome war machine ever put together by any nation anywhere. Within a few months, an armed force of twelve million men was demobilized into a bare fraction of the original. Given the record, no one could possibly construe that the American victors were arrogant or selfish or power-mad. Their actions spoke louder than the hollow accusations of their critics.

But this was not to be enough. For the dream ship of the American people was to be shattered on the rocky coast of reality. The new victors were soon to discover that the responsibility of the victor fell heavily upon them in a world that really hadn't changed very much in spite of the price paid for the war. The ugliness of power politics was disillusioning in a society where man had conquered the unconquerable, had achieved the impossible, and had performed the incredible. Despite the miracles of medical science and the breakthroughs in technology, the new wonders of inventive genius, and the new luxuries of everyday living, man soon discovered that these same great strides forward had not been matched by similar strides in the realm of international relationships.

Though he had scored high in other realms, man flunked his course in international relations. In the world there was neither law nor order nor stability. In fact, if Adolph Hitler were suddenly to return to earth following the war, he would have found no material change in the mechanisms affecting the nation-state system. If "Kaiser Bill" were to return, he would have found the international community strangely familiar. Or to go back a century and a half, even if Napoleon Bonaparte were to return to earth, the international climate would have seemed less strange to him than one might think. It was an old problem set in a new day—that of a lawless community of nations, each an independent sovereignty in its own right, regulated by the open-ends of anarchy and disciplined by the ruthlessness of survival of the fittest. Remembering the fondest dreams of Woodrow Wilson and the old League of Nations, the present had to represent a bitter pill for those who had striven toward peace on earth.

It is equally harsh to note that the only substitute for war which civilized man has yet worked out is the balance of power. One hesitates to use that phrase from the vernacular of the political scientist. It stands in such an unsavory light. Yet, however wrong or uncivilized it may seem to some people on moral grounds, it nonetheless is the stark fact of international life—perhaps the basic fact. It contradicts our ideals. It violates our hopes and shatters our dreams. Nevertheless, it is where we are now. Even as the balance of forces has preserved the peace, wars do violence to the structures of balance. After every one of the modern wars of history, a new balance had to be struck among the victors. Sometimes this new structure achieved only a fleeting peace; at other times, a protracted one as that "golden century" which followed the Congress of Vienna in 1815.

Thus, American responsibility for the shape and form of a new world began amid the debris of World War II. In building a better world, we had to begin where we were—not where we should have been or where we would rather have been or even where we some day might be. We had to start in the "here and now." We had to start where we were.

Frightening and disillusioning as the struggle for the balance of power is to America, it is old hat to Europe. Because it is so new in our own national experience, we tackle its implications with great uncertainty. Yet the hard fact remains that World War II imposed upon the United States a responsibility for striking a new balance in the world—a balance even more complex and more awesome than any ever struck by the old, imperial powers of Europe.

World War II was a different kind of war. Not only did it destroy three great powers, each of which in turn left a vast political vacuum in its wake, but even two of the victorious nations (England and France) were left so crippled by the conflict that they could no longer continue their historic role as a part of the make-weights on the scales of the balance of power. Perhaps never in history has so much violence been done to the old infrastructure of world stability. In East as well as West very few of the vestiges of the past were left intact.

It was into this chaotic setting that history thrust the United States of America. Perhaps never in modern times has one nation emerged from a world war with such great power and such frightening responsibility for the wise use of that power as did the USA. And as history long since should have taught, unless and until the world is brought back into balance following a war, few—if any—meaningful strides can be taken toward an improved world community.

The quest for the new balance of the world has been the substance of what we loosely call "the Cold War." From World War II there emerged only two great powers capable of contesting the shape of the new balance, the USSR and the USA. This sharpened the conflict. In earlier instances, the great powers sought to strike a balance among three or five or more nations. This was an immeasurably simpler undertaking than drawing a fine line between only two poles of power.

The process was further aggravated by the Atomic Age. The fact that man acquired for the first time the capability of destroying himself *in toto* made even more frightening the normal processes of struggle for the new balance. At times, the prospect of any kind of a future seemed virtually hopeless. Robert Oppenheimer once likened the Soviets and the Americans, with equally horrendous capabilities of destruction, to "two scorpions in a bottle." The mutual quest of both powers, however, came to be that of a balance of terror. But the important point lay in the word "balance," whatever its dimensions.

For the United States, the basic policy proposition was to prevent any one nation from ever again dominating Europe as Hitler's Germany had almost succeeded in doing. The new threat was posed by the Soviet Union. The basis of policy was to be that of containment of Soviet expansionism. Although somewhat later "containment" became a dirty word in the political arena, it still remains the best description of a policy which sought to restrain Russian ambitions.

It is interesting to note, from the vantage point of hindsight, that the esteemed journalist-pundit Walter Lippmann saw no hope whatsoever in a policy of containment. In his little volume, *The Cold War*, which appeared in 1947, Mr. Lippmann wrote:

> "They (the Western Europeans) realize, even if we do not realize it, that the policy of containment in the hope that the Soviet power will collapse by frustration, cannot be enforced and cannot be administered successfully, and that it must fail. Either Russia will burst through the barriers which are supposed to contain her, and all of Europe will be at her mercy, or, at some point and at some time, the diplomatic war will become a full scale shooting war. In either event, Europe is lost."[1]

Hardly had the firing ceased when the first trappings of cold war appeared. The closing acts of the campaign in Europe in particular produced some delicate and tense moments when the areas of occupation by the Allied Forces resulted in tests of strength or policy intentions between the war-time Allies, Russia and America, who were soon to become peace-time enemies.

That the Russians should launch at once into a program of aggression and peripheral probings could have been a surprise only to the naive. But the man-on-the-street in the United States was naive in the realm of power politics. And so it came as a shock to many that our great war-time trust in the camaraderie of the Reds should so soon be displaced by new suspicions and rivalries—in fact, by flagrant deeds of force. Too quickly some pundits blamed it all on the "national Communist conspiracy." Had they but taken the time to thumb through a Russian history book they might have foregone this gross oversimplification.

Nearly 100 years before, Lord Palmerston in London—speculating on the anxieties of his countrymen toward the intentions of the Russian czar in the Crimea—noted that there wasn't much to guess about. He noted the pages of Russian history were sprinkled with the instances in which the Russian Government constantly pressed outward along the periphery of its massive land frontiers probing for weaknesses. When they located soft spots, he explained, they broke through to add another scrap of territory to their domain. But where they were resisted, they were quick to pull back—perhaps to search elsewhere for a new opening.

In looking back upon the post-World War II years, one observes the continuation of this tendency of the great Russian bear—a trait that was as much a part of the czars as it was later to be of the commissars. It would appear to have more to do with Russian national interest than with ideology. This is not to downgrade the implications of the world revolutionary dialectic of the Communists, but rather to place it in proper perspective.

The specter of the new Soviet aggressor first appeared on the horizons of Teheran in the Middle East in 1946. There, where the tiny government of the Shah stood in diminished proportions to the colossus to the North, the Russians mobilized along their mutual frontier. The prize, of course, was the oil reserves of Iran as well as the land routes to the East which might thus open up—outflanking, in effect—the Indian land mass on the subcontinent of Asia. The

Americans, however, quickly committed themselves to Iran; and the Russians backed down.

Next, it was the strategic Eastern Mediterranean—Greece and Turkey. For centuries the Russians had striven to break out of the Turkish Straits. And now the commissars of the People's Socialist Republic, as the imperial czars had before them, bore down upon both Turkey and Greece.

In the first instance, it was a case of naked power pressure; in the second, it was the exploitation of a civil war with the offer of outside help to the guerrillas in Greece who, even in the American lexicon of political ideology, stood for all the right principles. Our showdown with the Russians evoked the Truman Doctrine, in which the United States committed itself to both Greece and Turkey. As the Americans stood up, the Soviets backed down.

Confrontation in Berlin produced similar results. What had been a temporary agreement to accomplish a transition of troop occupations in conquered Germany from war to demobilized peace found the Allies frozen in a divided Berlin. The French, British, and the Americans stood on one side, confronted by Soviet intransigence against a united Berlin on the other. Two Berlins, as two Germanys, became one of the first legacies of the newly divided world.

Berlin itself was a freakish consequence of military jousting by Allied troops at the close of the war. It emerged as an island of Western European military presence in a sea of Soviet-occupied territory. It was conspicuously vulnerable to the whims and the long-range intentions of the Russians—a vulnerability which they sought to exploit in 1947 and 1948 when the surface supply lines from West Germany into the city were cut off. Apparently, the Russians were confident that Berlin would wither on the vine and be forfeited to them.

But the American airlift completely changed the course of events. Once again the result was that, as the Americans stood up, the Russians backed down. This perhaps was the high-water mark of the Cold War stresses and strains in Europe. It was the critical test.

Tens of thousands of American soldiers were still in Europe, and although American officials repeatedly declared their intention to stand by their Western European allies in time of crisis, the memories of similar pledges after World War I haunted every

European capital. Few, if any, looked forward to the prospect of being "rescued" again from the grip of an aggressor. Europeans needed to know if the Americans would stand with them to prevent such a takeover, rather than follow through later in a massive rescue operation as they had against Hitler. It made a difference to many of them. Rather than wait for rescue, some of them preferred to work out an accommodation with the Russians and live under Communist influence if necessary.

But the American airlift changed all that. It removed the great question marks. It allayed the deep uncertainties about what the United States would do. If the Blitz was Britain's finest hour, as Churchill described it, Berlin indeed was America's finest test in her new role as a world power. And as Churchill observed, "If you Americans had acted this time as you acted after World War I, Russia would be on the Atlantic Coast of Europe today."

Berlin indeed turned the tide in the Cold War in Europe. Whereas Italy and France seemed to be inescapably plunging toward Communism in the aftermath of the war, they now experienced an about-face and not only rejected the one extreme but returned to a newly structured and more responsible government. The other areas in the West soon showed the new spirit of hope which the American presence seemed to invite. Before long the Marshall Plan had the factories and the highways of the western portions of the Old World very much back in business.

The new successes of Europe were not without their price; for, as stability and prosperity returned to all areas, the resurgence of nationalism and petty rivalries also began to dominate the political scene. The significance in the change, however, lay in the fact that the new problems of Europe were far preferable to the old problem of whether the Soviet Union would take over the continent. The new stability of Europe produced the surfacing of second- and third-rate crises; but none of these threatened to "blow up" the world.

And now, after twenty years, the fabric of the Iron Curtain is badly tattered. The satellite countries in Eastern Europe are painfully finding their own way and are slowly loosening their ties to Moscow. Bridges are being built to the East. "Titoism" has become a common cliche of world politics denoting a successful defiance of the Soviet monolith.

Earlier in this chapter reference was made to the dismay expressed by some experts about the prospects of the successful policy of containment of Europe. Perhaps it is appropriate at this point to look backward and recall still another statement made by the distinguished observer Walter Lippmann:

> "My objection, then, to the policy of containment is not that it seeks to confront the Soviet power with American power, but that the policy is misconceived, and must result in a misuse of American power . . . it commits this country to a struggle which has for its objective nothing more substantial than the hope that in ten or fifteen years the Soviet power will, as the result of long frustration, 'break up' or 'mellow.' "[2]

Positive as Lippmann was of the futility of containment, history has dared to contradict him. The American policy of containing Russia in Europe became a striking success. By sharing her national treasure, committing her military strength, and risking even nuclear war, the United States in fact waged a successful peace in the West.

Perhaps a more effective way to comprehend the success of the American containment of Russia would be to look at a map of the world. With a piece of chalk, one can begin on the frontiers of Finland and draw a line down through Eastern Europe, veer further to the east above Greece and Turkey, and in fact thereby describe the new balance in the West. The delicate line of balance was soon extended above Iraq, Iran, Afghanistan, Pakistan, and India, enfolding in the process the temporary frontiers of the mid-East and the Indian subcontinent.

Such a line remains vulnerable, however, to the elements of peaceful change. Communications, trade, and tourism all exert erosive—as opposed to abrasive—forces on the line. Indeed, who would deny that East and West in Europe are edging steadily closer? To put it another way, even in the stark terms of Cold War, what general in the Kremlin would dare to count on the legions of the satellite countries in Eastern Europe if there were to be a massive showdown between East and West? Time is taking its toll. It is on our side if we continue to use it wisely.

The containment of Russia was a notable success of American policy in the post-War. That success in itself epitomizes the "Good News from Foggy Bottom."

CHAPTER II

The Critical Balance of Asia

The real significance of Vietnam is captured best when measured in the context of the balance of Asia. For that story one must turn back to the end of the War in the Pacific.

August 14, 1945, may some day mark the beginning of the Age of the Pacific in history books. On that date when Japan surrendered, new historical forces were unleashed—forces which for generations had been locked up in the mysterious depths of the ancient Orient and amid an assortment of Western colonial structures.

For better or for worse, World War II thrust Asia front and center. This circumstance alone was to say much to the peacemakers of the world in general, and to the would-be architects of peace in the United States in particular.

Foremost among the new facts of international life was to be the Asian factor on the power balance scales of the world. The achievement of a new balance of Europe was not enough. The second World War had woven the East inextricably into the fabric of the power politics of the West. Whereas in the "good old days" a balance had been struck at a Congress of Vienna, or at Versailles, or The Hague, it would never be again.

At the very least, the defeat of Germany and Japan had verified the simple truth of Christopher Columbus' theory that the world indeed was round. The war, moreover, not only established its roundness but dramatically emphasized its rapidly shrinking size.

Science and technology had placed the remote East within commuting distance of the capitals of the Western World, and thus a new balance of stability—if it were to be realized after the war—had to encompass East as well as West.

That is not to say that the Far East was never a significant weight on the scales of world political balance. Rather, it says that due to World War II it acquired a new and complex and more difficult dimension.

For centuries Asia had been the target of conquerors. The forces of Alexander the Great conquered a large portion of southern Asia over 2300 years ago. The Huns invaded and subjugated the Chinese, destroying the first Chin Dynasty in 316 B.C. The complete subjugation of the area of modern China and much of Asia came in the 13th Century with the driving victories of the Mongols under the leadership of Genghis Khan. Invaders of the Asian mainland seemed to follow a general pattern through the ages. Taking power during periods of disorder, they had the tactical advantage due to their superior military power based largely on cavalry. Often the invaders allied with native tribes in order to further their conquests.

In a sense, their ambitions tied the visions of treasure in the East to the politics of capability in the West. But the first real intertwining of the two was the expansion of Europe in the 15th and 16th Centuries. The advent of colonial empires to build and enrich the power of the capitals of Europe launched a new age in political as well as imperial competition. That age, begun by the Portuguese and the Spanish, ultimately included the Dutch, French, British, and—in a later day—the Germans, Americans, and the Japanese. The old imperial wars always led to treaties or peace conferences in which the riches of the Orient became the trading stock.

By the 20th Century, however, Asia had become a more potent factor in the balance of power in the world. This would be the century that ushered in the bold dreams of Otto von Bismarck and Kaiser Wilhelm of Germany. And it is the century that brought the United States into the East through the back door of the Spanish-American War. The fact that a decadent Spanish kingdom had rotted away at its base gave the Americans, quite unexpectedly, the legacy of the old Spanish empire in the Pacific—namely, the Philippines.

From then on, President Theodore Roosevelt and the United States became calculated factors in the balance of Asia. The Boxer Rebellion in China, the new trade routes between the West and the East, the defeat of Germany in World War I and the necessary abandonment of her colonial outposts in Asia, and the rapid rise of Japan quickly influenced the new shape of the politics of the Far East.

By the 1930's Japan had easily become the dominant force in eastern Asia. Whatever balance of forces remained rested tenuously on Japan, China, and less clearly upon the shoulders of a conglomerate of colonial nations. As the efforts of the diplomats of the 1920's and 1930's disclosed, the interests of the United States were intertwined with the politics of the East. For better or for worse, the USA was not only an Atlantic power but a Pacific power as well.

This, then, was the setting on the eve of World War II. Already events were straining the validity of Rudyard Kipling's couplet, "East is East and West is West and never the twain shall meet." The meeting and the merging of cultures, races, and politics were fatefully under way even as the new, westernized Japan moved into Manchuria, seized the lucrative territories of coastal China, and methodically planned to grab the rich prize of Southeast Asia.

On December 7, 1941, the entanglements of rival interests between Japan and the United States were stripped of all of the niceties of diplomacy or hypocrisy or pretense.

Perhaps no war in history had ever left a continent in such disarray as World War II did eastern Asia. Completely shattered were the old structures of power and whatever stability had once prevailed. The strongest nation in the East lay utterly destroyed. The largest country in Asia was thrust into an upheaval, the dimensions of which remain uncertain even today—more than twenty years later. One by one the vast colonial empires were forfeited by the rulers to the ruled. More gracefully than the others, England pulled out of the Asian subcontinent—India, Burma and her centuries-old stations in the Malay States. Much less gracefully, the Dutch were forced out of Indonesia. Belatedly, in disrepair and near disrepute, the French backed out of Indochina.

But these are only the outward political manifestations of the debacle. The disorder and ruin left in the wake of war were compounded by the awakening among tens of millions of Asians themselves. Adlai Stevenson first described it as the revolution of great expectations. Colonial subjects, as well as semi-civilized tribesmen, were thrown face to face with the conquering soldiers of the West. American GI's penetrated even the remotest areas. The contact was infectious. The peoples of the East, for the first time, verified what some of their leaders had suspected all along: that they had been cheated out of what was rightfully theirs by the white overlords.

Understandably, they determined to make up for lost time. In their leap from their ancient past into the future, they sought every possible short cut. They felt that too much time had already been wasted. Their quest was for the prestige of national independence, for more of the benefits of good living, and for the personal dignity of the individual. They were not about to believe the departing warnings of their former masters that they were not yet ready for independence. They intended to stumble through the painful processes of rising to the responsibilities of plotting their own destinies. Thus, along with the old balance of Asia, Rudyard Kipling's philosophical capsule of the mysterious East lay shattered. East was West, and West had become East. They were irrevocably joined. Figuratively speaking, they were romping in each other's backyards, sitting in each other's laps, and stepping on each other's toes. To pretend otherwise would only be an exercise in self-delusion.

The United States has a deep responsibility to restructure a new balance of Eastern Asia. After a long and bloody war in the Pacific, the temptation to be rid of it all is understandable, if not justifiable. After the signing of the Treaty with Japan on the battleship *Missouri* in 1945, we might well have chosen to go home and pretend that Asia had disappeared in the mushroom clouds that rose over Hiroshima and Nagasaki. To have done so, however, would have been irresponsible to our interest and morally reprehensible to our obligation as the principal victor of the war of the Pacific.

The United States is not only a Pacific power but an Asian power. We are committed there by our own history. Since Caleb Cushing's treaty with the Chinese in 1844, and our special role in opening the door of Japan, in our acquisition of Alaska in the Northern Pacific, of Hawaii in the Eastern Pacific, and of the Philippines in the Western Pacific, we have been irreversibly involved. What happens in Eastern Asia not only can make a great difference in our future, it has already begun to do so. Our new role in the world as leader of most of the independent nations was the result of our participation in World War II, a war we became involved in because of Japan's attack on Pearl Harbor. The politics of Asia, in other words, triggered the events which catapulted us into our position of great power.

Hopefully, we should have learned that wars do not bring peace. They only win the chance to build a newer, peaceful society. The silencing of the guns does not automatically signal the arrival of peace. Peace has to be planned and pursued. Unless or until we learn to wage peace as vigorously as we always manage to wage war, it remains doubtful whether we will ever achieve peace in our time. From this thesis must come the corollary that the best way to capitalize on the victory in the war was to prepare to take the risks and pay the price for *waging peace*.

The totality of the devastation of Asia has already been described. Suffice it to say that the ruins were largely the doing of the United States. While it was common to refer to the "Allied effort" in the war, it is well to recall that, in the war of the Pacific, Allied participation was largely token. The United States produced the victory there. We destroyed Japan; we witnessed the discombobulation of China; we shattered the centuries-old underpinnings of the colonial empires of Britain, France, the Netherlands, Germany and Japan.

The consequence was a massive political vacuum which lay as a temptation to an assortment of predators who always manage to find in ruin the opportunities for self-aggrandizement or national gain.

In those days some of us dared to hope that the newly independent government of India might become the force of balance in restructuring the new Asia. Prime Minister Nehru, however, thought otherwise—at least until it was too late. In all fairness to the late, distinguished leader of India, it should be noted that he was wrestling with this question.

I remember well a conversation I had with him in his study during a visit in New Delhi in 1959. One of the topics discussed was India's role in Asia. After I had asked him why India refused to face up to the problem posed by her neighbor China, his response was, "Mr. Senator, as new nations, we all have to grow up to our responsibilities. Ours at the moment in India are those of coming to grips with our tremendous, if discouraging, internal questions of economics and population and politics. You will forgive us if we feel we do not have either the time or the energy left to worry about the outside world." And then, it seemed to me, the Prime Minister acquired a twinkle in his eye as he continued, "Perhaps you Americans will understand our position. For more than 100 years you were so obsessed in your history, with your internal development, that you rarely looked outward. In fact," he said, "as recently as the 1930's you were militantly isolationist. It took a direct attack on your territory by Japan to shock you into the realities of world affairs. Perhaps the same thing will first have to happen to India before my people rise to external needs."

Nehru ventured the thought that something like an attack by the Chinese on Burma, thus laying bare the eastern flanks of India, would be the most likely incident in the offing. Tibet, to him, did not seem as probable at that time.

The important thing to note, however, was his readiness to compare his country's public psychology to the American transition from isolationism to world commitment. It suggests that he was coming closer to accepting a meaningful role for India in all of Asia than the record of his deeds would suggest.

The hard fact in Asia which emerged was that either the United States must take on the responsibility for putting the meaningful pieces back together again, or forfeit this process to predatory soldiers of political fortunes, thereby taking the risk of the shape and combination of pieces which those with different designs toward world peace than ours would undertake.

What this says is that the United States was already committed by deed as well as by history to participate in the rebuilding of Asia. And it was even more deeply committed by the force of political morality. Not only as the principal victor in Asia, but as the only great surviving power in the East with the capabilities of rebuilding, we had acquired a moral obligation to humanity that defies assessment in strictly material terms.

This is the "Why" of American policy in Eastern Asia. This is the answer to those of our critics today who try to argue that we have no business meddling in the Orient. We not only have business there, we have the awesome responsibility imposed upon us by the circumstances which brought us there in the first place.

If we look ahead, we do not have to indulge in fanciful speculation to realize that Asia will be the substance of the world of tomorrow. While our history until now has been dominated by the culture and the institutions of Western Europe, it will not always be so. Asia is where the world is. It's where the people are. It's where much of the future of the human story will be written.

One way to capture this overhwelming fact of our time is to imagine for a moment that we place a hundred people on a small stage in front of us. The hundred would represent, in proper proportion, a cross-section of the more than 3 billion people now on earth. Who would they be? Of the hundred,

   1 would be from Australia, New Zealand, and the South Pacific
   5 would be from the United States and Canada
   6 from the Soviet Union
   8 from Latin America
   9 from Africa
  15 from Europe
  56 from Asia

This is the world that already is. The world that is coming is an even more Asian world. And as a Pacific power, the United States has a very large stake in the shaping of that new world. It is in our basic national interest, therefore, to participate in the process of re-building it.

What is rebuilt and, certainly, how it is rebuilt can make a difference. The often unfathomable mysteries of the East do not make the task any easier. Neither, however, do they absolve us from undertaking to do so.

In approaching the new Asia, we are entitled to apply the lessons of history. I would be the first to caution against applying the experiences of Europe to the problems of Asia without careful reservations. As the British historian Arnold Toynbee has said, "History repeats itself only when man makes the same mistakes over again."

Even so, it is appropriate to note that there are common ingredients in the politics of both East and West. In both, the political components are sovereign nations no longer separated by colonial empires. In each area the nations entered World War II because one single power threatened to dominate the continent— Germany in Europe, Japan in Asia. Both regions, moreover, experienced a series of acts of aggression that seemed to be so small in their beginning as not to warrant larger concern. In both cases, the hope was expressed that a little bit of aggression would appease the aggressors. Finally, both areas were left so shattered by the war that no combination among them was capable of rebuilding amid the ruins. Both were at once vulnerable in the immediate post-war period to exploitation by a new generation of potential aggressors.

These common denominators entitle us to extract from the old history of Europe meaningful guidelines for American policy in shaping the new history of Asia.

From these facts, we can select some pertinent lessons of history to be applied to our efforts in Asia. Until better guidelines are offered, these ought to be heeded. Within their confines are the answers to those who today ask, Why not go home and forget about it?; or, Why does China make a difference to us?; or, Why Vietnam 11,000 miles away?; You don't believe Mao means what he says, do you?; or, Isn't Ho Chi Minh a frustrated nationalist?

Those questions have a haunting ring because they sound so much like the questions a college generation 30 years ago was raising about Europe—3,000 miles away: Who cares about Hitler? *Mein Kampf* is only a book; it is no threat to the future. Austria and Poland are too insignificant to provoke war. Isn't German Nationalism as legitimate as our own? What can they do to us thousands of miles away?

The criticisms voiced today leave me with the strange feeling that this is where I came in a generation ago. Each generation has to come to grips with the need to evaluate the incidents of its own time. People in the 1930's who thought we could hide, or could bury our heads, or that Hitler would go away, or that Japan had no larger ambitions, or that Austria or the Sudetenland or Poland were too small to cause a world war, have been replaced by the people in the 1960's who now, through the 20-20 vision afforded by hindsight, see the larger meaning of the smaller developments of yesteryear.

Today's critics, moreover, are even grudgingly willing to believe that "Fortress America" is unrealistic, and they would extend it from the three-mile limit off our coast all the way to Western Europe. In doing so, the current generation proudly boasts of its new enlightenment. They have caught up with the changing world, they say to us, because they realistically extend the boundaries of our concern all the way across the Atlantic to the Old World.

The real tragedy of those who think this way, of course, is that they're so busy catching up with the cruel truths of the last world war that they remain blind to the harsh facts of today which, if ignored, could lead us to the next world war. Little Vietnam and Thailand are just as important for the future as were Austria and Poland in the 1930's. To abandon them would hold as grave a portent for the future as that of the 1930's.

Now, in 1968, because of the ever-present prospect of nuclear war, the decision is more desperate than that which was avoided in 1938. This is why we strive to come to grips with the realities of the present in foreign policy, why it is so desperately important that—if possible—we be right the first time. Because of the nuclear threat, we may not have the luxury of a second chance if we permit the first to slip between our hesitations.

The first lesson of recent history is that no one nation should be allowed to dominate the continent of either Europe or Asia. In the perspective of history, it was this concept that triggered the Napoleonic Wars at the beginning of the 19th Century. It was this principle which dominated the events which erupted in both World Wars I and II. And since the emergence of the United States as the leading power in the world, this same principle has been the nub of American post-war policy in Europe.

Aimed as it was at the Soviet Union, it came to be called the policy of containment. The success of containment is now a matter of record. The line which separates Eastern Europe from the West extends far beyond the boundaries of the Old World. From Greece and Turkey it has been sketched eastward across the Asian land mass almost to the China Sea. One reason is that the policy of containing Russia could not be translated into the politics of Eastern Asia. Even as it is daily more apparent that the Soviet Union in middle Asia (Pakistan, India, Afghanistan) is as interested as we are in maintaining a status quo, the politics of Eastern Asia continues in a state of flux with the uncertainties looming large. It is for this reason that American policy moves in transition from West to East to become one, also, of the containment of China.

A second lesson from history is that there is never a cheaper time or place to stop an act of aggression than at its beginning. The illusory qualities of Neville Chamberlain's symbolic umbrella at Munich are now a tragedy of the 1930's. We learned, both with Hitler and with the Tojo Regime in Japan, that you can't appease an aggressor with someone else's territory. To do so only whets his appetite.

Historians even today speculate on what might have been the history of the Far East if the Allies—England, France, and the United States—had dared to stop Japan in Manchuria in 1931. We can't know for certain. What we do know is that we did not buy useful time or lower the cost by forfeiting Manchurian real estate to the Japanese warlords.

Similarly in Europe. The hope of Munich, that yielding to Hitler's territorial demands in Czechoslovakia and Austria would somehow satisfy his hunger, was dashed on the rocks of war in Poland.

What would have been the course of politics in Europe, on the other hand, if the Western Allies had stopped Hitler's Panzer divisions at the Rhineland in 1936? Since the war, historians have told us that, as Hitler's legions approached the Rhine in that year in violation of the Versailles Treaty, they marched under sealed orders to withdraw and retreat if they met resistance. But they were not halted. While we can't be certain what would have happened to the Wehrmacht had it been stopped at the Rhine, we do know what did happen when it wasn't. Adolph Hitler moved on to new conquest, boldly defying the hopes of his peaceloving neighbors. And the world was plunged into war.

A third lesson is that, in striking a new balance, it is in the national interest to withhold from the potential enemy the sinews of power for a new war. For example, the major prize in Europe after the defeat of Hitler was obviously the Ruhr Valley—Germany's industrial heartland. In dividing Germany after the war, the industrial power fell within the zones of the Allies. And so in Asia. The war in the Pacific held two chief prizes for the victors—the industrial power of Japan and the rich resources of Southeast Asia.

Each prize constituted the extreme ends of a long defensive arc which curved all the way from the Sea of Japan to the Straits of Moluccas. Japan was saved from the Communists' military thrust by the war in Korea; the raw materials of Southeast Asia are the prize at stake in the war in Vietnam.

A fourth lesson, taken from events of the past 20 years, is that we have found it possible to live in a divided world. In hindsight, the dialogues of the 1940's over "we or they" seem unreal and even ridiculous. Pontification at all levels proclaimed that Soviet Communism and American Capitalism could never co-exist. A policy of live-and-let live was no policy at all, it was argued. It only temporarily slowed the sands of time that were running out against us. The corollary to this theory, of course, was that war between the USSR and the USA was inevitable. Therefore, the next stage of public dialogue had to do with preventive wars.

What the "preventers" blithely ignored was that you don't prevent a war by starting one. They also forgot, if they had ever known, that there have been dozens of "inevitable" wars talked about that were never fought. Historians remain reluctant to pronounce the inevitability of cataclysmic events. Even the folly of debating whether there could be coexistence between the capitals of world Communism and world Democracy was conspicuous at the time because it occurred at a time when coexistence was fact.

What has emerged after more than twenty years is indeed a divided world—a world subdivided into divided countries and even divided cities.

The dividing line of the world, as we have already seen, reflects the demarcation line of the new balance of power around the globe. The specific dividing lines on a smaller scale, however, reflect some of the existing conditions at the end of the war. Intended originally as transitional or temporary lines, those drawn in Germany or Korea had a tendency to become permanent—frozen by the cold facts of balance of power.

The late Adlai Stevenson phrased it best: "If we had our own way, it would be one world, not a divided world. But a divided world," he concluded, "is better than no world." And what we understand now is that a divided world and even divided countries do achieve moments of stability and defer greater violence so that time itself can diminish the sharpness of the lines of division.

Given the presence of large numbers of Soviet troops in Eastern Germany and American troops in Western Germany at the end of the war, a divided Germany won the time for the power and pressures and tensions of mutual distrust on both sides to abate. The same is true in the City of Berlin. It is already appearing on both sides of the 38th Parallel in Korea; and some day, we can be sure, it will be the case in two Chinas.

Having learned that we can live divided, we experience another option available in the tightest cases of crisis; namely, that of dividing a nation in lieu of a larger war. This is reflected in the two Vietnams.

The fifth lesson of history, derived from our experiences in Greece and Turkey, is that it is important in policy projects to put first things first, both chronologically and in terms of the weight of priority.

A case in point is the Greek civil war in the late 1940's. In Greece at that time a great many internal quarrels and frustrations came to a head very soon after the war in Europe ended. Resentment against a less than democratic government, criticisms of royalty, and military cliques of war-time black marketeers and the landed gentry combined to foment organized uprisings in the rural regions of Northern Greece. All of the makings of civil war were present in Greece. But so was something else.

Across the border in Bulgaria, Yugoslavia and Albania, the Communists, under the direction of Moscow, saw in the internal strife of Greece an opening into which they might move and which could be exploited to the advantage of historic Russian desire to get a warm-water port in the Mediterranean. Therefore, what started out as a Greek internal quarrel mushroomed into an ideological conflict for Southeast Europe. The stakes for the Russians were high, principally the control of the Eastern Mediterranean.

American presence was injected into that crisis by President Truman. The result was the Truman Doctrine with open assistance to both Greece and Turkey. What such a policy involved was support for a status quo that failed to meet the legitimate demands of changing times. It became a matter, however, of first things first.

Had the Greek government not been sustained, the Soviet Government almost certainly would have moved into a position of dominance on the Balkan Peninsula. Therefore, by interceding, the Americans not only stopped Soviet penetration, but—in doing so—won time and the chance for the Greeks to put their own house in order their own way. (A process which still goes on as this is being written.) This would have been impossible to achieve had the order of priorities been reversed.

The principle of first things first reflects the immediate and successful experiences in our own pursuit of a policy aimed at restoring a favorable balance of forces around the world.

To recap the lessons of the recent past which may be applicable to Asia now:

1. No one nation should be allowed to dominate Asia.

2. The cheapest place and time to stop aggression is at the beginning.

3. Withhold from potential enemies the sinews of power (industry and raw materials).

4. Where necessary, a divided nation or region may be the least evil of several unpleasant alternatives.

5. It is important to put first things first, thus stopping outside aggression before internal reforms can be achieved.

The foregoing lessons from history, applicable to current events in Asia, constitute rational guidelines for the policy decisions of the United States in that distant part of the world. Within those lines one finds the principal underpinnings of the Far Eastern policy of the United States today.

And along their course, we discover the "Why" of Vietnam.

CHAPTER III

Vietnam in Perspective

The war in Vietnam has galvanized dissent and provoked a bitterness rarely equalled in our history. Not only has it divided the American people, it threatens to divide much of the free world as well. It is imperative, therefore, that U.S. policy in Southeast Asia be understood and fairly evaluated in the light of the events which brought us there.

To understand the war in the Far East, it is necessary to relate it to the historical forces which preceded it. These include the beginnings among the Vietnamese people themselves many centuries ago. The meaningful past must be related to the troubled present. Vietnam must be viewed in the perspective of history.

The Vietnamese people have a recorded history of over 2,000 years. They originated in the valley of the Yellow River in North China and were slowly driven southward by pressure from the Han Chinese. By the Second Century B.C., they were a tribal people inhabiting the Kingdom of Nam Viet ("Nam" meaning to the "south" of China and "Viet" being the name of the Vietnamese people) in the Red River Delta of what we now know as North Vietnam.

In the First Century B.C., Nam Viet was conquered by the Chinese and administered as the southern province of Giao Chi, later Annam. Despite a distinct pattern of civilization, the Vietnamese were dominated by China for ten centuries. This domination was marked by continual uprisings, the most serious led by two women, the Trung sisters, in 39 A.D. They were put down by an illustrious old warrior, Marshall Ma Yuan, who destroyed most of the local institutions which had insulated the people from direct impact of the Chinese administration. The Vietnamese people were then forcibly integrated into the Chinese world.

Yet these drastic measures saved the Vietnamese from extinction as a separate people. Their conquerors inadvertently provided them with the social and administrative institutions which were to give them the strength they needed to survive—even against the Chinese themselves.

As a result of several factors, including population growth, the Vietnamese worked their way south toward more rice land. The Nam Tien, or "March to the South," began in the Tenth Century and ended many hundred years later when the Vietnamese reached the southernmost point of the Mekong Delta in what is now South Vietnam.

The 10th Century is also important for the fact that Vietnam emerged as an independent state (939 A.D.) until the end of the 19th Century. However, the country continued to suffer from Chinese invasions, particularly in the 13th, 15th, and 18th Centuries. During this time, Vietnam extended its own boundaries; invaded the Mekong Delta of the Champa Empire; entered the languid Kingdom of the Khmer (Cambodia); went on forays west into Thai territory; and sent expeditions into the "Plaine des Janes" of northern Laos.

As the Vietnamese expanded to the south, they finally set up two rival centers of power. One power center was established at Hanoi, and the other appeared in the southern half of the country. With the aid of early European colonialists, notably Portuguese and Dutch, the Nguyen rulers of the south became an independent kingdom. From this southern repository of power the rulers expanded into the Cambodian areas of the Mekong Delta. It was a slow process which finally conquered the area around Saigon by the beginning of the 18th Century and settled the entire delta near the close of that Century.

On and off for more than 900 years, Vietnam maintained its precarious existence as an independent state by paying tribute to the

Middle Empire of China and by going on its own military adventures. It was not until the establishment of French protectorates over Tonkin and Annam in 1863 that the latter tendencies were curbed.

But it is interesting to note that, *several hundred years prior to a European presence, dynastic power struggles divided North and South Vietnam along a line that approximates the present 17th Parallel.* The massive stone walls that were erected in the 1630's across the plains of Quang Tri divided Vietnam into an upper and lower kingdom for one hundred and fifty years.

In 1673, however, a united Vietnam came apart largely due to dynastic rivalries. The troubled country was divided into three separate entities—Cochin-China (the Mekong Delta); central Annam, which included the central and coastal areas of what is now South Vietnam; and Tongking (North Vietnam today).

Two of the regions were reunited in 1789, but it was not until 1802 after a temporary French intervention that the Emperor Gia Long united the country for the first time from the Gulf of Siam to the Chinese frontier. Founder of the Nguyen dynasty (of which Bao Dai was the last ruler), Gia Long named the country Viet-Nam, made his capital at Hue, and began a vast program of national rehabilitation.

This period of unity and quasi-independence was destined to be brief. Once again the French intervened after local persecution of Christian missionaries in the middle of the 19th Century. By 1867, France occupied the southern part of Vietnam and established the colony of Cochin-China.

From this new colonial base, the French then pressed outward toward the north, establishing some measure of control as far away as Hanoi. By 1882, France had conquered the bulk of the Red River Delta (in North Vietnam). In rapid succession she added Cambodia (1884) and Laos (1893); and by the end of the 19th Century, the assortment of French colonies and protectorates in Indochina had been merged into an Indochinese union under a governor-general.

From the outset, the purpose of the French administrative system was to downgrade local responsibility and upgrade centralized control in France. The contrast between the north and the south in this new French kingdom has something to say about what was to follow later in the 20th Century.

In the north (what is now North Vietnam) the Red River Delta land was developed by small farmers. They never developed enough, however, to meet their own food requirements, leading them to the importation of rice from the delta regions of the Mekong River.

In the south (the Mekong Delta of South Vietnam) the more fertile acres were controlled by landlords in the form of large estates. Labor was provided by tenants and work gangs. The French themselves introduced the large rubber plantations and the mining companies which were developing some of the raw resources of Indochina.

The early years of French administrative control saw few major efforts on the part of the native population to overthrow colonialism although small uprisings occurred from time to time. But already an interesting young Vietnamese was on the scene, though too young to be recognized as yet. He was Nguyen Tat Thanh, born in 1894. This new personality at the turn of the century ultimately went to Paris to study and later organized the first Vietnamese communist group in 1917. He finally took the name Ho Chi Minh.

"Ho" is supposed to mean "the enlightened one." Very little is known about his early career. It is believed, however, that he joined Comintern (Communist International) in 1920, studied and trained in the Soviet Union, and finally was sent to China where he worked closely with Michael Borodin.

By 1930 Ho combined several of the dissident groups in the French Indochinese area into the Vietnam Communist Party. Out of this organization came a whole series of popular front groups, the most familiar one of which was the Viet Minh.

The French administered control of all Vietnam, Laos, and Cambodia as Indochina until Japanese troops moved into northern Vietnam in 1940. This was the first step of Japanese conquest of Southeast Asia. In 1941, the Japanese moved into Southern Vietnam and remained there until their surrender to the Allied Powers in 1945.

During World War II, the Communist Party in Vietnam became the core of the resistance movement against the Japanese. By demanding free elections, land for the people, and complete independence, the Viet Minh attracted the support of a great many nationalists—both north and south. A resistance army organized around guerrilla cadres and under the command of one of Ho Chi Minh's colleagues in the Communist movement, Vo Nguyen Giap, commanded the military phase of the resistance.

Near the end of the war in the Pacific, the Japanese took over all of Indochina including the south. In August, 1945, a Communist-led uprising broke out. The Viet Minh, armed with American weapons and receiving some tactical assistance, continued to fight on. In September, 1945, the independence of the Democratic Republic of Vietnam was proclaimed with Ho Chi Minh as its leader. The government of the new state was moved to Hanoi.

Meanwhile, it had been agreed at the conference which the Allies held in Potsdam that British troops already in the Far East would occupy the south of Vietnam and that Chinese Nationalist troops would temporarily move into the north of Vietnam until French forces could be rushed to the area. The Chinese permitted Ho to hold elections and to form a government. The British, on the other hand, refused to deal with the Viet Minh committee that had been temporarily in charge in Saigon when the war ended. They proceeded to turn Saigon machinery back to the French.

French soldiers arrived in Indochina in March, 1946.

A prolonged three-way struggle ensued among the Vietnamese Communists led by Ho Chi Minh, the French, and the Vietnamese Nationalists nominally led by Emperor Bao Dai. The Communists sought to portray their struggle as a national uprising; the French attempted to reestablish their control; while Bao Dai's Nationalists, who chose to fight militarily with the French against the Communists, wished neither French nor Communist domination.

The French signed an armistice with Ho Chi Minh which recognized the Republic of Vietnam as a free state with its own government, parliament, army, and finances. But all of it was to become a part of the French Union.

It was indicated, moreover, that a referendum should be held in Cochin-China (South Vietnam) to determine whether the south would remain an autonomous republic under French authority and separate from the Hanoi regime. Efforts to resolve the differences between the north and south at this point got nowhere.

With the breakdown of the negotiations between Paris and Hanoi, a war between the Viet Minh and the French got under way; it was to stretch out for eight years. The conflict followed the familiar pattern.

The Viet Minh's most successful theater of operations was in the countryside, especially the hill-tribe regions, while the stronghold of the French remained in the urban areas and the lowlands. Although Vietnam was loosely thought of as a single country, there emerged in fact during these years *two* Vietnamese regimes—the French-sponsored state of Vietnam in the South and the Viet Minh-controlled Democratic Republic of Viet Nam (DRVN) in the North.

After the victory of Mao Tse-tung over the Chinese Nationalists in 1949, the Chinese Communists operating out of Peking began to extend specific support to the North Vietnamese. Training centers for Viet Minh guerrillas were created just over the borders which North Vietnam shared with Communist China. Other troops were trained in and equipped with modern weaponry from the Soviet Union. Technicians from China manned anti-aircraft guns. Chinese military advisers moved in elsewhere with the Viet Minh.

Finally, the French moved a large force of troops to Dien Bien Phu, a fortress which lay along the strategic routes into Laos. During the assault by General Giap on this French stronghold, the Chinese Communist government supplied heavy artillery and trucks in addition to their other assistance.

The French government was increasingly unable to win the confidence and the support of the non-communist nationalists in Vietnam. At the same time in Paris, the French government was in deep trouble over the status of its war in Southeast Asia. Heavy losses of men and material provoked a rapidly escalated criticism on the homefront.

At this same time there was growing concern both in the United States and in Great Britain that the implications of the conflict in Indochina extended far beyond the borders of that particular region. In both of the English-speaking capitals there were those who saw in the struggle in Southeast Asia a potentially serious threat to the security of a large part of the Asian mainland.

In the Soviet Union, moreover, the Politburo apparently wanted a relaxation of international tensions because of the need for adopting ambitious domestic programs for economic development. Thus, the coincidence of the apprehensions in London and Washington coincided with a quest in Moscow for an easing of international pressures. It was the combination of these circumstances which set the stage for the Geneva Conference.

On February 18, 1954, at the close of the Berlin Conference, the Foreign Ministers of France, the United States, Great Britain, and the Soviet Union called for an international meeting to discuss both Korea and Indochina. The conference was to convene in Geneva on April 26, 1954.

With the confrontation between the French and the Viet Minh at Dien Bien Phu in the spring of 1954, a long and sometimes stormy colonial era had come to an end. What was to happen because of the defeat of the French and the rivalry of the competing forces among the Vietnamese would constitute the main threads of the history of the new Vietnam between 1954 and the present. Tied to those threads was the postwar foreign policy of the United States in the Far East. How the Americans got there and why they were there can only be understood in the context of what happened to the world system as a result of World War II.

Forces had been set loose as a result of the defeat of Germany and the collapse of Japan which were to engulf the United States in a new series of crises and responsibilities. The price of victory in World War II was to extract from the government of the United States and its people a new, costly, frightening, and sometimes violent commitment in the quest for a more peaceful world to replace the age of dictators which had precipitated World War II.

To understand Vietnam, it is necessary to understand the events which projected the Americans into this new role.

Chapter IV

The Far East Policy of the United States Since 1945

Does the United States have a Far East policy? In view of what some critics have been saying, it may come as a surprise to many that we have a policy for Eastern Asia. *That* there is and *what* it is, become the central theme of this chapter.

First of all, that policy has as its postulate that no one nation ought ever to be in a position to dominate the Far East. This is as important to Eastern Asia now as it was to Western Europe at the end of World War II. Parenthetically, it is as important to the Soviet Union that this precept be adherred to as it is to the United States. And surely it is as important—in relative terms—to India, to Indonesia, to Japan as it is to the tiny countries of Southeast Asia. In these difficult times the great question mark of China hovers over the capitals of many nations of the world.

This is not new. Almost as far back as one cares to go in the history of Asian politics one finds China to be the source of apprehensions among her neighbors. It might help to dispel a few false notions even now to suggest that it wouldn't matter a great deal whether Peking were occupied by Mao Tse-tung or Chiang Kai-shek. The historical fact of China is the over-riding issue. In land mass and population, as well as in aggressive economic and political activity, China is a veritable giant among pygmies in Eastern Asia. The overseas Chinese, still numbering 15 or 16 millions, connote another manifestation of the China which the Orientals view with misgiving.

The small countries on the rim of China have had cause to be uneasy about an entire succession of regimes in China. From the Chin dynasty down to Mao Tse-tung and Lin Piao this has been true.

While many Americans when thinking of Asia tend to think only of Chinese, we ought to recall the weight of Secretary of State Rusk's reminder that, while there may soon be a billion Chinese on the Mainland, there will also be a billion non-Chinese Asians who will have a stake in what happens in the Far East.

I have made three trips to the rim of China—the first in 1959, the second just three years later, and the third a little over a year ago. On each tour, spokesmen for the governments located in the shadow of Mainland China expressed concern about Chinese intentions or where they were heading. These governments stretched all the way from Pakistan and India around to Korea and Japan. The apprehensions now felt by the Soviet Union, which is the principal neighbor of China to the north, need no additional embellishments. Whatever uncertainties linger in our thoughts about Chinese intentions, and however some critics choose to rationalize the new China, the fact remains that in Asia nearly a billion non-Chinese Asians live in fear of China.

If the critics do not recognize the implications of a Chinese policy of violent world revolution, the non-Chinese Asians do—those in Malaysia, the Philippines, Japan, Thailand. Even Ho Chi Minh is not unaware of the threat of a nuclear-armed government in China, and that is perhaps one reason he obtains as much of his war material from Russia as he does.

Those who would blithely assert that China is not an expansionist power must erase from their memories the action China has taken along the 2,000-mile border she shares with India, as well as Peking's conquest of Tibet; its interference in Indonesia, Laos, Burma, and similar border areas.

Is the Chinese threat the figment of her imagination? Secretary of State Dean Rusk has phrased it best: "We are not picking out Peking as some sort of special enemy. Peking has nominated itself by proclaiming a militant doctrine of world revolution, and doing something about it. This is not a theoretical debate; they are doing something about it."

The fact of China's intentions is, fortunately, recognized by her Asian neighbors.

The Tunku of Malaysia says, "China remains the heart of the problem in Asia."

From the newest and smallest republic in Southeast Asia—Singapore—Premier Lee Kuan Yew notes, "It is fear of China that dominates all of the small nations in Asia."

President Marcos of the Philippines put it this way, "The central fact of life here in Asia is Red China . . . Vietnam is merely the theater where the intention of Red China may be reflected."

The fears entertained by the leaders of Asia toward Mainland China are not without some substance. China's drive into Mongolia, thus increasing friction with the Soviets, is one manifestation.

A second is China's push into the Northeast of Asia. This move was not without provocation because of the turn of events in the Korean War. The fact is that the Chinese are there and are on the move.

A third was the Mainland's quest for Formosa and the islands in the Straits. To be sure, the Nationalist Chinese did violence to the nationalism of the native Formosans. It only serves to underscore the point again that the issue is China, whether Mao's or Chiang's.

And fourth was the conquest of Tibet in 1960. It shocked many otherwise complacent Asians.

In Southeast Asia the influence has involved meddling. The Chinese role in the PKI in Indonesia was much more substantial than "moral" support. The Indonesian revolution was engineered and directed from Peking. The ties between Ho Chi Minh and Peking antedate by many years the outbreak of hostilities between North and South Vietnam. And in Burma, Peking has appeared as well. More recently, the actions of the Mainland Chinese in Hong Kong and along the nearby frontier underscore the cause for the fears entertained by her neighbors.

It remains important, however, that we neither distort nor exaggerate the Chinese threat. China is beset with great problems of her own, and she has many needs which the current regime has failed to satisfy. The present political discontent inside her boundaries continues to defy accurate assessment. The best of the China-watchers remain unsure.

Certainly no rational individual can make a case for attacking China in order "to prevent something worse later on." Her nuclear capability still lies in the future. Her present capabilities are no excuse for panic; but neither do they invite relaxation or complacency.

Perhaps we can learn from our long experiences with the Soviet Communists not to make the Chinese "ten feet tall" or consider them specters lurking behind every potential crisis in Asia. In recent months the Chinese have suffered enough setbacks to warrant a more cautious reevaluation of their capabilities than the headlines suggest.

Most notable among these developments is the widening breach between Peking and Moscow and along her long border with India where China suffered a humiliating experience in 1962. In her showdown with New Delhi, the capital of a country that had practiced pacifism and preached non-violence, China served an ultimatum which the Indians blithely ignored. It would be difficult to exaggerate the humiliation experienced by any sovereign power that has to swallow its own ultimatum. A good many of the China specialists believe that this break is irreparable.

Elsewhere on the international scene, China has been quite literally thrown out of Africa. And in the United Nations, of which she is not a member, she finds today only one nation that speaks up in her behalf—tiny and insignificant Albania. Yet, little more than a year ago, there were seventeen or eighteen voices in that world organization ready to speak out for China. And more recently—perhaps the most humiliating blow of all—the Chinese experimental venture in Indonesia fell apart at the seams.

That today China is undergoing the internal convulsions caused by the muscle-flexing of the Red Guards suggests it may be some time until China is able to put her own house in sufficient order to merit being viewed as a major power threat.

If it is fair to contend that the China policy of the United States during World War II was just to keep China in the war against Japan, it would be equally fair to note that our immediate post-war policy was that of trying to figure out what kind of a China was emerging from the war. The commitment to Chiang Kai-shek and his Nationalists was a deep one stemming from the war-time alliance in Asia. And when Roosevelt and Churchill had elevated the Generalissimo to heights probably beyond his due as a real force in Asia by calling him to the Cairo Conference in 1943, they added a much deeper complication to the problem of dealing with China than perhaps even they realized at the time. Crossing one bridge at a time, however, is not an unknown principle in war-time diplomacy.

The war against Japan had tended to gloss over the multiplicity of internal problems of China as well as the tenuous hold which Chiang Kai-shek had on the Mainland. The long and bitter contest between Chiang and Mao Tse-tung had been only temporarily set aside during the attacks by Japan. In the long march of the autumn of 1934, in fact, Mao and his followers had trekked to the remotest of the northwest provinces where they settled and established a new socialist state with Yen-an as its capital. The onslaught of the Japanese along the coastal provinces, moreover, ultimately drove Chiang beyond the barriers of remoteness in the southwest of China at Chungking. Therefore, as the Japanese were pushed slowly out of Eastern Asia, there began the race between the Nationalists and the Communists to fill the vacuum created by the Japanese retreat. Open civil war was inevitable.

To begin with, the Government of the Republic of China had the advantage of status due to the victory against Japan, while the Maoists had only the memory of privation and suffering during their isolation in Sinkiang Province. Chiang Kai-shek, moreover, had the additional and immeasurable advantage of hundreds of millions of dollars worth of American military supplies. In addition, Chiang held all of the major cities and seaports along the east coast while Mao had access only to the countryside. For some observers yet today it remains a major mystery how, with the discrepancy and advantages between the two sides, the Nationalists could possibly lose the country. The answer lay in part in the hearts and the minds of the Chinese people.

Mao Tse-tung skillfully played on the hopes and frustrations of the overwhelming numbers of Chinese who felt they had waited too long and that, under Chiang, events had moved too slowly. In a contradiction of Marxist techniques, Mao Tse-tung quite literally conquered the new China without a single, major city under his control. Chiang lost it because he failed to inspire the confidence of not only the man in the street but the hundreds of millions in the countryside.

The internal war for the control of China, which in a sense had been going on since Sun Yat-sen had begun the revolution in 1911, was to be waged to its conclusive stage more violently between 1945 and 1949. The role of the United States during that strife and our policy toward it remain highly controversial issues even today.

Suffice it to note that the popular caption applied to the Truman policies, as drawn and executed by his Secretary of State Dean Acheson, was described by the phrase, coined by the Secretary, "letting the dust settle." Militants in America believed that the United States should involve itself more deeply with both arms and men to insure ultimate victory by Chiang Kai-shek. Others, however, including the President and the Department of State, were convinced that a direct intervention in the interior of China could lead to far graver problems with far more serious implications from which it might be impossible to extricate the national interest. There was no certainty, as it was frequently pointed out, that such an intervention could guarantee the survival of the Nationalists. Nor could they be certain this would be a good idea even if possible.

Finally, it was highly doubtful that the American people were prepared to condone a commitment of sufficient manpower to do the job. Military experts thought the intervention would require as many as 2.5 million troops. Coming so soon after the War itself, a commitment of those dimensions would not likely have been approved by public opinion in the United States.

For this combination of reasons, then, American policy toward China remained one of "wait and see."

Only when Chiang Kai-shek was driven from the Mainland and had taken refuge on the former Chinese-held island of Formosa did American policy assert itself in a positive way. The Seventh Fleet of the American Navy was stationed in the Formosan Straits directly astride the paths between the rival Chinese forces. The presence of the Fleet, aimed at cooling off the two protagonists, became increasingly more permanent as time passed and as efforts to reconcile the difference between Mao and Chiang failed.

The upshot, of course, was the emergence of two Chinas—just as there had emerged under similar circumstances in post-war Europe two Germanys, two Berlins, and, in fact, two Europes—East and West.

That an American force—the Seventh Fleet—became the boundary line separating the two Chinas only served to intensify and emotionalize the role of the United States in Eastern Asia. Equally intense was its impact on the domestic political front in the States.

The pro-Nationalist and anti-Nationalist groups within the country often shed considerably more heat than light on the difficult questions hovering over the Straits of Formosa. There were times when it seemed that American advocates were more concerned about what was done to Mao Tse-tung than they were about what ought to be done in the best interests of the United States.

It would seem fair to say now in hindsight that two factors loom large as justification for American policy toward Taiwan during those tempestuous years. One was the residue of moral decency, if not responsibility, to protect a war-time ally from annihiliation. This involved the positioning of the American Fleet between Taiwan and the Mainland for as long as the Peking Government remained a threat to the island fortress of the Generalissimo or until the latter passed on.

A second factor, no less important, was the tactical advantage of keeping the Army of the Nationalists close to the flank of the Chinese Communists where their mere presence served as a source of worry and required the Mainland Government to commit large forces to the coastal defenses directly opposite Formosa. This was no small advantage. Whatever the cost of subsidizing the half million Nationalist troops, their existence—scarcely 100 miles from the Chinese shore—pinned down large numbers of Mao's limited army. Some estimates of the latter numbers ran as high as 1,200,000. This was a considerable shackle to the mobility of Peking's new political and military muscles. It was achieved, moreover, without new bloodshed or wanton destruction. It also won time.

The problems that the two Chinas pose for the peace in the world should not be judged out of context. The fact that one China would theoretically be better than two should not obscure the fact that such an observation would have to be qualified by the simple cautionary question, "What kind of China?" Even now—nearly twenty years after the demise of the Nationalist Government on the Mainland—the shape and the form of the new China remain fraught with uncertainties. Something, therefore, can be said for the time gained by the temporary impasse enforced by an American policy of two Chinas.

The two Chinas illustrate another expression of the balance of forces which had already drawn arbitrary lines of demarcation between the two Europes, the two Berlins, and the two Germanys. At the very worst, it remains a place to begin, somewhere short of the price of large-scale war and the heavy bloodshed of a major military campaign into the interior of China.

From this beginning, then, the China policy of the United States has remained consistent; namely, one of containment rather than destruction. The decision in the Formosan Straits with regard to the two Chinas set the tone and the guidelines of the Far Eastern policy of the United States. That there has been no serious deviation from it in nearly twenty years at least attests to its consistency and to its substance and validity as well.

Korea was destined to raise still new issues of policy. The peninsula of Korea not only represented the further outposts of Northeast Asia, but was the closest mainland thrust toward Japan. It had on several occasions represented significant, strategic importance in the early power-political conflicts in that part of the world. What happened to Korea and what kind of Korea emerged after World War II would make a difference to Japan in particular and, perhaps, to the Soviet Union and China in general. If it might affect the delicate balance of political interest, it was destined to make a political difference to the United States as well. Because it represented so early a major Japanese foothold on the mainland, it became a focal point for the repatriation of Japanese troops and the whole disentangling process of demobilization. This was a process that had been frozen by the tardy injection of Soviet troops into the war of the Pacific. Their presence increased the difficulties of restructuring the political vacuums left by the withdrawal of the Japanese and of balancing anew the competing outside interests; namely, the Russians and the Americans.

The setting was complicated still further by the race between the Mao Tse-tung troops from the northwest and the Chiang Kai-shek troops from the south toward the critical corner provinces bordering on Korea. It was in this setting, then, that the Allies in Asia agreed to a temporary demarcation line along the 38th Parallel in Korea.

As in the earlier instance of Germany and Berlin, the line was to be "temporary." Its purpose was to make separate zones of responsibility for repatriation and readjustment in the wake of the Japanese withdrawal. It was designed to intensify and speed-up the processes of getting Korea back to normal.

The result, however, was to be quite different. The 38th Parallel came to delineate the rival conflicts of interest between Moscow and Washington and to crystalize the factions of power as the two giant victors of World War II contended for the shape and form of the new balance of the world.

In that context in Asia, postwar Japan was the obvious prize. Just as the Ruhr Valley of Western Germany had been the key target of both the Russians and the Allies in their jousting for the new balance of Europe after Hitler, so the control of the industrial plant of Japan became the main goal of the Soviet Union in the Pacific. While the United States did not itself need the Japanese industrial output, it was determined that that capability should not fall into the hands of the Russians. To have permitted it to do so would have materially affected the American interests adversely in the new balance of Asia.

Korea was the major test of Soviet intentions toward Japan. It was the American policy to deny them success in that thrust. To hold along the 38th Parallel was in effect the dividing of the conflicting spheres of interest for both Moscow and Washington much the same as those conflicting interests had been divided in the two Germanys in Europe.

The 38th Parallel in Korea contained one other ingredient not present in the dividing lines in Europe, however. Its definition and drawing was within the context of the operations of the United Nations. It was, in effect, a creature of the new world organization. This injected into the controversial line a sort of worldly presence. On June 25, 1950, when the troops from North Korea forcibly crossed the 38th Parallel into the South, the theoretical dream of a revived and reunited Korea was shattered.

The issues in this newest breach of the postwar peace were simple. The most obvious was that the action constituted an open affront to the prestige of the new United Nations. Less conspicuous, but probably more fundamental, was the challenge that the new aggression posed to the chances of stability and orderly change in Eastern Asia. And finally, in the shadows of these two questions lurked the ever-present elements shaping the new balance of power around the world. It brought into sharp conflict the rival concepts of the Soviet Union and the United States in structuring the new profile of an old Asia.

For the Americans, the issue involving the United Nations seemed to loom the largest so soon after the creation of the new world organization at San Francisco in 1945. The hopes for the UN were almost unbounded. Its credentials among the citizens of the land were the highest. The general public, then, grasped the question of sustaining the prestige of the United Nations far more quickly and tightly than they fathomed the implications of the test for stability and peaceful change.

At the beginning of the Korea War, President Truman quickly exercised the precaution of consultation with the leaders of both major political parties. The anticipated dimensions of the conflict were loosely sketched, and the need for paying the price was generally agreed upon before it was even under way.

As the violence in Korea mounted and the casualty lists lengthened, the impatience of the American public soon began to manifest itself. The sheer fact that the remobilization of sufficient troops to do the job would take time did not slow down the critics who demanded immediate action. As the war entered its second year and then its third, the crescendo of strident voices dominated the national scene. Some cried for use of atomic weapons, leaving aside the moral question implicit in the demand, and not bothering to note that there were no targets of sufficient magnitude. Politicians

began to coin flippant cliches to substitute for their own inadequacies in marshalling a hard case of criticism against the war. The
"no-win" policy and "there's no substitute for victory" were two of
the cliches which quickly became substitutes for thinking.

The question which disturbed the policymakers the most, of
course, was that of China. Would the Chinese stay out? Or, was war
with China the real war which should be waged at this time? These
were uncertainties that could not be answered with finality. The
options, however, could be weighed with some degree of measurable judgments. Once it was determined that, if possible, China
should not be provoked into war and that the conflict should become a limited one for limited objectives, it became possible to
define in more public ways what the war was all about.

It was a war, the Administration said, to deny success to an
aggressor. It was a war to establish the integrity of a line drawn by
the United Nations. It was a war to guarantee stability and to insure
the chances for peaceful rather than violent change. The longer the
fighting continued, however, the louder the demands became to
"win or get out."

Some self-appointed patriots, who obviously had not bothered to
read history books, proclaimed that the USA had never lost a war
and should not begin in Korea. Some of the military spokesmen
involved in the conflict rankled with impatience at the kind of
restraints imposed upon them by "that man" in the White House,
President Harry S. Truman. The President was accused of forfeiting
the lives of American soldiers when he ordered the military not to
cross the Yalu River separating the northernmost boundaries of
North Korea from Chinese territory. More and more, in fact, the
conflict came to be called "Mr. Truman's War," a phrase which
would cause the history buffs to hark back to another war 140 years
earlier that was referred to as "Mr. Madison's War." (Today—"Mr.
McNamara's War!")

One of the Senate's most distinguished and prestigious members, Robert A. Taft of Ohio, solemnly pronounced the Korean
conflict as "an utterly useless war."[1]   Once again, the history
buffs would remind themselves that in "Mr. Madison's War"
in 1812 another very distinguished American Senator, Daniel

Webster, condemned the War of 1812 as "ruinous . . . premature and expedient."

The momentum of criticism mounted steadily. It was predictable, therefore, when a part of the focus of criticism shifted to the Government of South Korea and its composition. President Syngman Rhee was upbraided as a dictator unresponsive to the will of the people, surrounded by a selfish military clique which fomented war for its own aggrandizement. President Rhee and the generals were collectively described as being the dupes and stooges of the wealthy landlords of South Korea who pulled the strings of power in Seoul with one hand while they tightened the chains of slavery around the helpless peasants with the other.

Among the American troops, the issue of the war became a very troublesome one. Obviously, the military had failed to define adequately the war's origin or goals for the individual soldiers. It has been said that troop morale was probably the worst of any in American wars—at least in this century. Desertions, mental breakdowns, psychiatric cases reached an all-time high in proportion to the total number of troops sent to Korea.

Some of the military leaders involved reflected their own frustrations by suggesting that we ought to go all-out in the war—meaning we should attack airbases and supply depots in nearby China from which the enemy in the north was obviously receiving the main source of its help. President Truman felt that the advantage which this might bring was outweighed by the risk of either direct warfare with the Soviet Union or massive intervention by the Chinese—perhaps even both. It was this uncertainty which set the stage for the ultimate showdown between the General of the Armies, Douglas MacArthur, and the President of the United States, Harry S. Truman.

MacArthur advised the country there were no risks of Chinese intervention—that his lines of intelligence assured him that the Chinese did not want war. But another five-star General, Omar Bradley, warned the President heavily against that kind of involvement, describing a war with China at the moment as "the wrong war, in the wrong place, at the wrong time, with the wrong people." Bradley saw the war more as a test of Soviet strength than as a showdown with Peking.

But more than the disagreement in interpreting enemy intentions or its implications, this new crisis represented one of those rare tests in our history of the meaning of the Constitution in its definitions of Executive Power in times of crisis. Students of the Constitution contended that the decision of the President as Commander-in-Chief was not only being called into question, but was being openly defied by General MacArthur. Therefore, superceding the issue of the dimensions of the war was this new issue of Presidential Power.

President Truman faced the issue squarely and courageously by summarily dismissing General MacArthur. This action went far toward stabilizing the Constitutional framework of Executive authority which is most important. But it also aggravated the emotions of dissident groups who were unhappy with the course of events in Korea. The cleavages produced by Korea probably did much to affect the outcome of the Presidential elections of 1952. But those same elections did little to change the nature of the war.

President-elect Dwight Eisenhower kept his campaign promise of going to Korea, but he failed to change the Truman thesis that this had to be fought as a limited war, with limited objectives. What's more, the new President—shackled with taking the consequences for other decisions which some of his cohorts had promised during the campaign—refused as the Chief Executive to "unleash Chiang Kai-shek." To have done so, he found out, would have been to spread the conflict in Asia in unlimited ways to unlimited places. It was not in the American interest to do so.

Even the voice of President Eisenhower, however, was not enough to stifle the critics who now demanded that the Americans put the Nationalist Chinese troops on the Mainland to confront the Communist forces of Mao Tse-tung. Thus, Korea was now provoking the prospect of a wider war with China.

Curiously, some of the same voices who condemned the action in Korea as committing too many American boys too far away, in the next breath advocated whatever commitment was necessary to put Chiang Kai-shek back in his homeland.

This contradiction of arguments was to become commonplace after Korea. It seemed to spring from the types of deep emotions invariably triggered by the big questions of Asia. Korea would not be the last of the platforms for those who wanted to have it both ways—depending upon which happens to fit their unreasoned feelings best.

The firing of General MacArthur stabilized, even so, the public concept of the presidency and the role of the Chief Executive in time of war as Commander-in-Chief. The election of General Eisenhower tended to stabilize enough public hostility toward the war to make its subsidence through a temporary truce agreement a reality. Some students of the Korea question doubt that a Truman, or even an Adlai Stevenson, could have sold the concept of a limited truce settlement to the Senate or to the public at large and that, therefore, the election of General Eisenhower achieved the Truman objectives in a way that fate might have denied to President Truman himself.

Be that as it may, the point is that the United States waged successfully its first limited war and prevailed in the ultimate truce in sustaining the principle over which the conflict had begun, the preservation of the 38th Parallel. Although a peace treaty has never been signed in Korea, an uneasy peace has prevailed—at least until recent months. The American presence remains along the 38th Parallel, moreover, very much as the American military presence remains in Europe—even though the shooting is only scattered. It is becoming the kind of continuing presence which we have learned to expect and with which we are learning to live.

The hope prevailed that, with the American presence and under an umbrella of American guarantee, South Korea at least might have a chance to restructure its own government, stabilize its own economy, and shape its own political future. Whether those tests could be met would have to be determined by the years which followed the truce at Panmunjom.

Hopefully, as South Korea might achieve stability, so also might time erode the deep difference between the North and the South. This, in any case, was the thesis which underlay the American presence. Peaceful change toward united Korea was to be preferred to violent change under the domination of an aggressor.

Following the Korea truce, there was a protracted period of time unpunctuated by major crises until 1960. It was as though the world were catching its breath in the wake of an intense period of

Cold War which had stretched across both Europe and Asia during the preceding fifteen years. Rather than the dawn of the millennium, however, the relative quiet of the late 1950's turned out to be the "calm before the storm."

The election of John F. Kennedy to the Presidency in 1960 coincided with the emergence of a new series of power-political crises. Whether it stemmed from the curiosity of the Russians to test the mettle of this new, young leader, or whether those on the other side felt that they had not only regrouped but marshaled sufficient fresh strength to renew the tests of the Cold War remains the subject of disagreement. The problem is to fit these new incidents of crisis into the perspective of this period of American foreign policy.

From the Kennedy-Khrushchev confrontation in Vienna in June, 1961 to the new and more critical crisis in Berlin in August, from the point of tension in Laos where 250,000 Chinese Communist troops massed on the Laos frontier to the nuclear-missile rattling by Castro and Khrushchev in Cuba in 1962, a new tempo of testing nerves in the arena of power politics was launched in the decade of the 1960's.

Whereas the American containment of China had been clearly marked in Eastern Asia as a result of the two Chinas and the two Koreas, this was only one side of that vast land mass held together loosely under the name of China. Containing the other three sides was partially a unilateral decision to be made by the Russians and partially to be regulated by the whims of Mahatma Ghandi's legacy—India—in the subcontinent of Asia.

The Soviet Union had deep historic roots of rivalry along the 4,150 miles she shared with China. The bitterness of their rivalry was attested to in the bloodiness of their common history.

By the 1950's the resurgence of these historic differences was conspicuous. It started by placing strains on Sino-Soviet relations and ended with all but an open break between the two governments. Particularly in the Provinces of outer Mongolia and Sinkiang, this took the form of open violence—shooting incidents between border guards and rather more substantial blood-lettings involving entire villages. The net effect was to restrain the outward movement of Chinese power to the north and west.

What would happen in the Himalayan mountain vastness of Tibet and the former Indian provinces of Nepal and Sikkim and Ladakh still had to be tested. The less-conspicuous Chinese thrust into Tibet in October, 1950 was to afford the first case study. On the record, one would have to say that the history of the newly independent India did not augur well for a military stance to thwart the expanding Chinese. Mahatma Ghandi, the inspiring Eminence of the Indian resolution, established his policies in the realm of non-violence and pacifism. The successor to Ghandi, Jawaharlal Nehru, was little different. He, too, seemed more obsessed with the principles of non-violence in Asia than with the prospect of a direct military confrontation along the 2,000 miles of border which he shared with China. The militant presence of Chinese troops looking through the Karakoram Pass into India above Ladakh or viewing from the Himalayan peaks near Nepal and Sikkim across to the alluvial plains of this rich part of India was a fact with which neither Ghandi nor Nehru had ever before had to come to terms.

Not so by 1962. Remembering Nehru's comments to me that it was probably going to take a direct assault upon India's borders to shock her into the facts of international life in Asia, (see pp. 17-18) it is interesting to note the quickness of his response to this new threat. He appealed to the United States for military assistance. Planes, guns, and other war materials were high on his order list.

Ultimately, a half million Indian troops were deployed along the Sino-Indian border. The Americans, reacting promptly, sent to their sometime-friend in New Delhi automatic weapons, light artillery, ammunition, and twelve aircraft to transport supplies and evacuate casualties. The concern over a common threat drove the often-quarreling Indians and Americans together in support of a common policy—that of containing China.

The result of this collaboration was the blunting of the Chinese thrust and the humbling of the Chinese in the Indian defiance of the Peking confrontation of October, 1962. Here, then, in the west and southwest of China a policy of containment was serving to curb whatever intentions the masterminds in Peking may have had.

There remained to be settled the status of the confusing political vacuum of Southeast Asia. President Eisenhower and his Secretary of State John Foster Dulles had already made public their misgivings in regard to the area—misgivings that turned out to be more prophetic.

The main thrust of strategic importance in the postwar Pacific area was to focus on the opposite ends of a long arc which stretched from the Korean-Japanese complex in the north to the rich raw material supply sources in Southeast Asia. If the industrial power of a future Japan was to be the key prize in Asia, the raw materials input for that industrial complex were certainly the second priority. It is not without point that Japan's principal move after the attack on Pearl Harbor was to occupy the key areas of Southeast Asia. Rubber, tin, oil, bauxite, and rice—among other resources—represented a rich prize of immeasurable value in the potential scales of power in Eastern Asia.

It was in these terms that the Government of the United States regarded the future disposal of the areas of Southeast Asia as of vital concern to its national interest.

In March, 1954, Secretary Dulles called for "united action" by the Allies and the employment of "whatever means" were required to meet the threat of Communism in Southeast Asia. "This might," he said, "involve serious risks, but these risks are far less than would face us a few years from now if we are not resolute today." One month later President Eisenhower remarked that the loss of Laos or Indochina could be compared to falling dominoes. He said, "You have a row of dominoes set up, you knock over the first one, and what will happen to the last one is the certainty that it will go over very quickly."[2]

Tiny Laos became the locale for a new type of threat—infiltration from without and subversion from within. Strong and direct assists from Peking made the crisis an explosive one. Even though the Sino-Soviet policy-makers were engaged in what was then called a "softline" policy, the tactics just mentioned were accelerated.

The Chinese set up camps and schools at Kunming and elsewhere for the sole purpose of instructing Southeast Asian nationals in the fine art of infiltration.

To see if that training was to be effective, they chose to test it in Laos and Vietnam, mainly during the period of 1949 through the Geneva Conference in 1962, although there was a slackening of their activities when Premier Souvanna Phouma attempted to form a coalition government with his Communist half-brother Souphanouvong and the Pathet Lao in 1957. The Communists stepped up their activity, however, with the collapse of the Phouma Government in late 1957; and subject only to priorities of aggression in Vietnam, they have continued to operate in Laos ever since.

The upshot of the testing in Laos was a "negotiated settlement" at Geneva in 1962. For those who may place their faith in such exercises, the fighting and the penetration of Laos subsided only on one side. The other side has not lived up to it. In fact, several thousand cadres, trained by Hanoi, still refuse to leave the eastern districts which lie along the Ho Chi Minh Trail.

Whatever stalemate may have been reached elsewhere in Laos is directly attributable to the United States' willingness to risk a commitment of 5,000 Marines which were landed in Thailand in May, 1962 and rushed to the Mekong Valley where that meandering river separates Laos from Thailand. This show of force at least prevented the total deterioration of the imperfect balance among three Laotian power centers.

The decision to chance a negotiated settlement that was unbacked by force of arms was governed in part by the realization that there were no good standing grounds in Laos—that the problems of supply and troop positioning were too much to the advantage of the other side. Whatever stand the United States should decide to make in that part of the world, it was thought, ought to be made along the China Sea where the American preponderance of sea power and air power could be operated to the maximum advantage. Laos, nonetheless, represented a further American thrust against the outward pressures of a restless China.

Just as the Seventh Fleet in the Formosan Straits and the 50,000 American troops along the 38th Parallel in Korea had represented the key underpinnings to the new containment of China, so our presence in Laos carried this policy further around her rim.

From the Plain of Jars in Laos it is but a short distance to Thailand, Cambodia, and Vietnam. The distance from the Meo tribesmen in Southern Laos to the Montagnard in Vietnam is indistinguishable. They reside irrespective of national boundary in all of that compacted region.

But before turning to Vietnam, this is an appropriate point at which to assess from whence we have come in Asia since the end of World War II.

Remembering again the debacle that was Asia in the wake of the War, we are better able to judge the distance we have travelled since.

Japan, in ruins. China, convulsed by contradictory movements. Korea, poverty stricken and divided. The Philippines, venturing upon an unlikely new political experiment in self-government amidst the ruins of Huk guerrilla warfare. Malaysia, torn by Communist guerrilla insurrection. And the rest of Southeast Asia, a gaping political vacuum bearing only the wreckage of outmoded colonial empires. By comparison, in 1945, the devastation of Western Europe looked hopeful and promising indeed when compared to the debacle that was Eastern Asia. In the perspective of the last twenty years, therefore, the changes in Eastern Asia are worth noting.

Japan, restructured by a constitution heavily influenced by the American conqueror, divested herself of centuries of imperial worship. She has now become the fourth largest industrial power of the world.

In China, the Communists have survived at least and appear to be there to stay in one form or another. After nearly twenty years, the Communism of the Mainland Chinese has become a fact of life. The tempestuous changes raging within her borders seem centered not on whether to keep the system, but rather on who is to command the system. The "other" China has become a stable, reformed regime on a prosperous Taiwan. Neither of the two Chinas is currently able to get in the other's hair.

South Korea has become a hopeful symbol of economic, social, and political reform. The redistribution of land ownership, the institution of the vast new educational system, the introduction of a growing industrial base in what used to be an isolated, rural outpost, and the emergence of stable government—with generals making the transition from the military to civilian control with some success— altogether constitute a near miracle.

That the outcome in Korea remains uncertain was pointed up by the Pueblo Incident in the winter of 1968. The flexing of muscles, the straining of tempers, and the testing of policies were all brought to the fore. Its outcome to date has pointed up the American determination to contain rather than to destroy the pressures north of the 38th Parallel and to stand by its earlier commitment to the government of South Korea.

Taiwan now constitutes a showplace of Asia, an excellent example of what can be done in an underdeveloped country. The Taiwanese now earn their way in the world, enjoy a high living standard in terms of their Asian neighbors.

Thailand, the only one of the tiny kingdoms in Southeast Asia to avoid colonial status, has not only maintained her historic independence but has begun to prosper as a modern self-sufficient, economic society.

Malaysia successfully put down the challenge of the guerrilla revolutionaries. She has also survived the challenge of her near-neighbor, Indonesia, and has achieved a relatively stable governmental structure.

Indonesia, the fifth largest nation in the world (population-wise), has successfully weathered the storm of an attempted Chinese Communist takeover. The union between the Indonesian Communist Party, the PKI, and the father of Indonesian Independence, Sukarno, has been thwarted in its efforts to convert the Indonesian experiment into a vast Communist state.

In Djakarta and, indeed, in the 3,000-mile long string of islands, it is a brand new ball game. The military junta even now makes its plans for the transition to regular elections and civilian controls. The new Legislature, with the junta, has tightened its economic belt and has started to come to grips with the runaway inflation and has already begun to set up incentives for foreign capital once again to return to the richly endowed Indies.

In retrospect, I suggest that the historians of the future will be likely to regard the war in Korea as the turning point of American policy in Eastern Asia. Korea becomes the "Berlin" of the Far East.

And to paraphrase the Churchillian comment on the American stand in Berlin, it might fairly be said that because the Americans stood on the 38th Parallel in Korea, the rest of Asia will have a chance—in the long run—to shape their own destinies and to enforce and to administer their own balance and stability.

From this point of assessment, therefore, it is possible to array the troubling violence of the present in Southeast Asia alongside the significant progress which American policy has made possible in Asia. What it says is that even now we are coming measurably closer to the end of what has been a long and tortuous road leading all the way from World War II to the present. This is the point along that road at which we find ourselves in Vietnam. Vietnam, as can be seen from this quick survey, is cut from the same cloth as Berlin, the two-China policy, and the two Koreas. This constitutes the crux of the answer to the question, "Why Vietnam?"

The more specific answers to the questions "Why South Vietnam?" or "Why two Vietnams?" lie in the diplomacy of the Geneva Conference of 1954. What happened at Geneva and, perhaps more importantly, what did not happen at Geneva, are factors which continue to stimulate many of the misconceptions in the dialogues on Vietnam.

It is important, therefore, that we take a close look at events at Geneva from May to July, 1954.

CHAPTER V

The Geneva Conference—1954

The Geneva Conference of 1954 was colored by the events in Korea. Not to relate the Korean War with the Geneva meeting is to fail to capture the atmosphere which prevailed in Geneva.

Soon after the July, 1953 armistice at Panmunjom, Korea, the Viet Minh in northern Vietnam began to receive large quantities of military equipment from both the Russians and the Chinese. Many advisers from Peking moved in at the same time. Although few recognized it at the time, the stage was already being set for Dien Bien Phu.

Both the Americans and the British proceeded with their plan for the Geneva discussions with a sense of impending crisis. The showdown was scheduled to begin on April 26, 1954.

In preparation for the Geneva meeting the United States sought to assess the implications of the strong military offensive by the Viet Minh which continued unabated as the April deadline approached. Secretary of State John Foster Dulles expressed concern that the only settlement to which the Communists at the forthcoming conference might agree would be one permitting them to take over *all* of Vietnam along with Laos and Cambodia. In other words, the Americans were apprehensive about the prospects for any kind of compromise or "give and take" that could reflect the basic differences between the two sides.

The Secretary of State believed, for example, that the future shape of all Southeast Asia would be largely conditioned by the nature of the compromise to be worked out in Geneva. If the Viet Minh groups in the North were to succeed through military successes in imposing their formula for taking all of the related territories, it conceivably would pose a threat to the existence of the rest of the countries in Southeast Asia.

With this in mind, Secretary Dulles undertook to lay the groundwork for the Southeast Asia Treaty Organization (SEATO) as a counter-development to the drive by the Viet Minh in northern Vietnam, Laos, and Cambodia. The United States approached the Geneva Conference determined to avoid, if possible, a Viet Minh-dominated Southeast Asia.

President Eisenhower in a news conference on April 7, 1954, expressed concern that the loss of Indochina to this new force of imperialism would cause other neighboring Asian governments to fall, as he put it, "... like a set of dominoes falling one against the other."

The United States delegate to the Indochina negotiations was instructed,

> "to assist in arriving at decisions which will help the nations of Indochina (Vietnam, Laos, and Cambodia) peacefully to enjoy territorial integrity and to expand their economies, to realize their legitimate national aspirations, and to develop security through individual and collective defense against aggression, from within and without. This implies that their people should not be amalgamated into the communist block. . . ."

Subsequently, Secretary Dulles (July 15, 1954) further explained the American goals. We went to Geneva, he said,

> "... concerned to find a way whereby we could help France, Vietnam, Laos and Cambodia find acceptable settlement without in any way prejudicing basic principles to which the United States must adhere if it is to be true to itself and if the captive and endangered peoples of the world are to feel that the United States really believes in liberty."

By the eve of the talks, United States officials had decided that an acceptable settlement for Vietnam would include:

(1) International control machinery set up and ready to function *before* the ceasefire came into force.

(2) Guarantee of "unrestricted movement in and free access to *all* of Indochina" for representatives of the International Control Commission. The United Nations was recommended for responsibility for supervising the Commission, although some other form of international supervision might be acceptable.

(3) Guarantees against abuse of the ceasefire and provisions for the security of both troops and people.

(4) Liberation of prisoners of war and of civilian internees.

(5) Examination of political and economic problems *after* conclusion of the armistice agreement.

In the final settlement, the United States viewed the international control machinery as critical to a successful compromise. It was the American judgment, moreover, that the settlement should contain no provisions for "early elections, or for troop withdrawals that would clearly lead to a takeover" [by force].

Geneva Conference–The Korean Phase (April 26-May 7, 1954)

The Conference opened in the Palais des Nations on April 26, 1954, to deal first with the problem of a permanent settlement in Korea.

The discussions were held in the midst of sudden intensification of the war in Indochina. The Viet Minh, apparently receiving greatly increased aid from China, had regrouped their forces around the French stronghold at Dien Bien Phu–a strategic point covering lines of communication linking northern Vietnam with China and Laos.

The French Commander at Dien Bien Phu surrendered to the Viet Minh on May 7, less than two weeks after the conference had begun in Geneva. The loss of this critical fortress precipitated general military collapse of the French in Vietnam. On May 8 the delegates at the conference shifted to a discussion of Indochina without reaching final agreement on Korea. (The Korean conversations dragged along one way or another until June 15 with no further success.)

Participants in the specific discussions on Indochina were France, the French-sponsored State of Vietnam (South), the Viet Minh's Democratic Republic of Vietnam (North), Laos, Cambodia,

Communist China, the Soviet Union, the United Kingdom, and the United States. The United Kingdom and the USSR, in the persons of Foreign Secretary Anthony Eden and Foreign Minister Vyacheslov Molotov, presided as Co-chairmen.

Other heads of delegations were: France, Foreign Minister Georges Bidault, (later replaced by Premier Pierre Mendes-France); State of Vietnam (South), Foreign Minister Nguyen Quoc Dinh, (replaced by Foreign Minister Tran Van Do); Democratic Republic of Viet Nam (North), Deputy Premier Pham Van Dong; China, Foreign Minister Chou En-lai; United States, Under Secretary of State W. Bedell Smith. (Secretary of State Dulles had appeared briefly for the opening ceremonies, but it had been understood from the outset that Smith would carry the responsibility.)

The official discussions of the conference were carried on during the eight plenary and twenty-three restricted sessions and lasted almost eleven weeks (May 8-July 21).

Major areas of debate revolved around the timing and supervision of the ceasefire; choice of areas for regrouping of military forces; foreign military aid after the ceasefire; general elections; the composition, procedures, and control of an international supervisory body; and the post-conference responsibilities of the nations participating in the truce.

So many of the major talks were carried on informally, behind-the-scenes, and off-the-record that it is impossible to spell out with careful detail the decision-making process as it emerged in its final terms at Geneva. What the record does show, however, is that the conference issued *separate* armistice agreements for the *three* Indochinese states–a conference declaration and two unilateral declarations each by Cambodia, Laos, and France. An amendment to the conference declaration by the State of Vietnam (South) and a unilateral declaration by the United States were noted by the conference but were not listed as official documents.

A comparison of the initial proposals by France, the Viet Minh, and the State of Vietnam with the final settlement agreed to does reveal in part the extent of the compromise achieved. When the Indochina talks began on May 8, France called for,

(1) Disarmament of all irregular forces [e.g. guerrillas],

(2) A regrouping of all regular forces in areas to be defined by the conference,

(3) Immediate release of all prisoners of war and civilian internees,

(4) Supervision of the implementation of the armistice agreement by an international commission.

The French then advocated that all of the states participating at Geneva were to guarantee the agreement. A violation, in their view, would call for immediate consultation among them "for the purpose of taking appropriate measures *either individual or collectively.*"

In contrast, the Viet Minh proposals included,

(1) Recognition by France of Vietnamese independence,

(2) Withdrawal of all foreign troops,

(3) Free elections supervised by *"local commissions"* without any "interference from the outside,"

(4) Agreement by both sides *not to prosecute* collaborationists.

The essence of the difference in the two sets of proposals rested on the concept of supervising the enforcement of the terms. The French stressed supervision by outside forces. The Viet Minh stressed local and internal agencies.

In Washington, Secretary Dulles said in his news conference on May 11 that the Viet Minh proposals added up to the same formula that had been used by the Communists in Germany, Austria, and Korea;

> "Namely, to compel a withdrawal of the forces which sustain a free society and to set up a system under which the Communists can grab the whole area."

Meanwhile, the State of Vietnam submitted its basic proposals on May 12. These included,

(1) Full independence for Vietnam,

(2) Guarantees for security,

(3) A united Vietnam underwritten by national control,

(4) Recognition of the Bao Dai regime as the only legal government,

(5) Acceptance of a single army by incorporating Viet Minh soldiers into the national army,

(6) Free elections under UN supervision *when the Security Council determined that the state exercised authority throughout its territory and that freedom really existed,*

(7) Amnesty for collaborationists,

(8) International guarantees of the political and territorial integrity of Vietnam.

Among the great powers, the United States and the United Kingdom delegates generally approved the French proposals while the Soviet and Chinese representatives backed the Viet Minh demands. Molotov went further, moreover, by denying that there was internal strife or civil war in Vietnam. He insisted that the Viet Minh was the only legitimate government.

Despite a number of accusations and distortions during the early meetings, all of the participants appeared anxious that a peaceful settlement be concluded. They all agreed in principal, moreover, that implementation of the ceasefire should be supervised by joint committees of the two sides and by a neutral international commission. They also agreed that the final settlement should be guaranteed in some way by the Geneva powers.

The delegates from the Communist governments strove further to apply the terms to *all* of Indochina rather than limiting them to Vietnam. Apparently they anticipated that the recent military successes of the Viet Minh might help them to achieve a takeover of both Laos and Cambodia as well. France, Great Britain, and the United States, however, insisted that the conflict in Vietnam could not be dealt with on the same basis as the Viet Minh invasions in Laos and Cambodia. And, therefore, the latter two issues should be kept separate. This was the principle finally agreed to by the competing sides at Geneva.

Understandably, the discussions seemed to bog down during considerations of controls over and guarantees of whatever agreements might be reached. During June and July, wide differences of opinion emerged on these questions:

Which countries should comprise the neutral commission?

Could a Communist nation be regarded as a neutral state?

Would UN supervision be enforceable?

Should the joint (military) committees operate under the control of the international commission?

Should the neutral commission have free access to all parts of the country at all times?

What role should the Geneva participants play as guarantor states?

As the debates over these questions seemed to be getting nowhere, the principal heads of delegations left Geneva—at least temporarily. The work of the Conference continued at lower echelons.

During this de-escalation of the diplomatic efforts, Prime Minister Winston Churchill and Anthony Eden came to Washington to meet with President Eisenhower and Secretary Dulles. A joint communication dispatched to the new French Government, dated June 29, stated the willingness of the two countries to respect an armistice for Vietnam which would preserve at least the southern half; did not impose any restrictions impairing the independence of the southern half in maintaining its own regime, especially in maintaining adequate forces for internal security to import arms and to employ foreign advisers; did not contain political provisions which would risk loss of the retained area to the North; *did not exclude the possibility of reunification by peaceful means;* provided for peaceful transfer under international supervision of Vietnamese civilians desiring to move from one zone to another; and established effective machinery for international supervision of the agreement. The new government of Mendes-France agreed that it would not accept new terms at Geneva which failed to meet those points.

By this time, it was clear what the core of American concern had become. As Dulles had said in his May 11 press conference, the formula insisted upon by the Viet Minh closely resembled the formulae of the Communist proposals which had sought to exploit divisions of eastern Europe at the end of the war. Whatever considerations influenced the details of the final compromise agreement, the government of the United States was determined that those details should not contribute to the takeover of Southeast Asia or, as a consequence, to a Viet Minh seizure of all of Vietnam. This concern became strong enough that at one point in mid-summer 1954 the United States actually contemplated withdrawing from the Geneva Conference or at least of receding to the position of "observer" and with a much lower level of representation at the conference table. Both the French and the British were told by Secretary Dulles that his Government could not be put in the position of approving "the sale of Indochina into Communist captivity." At the behest of the French, however, Dulles did agree that the Americans would not effect a dramatic withdrawal which might in other ways jeopardize the chance for some kind of settlement.

On the afternoon of July 18 Chou En-lai suggested to Anthony Eden that the controversial supervisory commission be made up of a representative from India, Poland, and Canada. As the British Foreign Secretary later wrote, " ... from that moment the tangled ends of the negotiations began to sort themselves out."[1]

By the afternoon of the 20th, Mendes-France and the Viet Minh delegate were able to announce that they had reached an agreement on a demarcation line. The Viet Minh had originally demanded that the line be drawn at the 13th Parallel, while France had insisted on the 18th. The DRVN, moreover, had also pushed for elections to be held within a matter of six months at the most. The compromise, however, drew the line along the Ben Hai River, just south of the 17th Parallel. It also stipulated that elections should not be held until July, 1956, two years hence. The agreement was signed by the Viet Minh and the commander-in-chief of the French forces in Indochina on July 21 (about 3 a.m.).

Although the State of Vietnam's delegate was accepted during the conference as an official representative, he had in fact had no voice in the closed discussions which hammered out the final armistice agreement. The final ratification was completed later that same day (July 21, 1954), being ratified by a voice vote only.

Tran Van Do of the State of Vietnam protested the "reject without examination" of the Vietnamese proposal for an armistice without partitioning the country. He also protested the "private" agreement reached solely by the French and Viet Minh as well as the surrender of certain territories north of the 17th Parallel to the DRVN. The spokesman for the State of Vietnam stressed, moreover, that his Government would not be bound by any agreement in which they had not participated. He reserved for his people their "full freedom of action in order to safeguard the sacred right of the Vietnamese peoples to territorial unity, national independence, and freedom." He singled out in particular the arbitrary fixing of a date for elections without the prior agreement of the State of Vietnam's delegation.

Under Secretary of State Bedell Smith submitted a unilateral declaration of the United States position. This stated that, while the Americans were not prepared to join in the final agreement, they would "refrain from the threat or the use of force to disturb them." Moreover, it would,

> *"View any renewal of the aggression in violation of the aforesaid agreements with grave concern and as seriously threatening international peace and security."*

Regarding the proposed elections in Vietnam, the United States statement said,

> "In the case of nations now divided against their will, we shall continue to seek to achieve *unity through free elections supervised by the United Nations* to insure that they are conducted fairly."

The declaration concluded with a reiteration of what it called the "traditional position" of the American Government; namely, "that peoples are entitled to determine their own future and that it will not join in an arrangement which would hinder this."

At the wind-up of the conference, Anthony Eden as Co-chairman said,

> "We have now come to the end of our work. . . . The Agreements concluded today could not in the nature of things give complete satisfaction to everyone. But they have made it possible to stop a war which has lasted for eight years and brought suffering and hardship to millions of people. They have also . . . reduced international tension at a point of instant danger to world peace. . . . All will now depend upon the spirit in which those agreements are now observed and carried out."

Later that same day, President Eisenhower stated in Washington,

> "The United States has in itself not been party to, or bound by, the decisions taken by the conference, but it is our hope that it will lead to the establishment of peace consistent with the rights and the needs of the countries concerned."

The final document is comprised of 47 Articles, divided into six chapters, and an annex.

Chapter I dealt with the establishment of a "provisional territory demarcation line" near the 17th Parallel in central Vietnam and a 5-kilometer Demilitarized Zone on either side of it. The forces of the Peoples' Army of Vietnam were to withdraw and regroup at the north of the line; and the forces of the French Union, to the south. The mutual withdrawals were to be completed within 300 days.

Chapter II instructed both sides to order and enforce a complete end to hostilities. Among the administrative measures in this section were the following of importance:

(A) "Pending the general elections which will bring about the unification of Vietnam, the conduct of civil administration in each regrouping zone shall be in the hands of the party whose forces are to be regrouped there."

This said simply that north of the 17th Parallel the DRVN was to be the responsible governing agency and that south of that line the State of Vietnam would be responsible. It should be noted that the only mention of reunifying elections to appear anywhere in the armistice agreement was in this simple statement.

A second key paragraph in Chapter II said:

(B) "Each party undertakes to refrain from any reprisals or discrimination against persons or programs on account of their activities during the hostilities and to guarantee their democratic liberties."

This was to assume greater significance as the subsequent activities in the north lead to the elimination of political opposition leaders and to the fleeing of other large groups of refugees to the south.

Still another significant passage specified,

(C) "Until the movement of troops is completed [within 300 days] any civilians residing in a district controlled by one party who wish to go and live in the zone assigned to the other party shall be permitted and helped to do so by the authorities in that district."

It is this section of the final Agreement which produced what later emerged as a determining separation of the two Vietnams. It also makes clear what was violated and by whom in thwarting the tentative agreements to hold free elections for purposes of reunification. It contains the root of the explanation for the failure to hold those elections; namely, the violation of these stipulated terms by the regime in the north.

Chapter III has been referred to as the heart of the agreement. In it, the introduction of additional armed forces or weapons into Vietnam was prohibited, although the rotation of troops and the replacement of worn-out material would be permitted. It was specified further that "no military base under the control of a foreign state may be established," and it bound the two Vietnams to insure that the zones assigned to them "do not adhere to any military alliance *or further an aggressive policy.*"

The Fourth Chapter contained instructions for the liberation and repatriation of prisoners of war.

Chapter V included the stipulation that the agreement should apply to *all the armed forces of either party;* i.e., regular and irregular. Each side was to inspect the Demilitarized Zone and the territory of the other zone and *"shall undertake no operation against the other party and shall not engage in blockade of any kind in Vietnam."*

The Sixth and final Chapter of the agreement set up two Commissions. One, the International Control Commission, was composed of India, Canada, and Poland with India presiding. It was to supervise the execution of the armistice agreement. It was *to have unquestioned access to all places* with fixed teams at ports of entry and mobile teams to operate along the sea and land borders, along the lines of demarcation, and in the Demilitarized Zone. The second, a joint commission composed of the representatives of the two opposing armies, was created to insure the execution of the provisions relating to the ceasefire, regroupment, and Demilitarized Zone.

The Annex to the Agreement simply contained specifications for the demarcation line, the Demilitarized Zone, and the regroupment areas.

As the Geneva Conference wound-up its deliberations, it adopted an Agreement summarizing the intent of the armistice points. The declaration stressed the importance of full independence and sovereignty for Cambodia, Laos, and Vietnam. It stressed, moreover, that the Armistice Agreement was meant to settle the military questions. "The military demarcation line is provisional and *should not in any way be interpreted as constituting a political or territorial boundary."* It was viewed as creating the necessary basis for a political settlement to follow.

A separate paragraph went on to specify the nature of the political settlement. It said in part that the final agreements "should permit the Vietnamese people to enjoy the fundamental freedoms guaranteed by democratic institutions established as a result of free general elections by secret ballot." General elections were to get under way two years hence with preliminary consultations on staging them to begin a year in advance.

The conclusions of the Conference left no one satisfied. Of the protracted deliberations, the best that can be said is that many look back upon them with relief—that they lay behind, not ahead. Among the compromises, it can be seen now with the advantage of hindsight that most of the ingredients for a peaceful solution to the crisis in Southeast Asia had been included. The terms of the military armistice were sufficient to cover the realignment of force and power during the gradual withdrawal of the French.

The Demilitarized Zone along the 17th Parallel, moreover, left no doubt as to the transitional responsibilities for carrying out the agreement of the Conference. And if the stipulations about staging "free" elections under "democratic" conditions were lived up to, the chances for a united Vietnam getting under way as an independent nation were promising indeed.

The test would be the willingness of the signatories to live up to the terms of the Agreements.

CHAPTER VI

Vietnam After Geneva—1954-1968

The obvious focal point of the Geneva Agreements was the move toward general elections for reunification of the country. What happened to the plans for those elections constitutes a very large measure of the disputes in the United States today over who did what to whom and for what reasons.

At the outset it ought to be remembered that both the Viet Minh, speaking for the DRVN regime, and the spokesmen for the State of Vietnam in the south were agreed upon one point—that there should be a united, rather than ᵃ divided, country. Their disagreement stemmed from who should do the uniting; which group should be the recognized governing authority. The Communists in the North specifically had obtained at Geneva only half of what they had demanded and what they felt they were in a position to insist upon because of the success of their military compaigns against the French. Their hopes for getting all of Vietnam under their control, therefore, rested on the opening providing for the staging of free elections.

In 1955 the DRVN Government launched a massive propaganda campaign for a general election on reunification "as agreed at Geneva." Hanoi chose to ignore the fact that South Vietnam had refused to associate itself with the final declaration largely because of the specifications for holding new elections. The new Diem government in Saigon steadfastly refused to consult with the Hanoi regime to prepare the way for elections in 1956.

While it is popular in hindsight to poke fun at Diem's opposition to free elections, his adamant position is not without point. The final Geneva Agreements had specified *free* elections under democratic conditions. In the North it was already obvious even to neutral observers that conditions of personal freedom did not exist.

What's more, political freedom in terms of opposition parties and groups was not tolerated. From the view in Saigon it made no sense to hold elections which were relatively free in the South at the same time that they were closed out in the North. The consequence would be no elections at all but would represent simply a device for delivering the South into the hands of its more populous neighbors in the North.

Even the brilliant Defense Minister of North Vietnam, General Giap, admitted the high-handedness of his government in eliminating political opposition. In an address to the Tenth Congress of the North Vietnamese Communist Party in October, 1956, Giap publicly acknowledged the emergence of a police state run by Hanoi:

> "We have . . . executed too many honest people. . . . Seeing enemies everywhere, we resorted to terror, which became far too widespread. . . . We failed to respect the principles of freedom of faith and worship. . . . Torture came to be regarded as a normal practice. . . . "

Under those circumstances the necessary preconditions for holding any kind of reasonable elections had failed to materialize. This is why it is important for those critics today to have another look in hindsight at the circumstances which shattered the Geneva Agreements.

It is one thing to argue that Vietnam should have been abandoned to whatever its fate at the hands of Ho Chi Minh, but it is quite something else to argue that free elections were not held because of some thwarting of the process by the policy of the United States. The American Government had reiterated again and again its interest in a united Vietnam, but it had also stressed that the unification must be accompanied by a free expression of the Vietnamese themselves. It takes a torturing of one's powers of rationality to believe that a free expression would have been permitted or could have been taken in the North. It is not without point, moreover, that—for better or for worse—the South has managed a succession of election tests. Even these efforts, however, have failed to satisfy the critics who chose to find in those tests elements of dishonesty or "rigging." The stark contrast between *no* elections in the North and at least an attempt toward an election process in the South should speak for itself. For critics to nitpick the details of abuse or the limitations of success in the South is to strain the whole point beyond either fairness or rationality.

What it says in fact is that country-wide elections could not have been held in 1956 and, therefore, the temporary military armistice which drew the 17th Parallel became a permanent, political separation of two Vietnams. It happened almost precisely in the same way that the transitional military lines separating two Berlins, two Germanys, and two Koreas were transformed into territorial lines and national boundaries.

The misgivings of Secretary Dulles expressed in May of 1954 seemed to have been borne out by 1956.

It is this fact of life in Vietnam which has to be the starting point for a reasonable assessment of the directions for American policy in that area. Nor should we forget that, throughout the Geneva Conference and following it, the Hanoi Government never deviated from its often-declared intention of "liberating" the South and taking it by force. At no point was there any indication that North Vietnam ever intended to abide by agreements, declarations, or truces which would give them anything less than *all* of Vietnam.

Consistent with this aim by Hanoi, a rash of violations of the Geneva Conventions occurred almost immediately.

Item—While nearly one million civilians left the north under the 300-day free movement provisions, the Hanoi Government *forcibly* prevented thousands, if not millions, of other from leaving.

Item—Several thousand effective North Vietnamese military groups and political agents were deliberately left in the South with orders to go underground.

Item—The Viet Minh caused incalculable destruction in the areas they evacuated.

Item—Large quantities of war material as well as military personnel were imported across the Chinese border for projects to increase the war potential of the northern zone.

Item—A note dated April 9, 1956, from the British Government to the Soviet Government complained that military divisions in North Vietnam had been increased from 7 to "no less than 20." (At the same time in the South, the last of nearly 200,000 French troops had been withdrawn by April, 1956, along with an estimated $200 million worth of war material. The national army of South Vietnam, moreover, had actually been reduced by more than 50,000 men.)

Item—As early as 1957, the North Vietnamese regime was deliberately infiltrating trained, ethnic southerners into South Vietnam to join the guerrilla forces already there. These troops were equipped with once-clandestine caches of arms and supplies furnished by Hanoi. This underground organization directed its activities toward terrorism and assassination of selected South Vietnamese civilians—government officials, security personnel, educators, and others in leadership positions.

It is well to remind ourselves that this is not a mere assertion by the South Vietnamese Government, by American intelligence forces, or by any other group with an ax to grind against Hanoi. It was documented in a 1962 report of the International Control Commission which had been created by the Geneva Agreements to supervise the carrying out of the terms of the Conference. The report reveals:

> *"There is evidence to show that armed and unarmed personnel, arms, munitions, and other supplies have been sent from the Zone in the North to the Zone in the South with the object of supporting, organizing, and carrying out hostile activities,* including armed attacks, directed against the Armed Forces and Administration of the Zone in the South. These acts are in violation of Articles 10, 19, 24, and 27 of the Agreement on the Cessation of Hostilities in Vietnam. . . . the PAVN (North Vietnamese Army) has allowed the Zone in the North to be used for inciting, encouraging, and supporting hostile activities in the Zone in the South, aimed at the overthrow of the Administration in the South. . . . in violation of Articles 19, 24, and 27. . . . "

Conspicuously absent is any record in those years of serious South Vietnamese violation of the terms of the Geneva Agreements. Nor is there any substantial evidence of efforts by the Saigon Government to subvert or in any other way to bring down the government of North Vietnam.

This fact also should be weighed again carefully and dispassionately by the critics of present policy.

By 1957 the Geneva Agreements had lost all meaning. They had been ignored and, in several instances, actually been torn to shreds by Hanoi. Consequently, it would be irrelevant to posture future arguments on policies in Southeast Asia on the basis of what was or was not agreed to at Geneva. There was nothing left of the Geneva declarations that could be said to have survived the Conference.

For these reasons it is meaningless to strain the argument that somehow South Vietnam *also* broke the agreements. International law has traditionally recognized the inherent right of self-defense against armed attack.

Another principle of international law is that substantial breach of an agreement by one party entitles the other to withhold compliance with an equivalent or related provision until the defaulting party honors its obligations.

It is in the context of the breach of agreements and international law that the stepped-up American participation in events in South Vietnam can be fairly evaluated.

Until late 1961, United States military equipment and advisers sent to Vietnam were well within the limits set by the Geneva Conventions. Only after increased infiltration from the North and stepped-up guerrilla terrorism in the South had become clear beyond doubt did our Government provide substantially greater levels of military assistance to South Vietnam. The Vietnamese Government, moreover, informed the International Control Commission by letter dated December 9, 1961, that it was requesting this extra aid for its legitimate self-defense. The Saigon regime went on to specify that, as soon as the acts of aggression from North Vietnam ceased, foreign assistance would no longer be needed.

For the critics who seek to fault both North Vietnam and South Vietnam (and they are few in number, for most of them fault only the South and ignore the North), it is well to measure again still another breach of the Geneva Accords practiced by the North alone. This breach has to do with the operations of the International Control Commission itself.

According to the Agreements, the ICC was to have *free* access to inspect the degree to which the two zones were living up to the terms of the compromise.

From the very beginning, however, authorities in the northern zone obstructed the Commission's activities by subterfuge and delaying tactics. The ICC inspection teams did not enjoy free movement and access in the North. Necessary documents were withheld from inspection. Consequently, serious violations of the Geneva Agreements by the North almost always were placed out of bounds for checking or inspection by the Control team.

The Government of South Vietnam, although not a party to the Geneva Agreements generally cooperated with the ICC and facilitated the Commission's work. The ICC representatives were allowed to investigate reported infractions, and sometimes they verified the complaints. Even though this type of verification reflected criticism on the Government of South Vietnam, that Government did not block the ICC's supervisory activities.

This, too, is a sharp contrast between North and South.

In retrospect, it should be obvious that, had the Geneva Agreements of 1954 been observed, there would be peace in Vietnam today. Because they were not lived up to, the fabric of agreement and compromise came apart.

How it happened and where the responsibility for its happening lay is rather clearly discernible on the record itself. The predetermination of the Hanoi Government to impose by force its goals in Vietnam with or without negotiations or agreements produced the state of affairs in Vietnam which confronts us at the present time. On this point the record is clear. In support of this conclusion the facts abound.

Whatever differences and disagreements may exist among us in terms of the size of the American commitment, let us at least be forthright enough to separate them from the allegations about conspiracies and guilt by the Government of the United States in the wake of the Geneva Conference.

As a result of the breakdown of the Geneva Agreements, two Vietnams became a fact of international life. The Democratic Republic of Vietnam with its capital in Hanoi and the Republic of Vietnam with its seat of government in Saigon were to be launched as independent countries.

Turmoil characterized political events in both North and South Vietnam in the early months following Geneva. Ho Chi Minh and his Lao Dong liquidated large numbers of the political opposition. In the South, the French-oriented puppet Bao Dai was replaced by Ngo Dinh Diem.

Following the proclamation of a Republic in late October, 1955 with Diem as President, a general election was held in March, 1956 for South Vietnam's first National Constituent Assembly and resulted in victory for supporters of Diem. Vietnam-wide elections were pledged "at such time" as conditions in North Vietnam would permit genuinely free voting. In July a draft constitution was approved by the Constituent Assembly, and two days later Vice President Nixon proclaimed on a visit to Vietnam that "the militant march of communism has been halted."

In January, 1957 the International Control Commission (ICC) reported that neither North nor South Vietnam was fulfilling obligations under the 1954 armistice agreement. In the spring Diem addressed a Joint Session of the U.S. Congress, and a joint communique was issued stating both countries would work toward peaceful unification of Vietnam. In October the U.S. Information Service and Military Assistance Advisory Group (MAAG) installations in Saigon were bombed, and some American personnel were injured.

An extensive plan for land reform was launched by Diem with the advice and under the direction of an American land reform expert, Wolf Ladijinsky. It was projected that the large holdings, particularly in the delta, would be regrouped and redistributed among more of the people. In the central highlands the plan called for the transfer of many coastal residents into the interior and settling of often nomandic hill tribes on agricultural plots. The land reform efforts were to experience stormy times during the years ahead.

The year 1958 was marked with increasingly larger Communist guerrilla band activity; and in July, 1959 such guerrillas attacked the military base at Bien Hoa, killing and wounding several U.S. personnel. In the second national election held in August, there was an overwhelming majority of supporters for Diem.

During 1960 Communist guerrilla activities increased in South Vietnam, and the period marked the first military coup attempt on the Diem regime which failed at the expressed satisfaction of the U.S. State Department.

After the reelection of Diem in April, 1961, President Kennedy on May 5, 1961, declared that the United States was giving consideration to the use of American forces—if necessary—to help the South Vietnamese resist Communist pressure. In May, Vice President Johnson visited Vietnam; and a joint communique was issued declaring additional U.S. military and economic aid would be given to Vietnam.

That autumn President Kennedy dispatched General Maxwell Taylor, his military advisor, to Vietnam. Following the General's return and consultation with the President, Kennedy decided to bolster the South Vietnamese military but not to commit U.S. forces. A state of emergency had been proclaimed by Diem.

The early months of 1962 were marked by increased numbers of military support personnel from the United States and the establishment of a U.S. Military Assistance Command under General Paul D. Harkins. Peking and the Soviets protested loudly the U.S. "buildup" and "demanded" U.S. withdrawal.

The period of April through October, 1953 proved to be a tempestuous one, culminating in the overthrow and execution of Diem on November 1. The Buddhist riots and demonstrations served, as President Kennedy noted July 17, to hamper efforts to press the war against the Viet Cong. On November 4, 1963, the United States recognized a new provisional government of South Vietnam and rejected a French proposal for a neutral, independent Vietnam. Maintaining the result would be a Communist take-over.

Following the assassination of President Kennedy on November 22, President Johnson reaffirmed United States intentions to continue support for Vietnam, with a strong emphasis on pacification to counteract the obvious Viet Cong buildup.

In early 1964, Secretary of State Rusk and Secretary of Defense McNamara reiterated their judgments that it was necessary and vital for the United States to remain as an active deterrent to the Communist push in South Vietnam. In the spring, President Johnson named General William C. Westmoreland to replace General Harkins, and General Maxwell Taylor was appointed Ambassador with Alexis Johnson as his deputy.

On August 4, two U.S. destroyers, *Maddox* and *C. Turner Joy* were attacked by North Vietnamese torpedo boats in international waters, and President Johnson ordered air action against the gun boats and certain support facilities in North Vietnam. The Gulf of Tonkin Resolution was subsequently submitted to and approved by the Congress. The action taken by the United States in response to the attack on the destroyers was the first incident of bombing North Vietnam.

From the overthrow and execution of Diem in 1963 until the installation of Premier Ky in June of 1965, the country was thrown into political turmoil that saw military coup following military coup. Many contend that the confusion during this period contributed almost exclusively to the inability to predict a successful "turning of the corner" of our commitment at that time.

The year 1965 was highlighted by the following events: In January South Korea dispatched 2,000 military advisers to South Vietnam. One month later Communist guerrillas attacked U.S. outposts, and our planes conducted strikes on targets in North Vietnam at the same time we evacuated U.S. dependents from South Vietnam. And despite threats from Premier Kosygin, who announced USSR willingness to aid the North if she were invaded, as well as similar statements by the Chinese Communists, in February the United States announced it had decided to open continuous limited air strikes against North Vietnam. On April 2 the United States announced its intention to send several thousand additional troops to Vietnam; and just five days later, President Johnson stressed our willingness to negotiate and suggested a $1 billion aid program for Southeast Asia. The next day this offer was denounced by Peking as "a trick."

United States bombing missions on the North were halted during the period of May 13 through 19; but the following day, the Soviets announced that construction of antiaircraft missile sites was under way around Hanoi. In early June the U.S. troop commitment in Vietnam was 50,000 which increased to 70,000 by June 16 and to 150,000 by October. On June 22, General Ky took control of the former Quat caretaker government and announced a series of reform measures. During the summer months, a build-up of U.S. forces continued, accompanied by intensive efforts to explore possible negotiation channels—through the United Nations, secret diplomatic overtures, and unofficial individuals.

Ambassador Taylor had by now been replaced by Henry Cabot Lodge. Domestic demonstrations against the war began that fall in a series of demonstrations, draft-card burnings, self-immolations, and other forms of protest. Ho Chi Minh continually and publicly rejected all purported "peace feelers," and the year ended with a November "peace march" on Washington and an uneasy "cease fire" over the holiday season.

Despite pessimistic events such as Russian Secretary Shelepin's visit to Hanoi in January, 1966 in which he arranged for increased Soviet military aid to North Vietnam, and Yale Professor Staughton Lynd's report on his unauthorized ten-day visit and interview with North Vietnamese leaders, by January 15 Premier Ky•pledged a popular referendum in October for a new constitution that would pave the way for elections in 1967.

The Senate Foreign Relations Committee began public hearings on Administration policy at the same time Secretary Rusk indicated that intense efforts to initiate peace talks were meeting with no success. By the end of January, Ho Chi Minh issued a message to world Communist leaders stating that the United States must accept Hanoi's four-point peace formula as the basis for ending the war and must recognize the National Liberation Front "as the sole genuine representative of the people of South Vietnam." The suggestion that the NLF be included in any discussions about negotiations was echoed on the Senate floor a few weeks later by Senator Robert Kennedy of New York among others.

The spring and summer of 1966 were marked with increased Buddhist demonstrations demanding the attention and energies of Premier Ky while American officials in Saigon estimated the rate of North Vietnamese infiltrations into the South at 5,500 men per month. By July 10 the Defense Department announced that U.S. forces in Vietnam would be expanded to 375,000 by the end of

1966 and 425,000 by the spring of 1967. In early August, Thailand proposed an all-Asian peace conference on Vietnam which was endorsed by President Johnson with the warning that "we do not want to make it appear that we are trying to direct or force it."

The conference, known as the Manila Conference, opened on October 24. And on October 25 the United States and five other nations assisting South Vietnam militarily offered to withdraw their troops from Vietnam six months after Hanoi disengaged herself from the war.

In the meantime, almost 81 percent of eligible South Vietnamese voters went to the polls to elect a 117-member Constituent Assembly to draft a new constitution and pave the way for restoration of civilian government by 1967.

With continued attempts to initiate a negotiated settlement coming to naught—including an invitation from the British to hold North-South Vietnamese talks on British territory (accepted by the South, rejected by the North)—Thailand on January 3, 1967, announced its intention to send 2,400 troops to Vietnam. (By June, 1967, U.S. Allies had a total of 54,000 troops committed in Vietnam.)

Further hearings by the Senate Foreign Relations Committee increased demands by several public figures for a halt to the bombing of North Vietnam. In the Senate, debate ranged between intensification of the war—urged by some—and "de-escalation"—demanded by critics. The Administration made it clear, through Secretaries Rusk and McNamara, that reduction of the bombing was solely dependent upon Hanoi's willingness to reduce her military effort in the South. Despite the hue and cry raised in the Senate over the continued bombing, a Gallup Poll in February indicated that 67 percent of the American people favored continued bombing of the North.

By March 27, South Vietnam's government had approved the new constitution; and it was promulgated on April 1, calling for election of a President and Senate on September 1, 1967.

News of further rejections of negotiation attempts dominated the headlines the next few weeks. United Nations Secretary General U Thant disclosed on March 28 that on March 14 he had proposed to both sides a "standstill" truce in Vietnam as a first step toward peace negotiations. The United States and South Vietnam approved the plan, but Hanoi rejected it. In April the United States proposed that both sides pull back military forces ten miles from the Demilitarized Zone as a first step toward peace talks. Two days later the North rejected the proposal, terming it a "trick." By late April, the United States was bombing powerplants and oil installations near Haiphong as well as MIG bases.

On April 28, General Westmoreland addressed a Joint Session of the Congress, asserting that "in evaluating the enemy strategy, it is evident to me that he believes our Achilles' heel is our resolve."

Secretary Rusk revealed on May 1, in a speech to the U.S. Chamber of Commerce, some twenty-eight peace proposals "made by ourselves and others" which had been rejected by North Vietnam. It was further disclosed that, in an unsuccessful effort to open negotiations with North Vietnam, the United States halted the bombing of the immediate Hanoi area from mid-December to late April, coupled with repeated statements to Ho Chi Minh that, if he took reciprocal steps, the United States would make further moves to scale down the fighting.

President Johnson appointed and dispatched twenty-two election observers to Vietnam on August 30. Despite increased terrorist activities on the eve of the elections, General Nguyen Van Thieu was elected President on September 3 as 83 percent of the eligible voters cast ballots.

The developments we have been tracing during this span of years in Vietnam were not limited to the military and political, for it was also during the period 1961 to the present that the strategic hamlet and/or Revolutionary Development Program really got off the ground.

The concept grew out of a variety of security and political measures adopted by local officials acting to a great extent on their own initiative to defend their areas from the growing Communist campaign of guerrilla warfare, terrorism, and intimidation. Diem's government gave the program its initial thrust, drawing on knowledge of the Communist insurgencies in Malaya and Indochina. In February, 1962, a high-level government interagency committee was established to coordinate, direct, and support the program on a national scale. And the following April the National Assembly passed a resolution declaring the strategic hamlet program a national policy.

The strategic hamlet program was the predecessor of the present pacification program to which President Johnson decided to give high priority at the Honolulu Conference. He appointed Robert Komer to administer and coordinate it with other allied efforts in the area.

The strategic hamlet program was conceptually sound but badly implemented. The basic concept was to concentrate the rural people in fortified hamlets in which civilian and military resources could be centered—to separate the people both physically and ideologically from the Viet Cong. While succeeding in some areas, the "quantity not quality approach" hampered real achievement.

The illusory aspects of the strategic hamlet program were exposed after the revolution in 1963, and by 1965 emphasis was placed on developing the organization to implement extensive efforts in 1967-71. The plan for 1965 corrected some of the weaknesses of the past, and its aim was improved military-civil coordination. Through Revolutionary Development Councils, an organizational framework was envisaged stretching from the national to district levels.

Civil RD activities began slowly in 1966—primarily because of the shortage of trained RD cadres, slowness in staffing the various RD councils and permanent bureau, and lack of aggressive local management in executing plans. However, the Minister of Revolutionary Development—by personal visits to all provinces—provided a great deal of direction and motivation. By mid-year, RD programs were being implemented; and local bureaus were staffed and began to function effectively. The first RD cadre class was graduated in May 1966 and deployed to the field shortly thereafter.

The 1967 program and the planning process for the 1968 program have revealed a growth in leadership in Vietnam. Heretofore the dearth of leadership has been the greatest inhibiting factor in revolutionary development. The participation of Vietnamese officials in the RD process in 1967-68 from local to national levels has been heartening. An increasing number of province chiefs, other province officials, district chiefs, and now, finally, local officials have come to appreciate the RD process and to utilize it. The focus of the program has turned to the only body which can meaningfully develop. a new spirit in the countryside—the people and their elected councils themselves.

The gains reflected the firm hand and direction of Ambassador Komer.

But all of these projections were to be suddenly set back by the massive Hanoi attacks on the major cities and towns of the Republic of South Vietnam which began on January 29, 1968 during the Tet holidays.

The Tet offensive was destined to have fateful consequences for the future of South Vietnam and the American presence. For many months the American Ambassador, Ellsworth Bunker, and the Commander of the Allied troops, General William C. Westmoreland, had been warning of an impending winter-spring offensive by the Communist forces. Captured documents at various levels spelled out the details of the projected assault, although no precise dates were affixed to the plans. Those in charge believed that the impending offensive might be the "do-or-die" effort by the other side. They also believed that it could be a direct forerunner to possible negotiations.

When it came, however, the Allied troops were surprised by its scope and its intensity. Part of its severe impact was achieved through the unexpected timing of the attacks which coincided with the Vietnamese national holiday in celebration of the new year, Tet.

By ordering his troops to achieve "total victory" and calling upon the population in the South to repudiate their government and to join the Communists, Ho Chi Minh apparently regarded the new move as the showdown in the war. His Order of the Day to the Viet Cong and to his own North Vietnamese regulars was to "move forward to achieve final victory."

The coordination of the attacks indicates that Hanoi planned for weeks, and perhaps months, choosing the Vietnamese New Year (Tet) deliberately in order to use the movement of the entire population as a guise behind which it might assemble its attack forces. This massive movement of the entire population is one of the oldest and most revered customs of the Vietnamese, during which it has been customary for officers and soldiers to leave their posts and to travel for many miles to visit their families. Weeks before Tet, Hanoi announced it would observe total cease-fire; but all the while its underground apparatus was storing arms and preparing to stab the Vietnamese in the back. The Republic of Vietnam, the United States, and Free World forces also announced they would observe a truce during the Tet period.

But as the New Year began, attacks by the enemy—particularly along the Demilitarized Zone—not only did not cease but increased in intensity. As it became obvious that Hanoi did not intend to live up to its declaration, the Allies publicly announced that the truce would not be observed in the DMZ.

Then Hanoi struck, concentrating its forces upon district, provincial, and national urban centers, entering sacred shrines, assassinating as many leaders as they could seize, and indiscriminately firing into civilian centers. This deceitful attack penetrated many urban centers, and for a few hours the shock value they had achieved enabled them to seize installations and to assassinate important civilian and military persons. It has been announced that in the city of Hue alone, 300 persons were assassinated. Throughout the entire country this scene was repeated on a smaller scale, mounting to a deliberate and planned attempt tantamount to genocide.

The Republic of Vietnam fought back, calling upon American and Free World assistance in certain locations where help was required. But the Government of South Vietnam led the counterattack and bore the brunt of its burdens. The South Vietnamese threw out the Communist forces in almost all the urban centers, although limited numbers held out for several weeks in a few isolated pockets.

The casualties on both sides were by far the heaviest of the entire war. Enemy losses ran several times those of the Allied military. In thirty days of fighting, the North is known to have lost more than 40,000 troops. Among the Allies, the Vietnamese military suffered nearly three times the losses of the Americans. The total Allied casualties were in excess of 4,000 but still many times less than the enemy.

How many civilians were killed is difficult to ascertain. Estimates range all the way from 2,000 up to 5,000. More than a half million South Vietnamese either lost their homes or were made refugees during the offensive.

These figures deserve attention. The South Vietnamese are suffering three times the casualties of the American and Free World forces. The Allies, it is estimated, are inflicting approximately seven times the casualties upon the enemy that they themselves are suffering.

While these enemy attacks were taking place on the military front, the political arm of the Lao Dong Party (The Communist Party of North Vietnam) announced its organization in the South of a special group, "The Revolutionary Armed Forces," to which ARVN defectors might turn. A second political organization was announced, "The Alliance of National and Peaceful Forces," designed to make it possible for South Vietnamese to defect from the government without becoming part of Hanoi's National Liberation Front.

Captured documents and interrogation reports indicate almost conclusively that Hanoi expected a massive shift in South Vietnamese population to the NVA/VC as the military situation deteriorated and the South Vietnamese Government crumbled. These documents and reports further indicate that sizable defections from the SouthVietnamese Army were anticipated. Although further general attacks were expected, we already know that the Viet Cong and the North Vietnamese Army expectations were not fulfilled. The population uprisings simply did not take place. No unit of the South Vietnamese Army defected. Even while the fighting continues, it is already clear that the Communist Party misjudged the temper of the people and of the Army who simply were not ready to join the Communists. Today, the new "organizations" announced by Hanoi have few defectors from the Army or from the people.

The effectiveness of the Tet offensive remains a point of dispute between the government in Washington and its Critical Establishment. It would seem fair to say that the offensive set back the recent gains by the Allies considerably. The pacification program in particular was partially disrupted. The director of the program, Ambassador Komer, has estimated that about one-third of the projects were severely damaged—if not wiped out, that another third were partially damaged, and a third remain largely untouched.

In assessing the seriousness of the Tet attacks, it is also well to keep in mind the failure of the North Vietnamese Government to take over. From the interrogation of prisoners and the marching orders found on the bodies of enemy troops, its seems clear that they expected to seize and hold major sections of South Vietnam. In these goals they failed. And in failing they paid an unquestionably high price in casualties. How high a price has not yet been determined with certainty, for there has been no clear indication of what kind of reserves the enemy forces still have available to be committed in the South.

Remembering the definitive pronouncements made by some critics—including Presidential candidates—that the attacks represented a defeat for the Allies, one finds it interesting now with the advantage of several months' hindsight to see how wrong they were.

It is increasingly clear that the North Vietnamese gambled a substantial portion of their real strength on the chance of seizing and holding key areas of South Vietnam. It is also clear that they hoped to tumble the Saigon Government. They failed in both.

The failure of the Tet offensive may well have hastened the decision of Hanoi to probe for possible peace terms. At least there is significant connection between the tenuous beginning of the Paris meetings so soon in the wake of the Tet offensive.

In a sense, President Johnson's renewed offer to Hanoi made March 31, 1968, on the night of his withdrawal from the Presidential race, may be viewed as an interrupted continuation of a probling effort for negotiations which had been under way as far back as January.

For three weeks, just prior to the Tet attacks, the Americans had refrained from bombing in the Hanoi-Haiphong area—giving the North Vietnamese evidence of our willingness to de-escalate and affording Hanoi an opening for demonstrating its desire to de-escalate as well. Hanoi's answer was obvious. She used the pause to escalate her infiltration of men and material providing the base of her coordinated assault on the cities of South Vietnam.

From the foregoing it is obviously too early to determine the next moves by Hanoi or the length of time that the violence of the conflict is likely to continue. If the timing remains in doubt, the need for American patience and determination to see it through becomes ever clearer. This requires the fullest understanding of why we are in Vietnam.

Chapter VII

VIETNAM: Right Place, Right Time

To understand Vietnam, it is necessary to understand that the issue is not Vietnam. What is happening there might have happened elsewhere—and almost did. It could have happened in the Philippines, where the Huks had represented a working base for a liberation-front type takeover. Or it might have happened in Laos, where some believed it would be easier to forfeit that country to Chinese pressures from the North and the Hanoi-trained legions in the east. Or it could have happened in Thailand, where National Liberation Front types had already made inroads in the five northeastern provinces bordering on the Mekong River. Or in Burma, whose northern provinces are even now infiltrated by guerrilla groups. Or in Malaysia, where ten years of guerrilla-type civil strife had been weathered. The point is that it just *happened* to *happen* in Vietnam.

The "Why" of Vietnam needs to be cast in the perspective of the pressures being applied to influence change in Eastern Asia.

The source of perhaps the greatest pressure lies in Peking. This does not mean Mao's Peking alone; it also means Mainland China. To be sure, Mao injects his own acute brand of aggressiveness.

The first dimension of the Chinese threat is China *as China*. This is historical in the Orient. The history of Indochina is replete over the centuries with efforts to repel China's ever-expanding pressures of influence. The Vietnamese overthrew Chinese rule in 939 A.D. The North Koreans tried to resist expansion of the Han Dynasty in the Second Century B.C. Japan was forced to defend against an armada of Mongols, Chinese, and Koreans in 1281 A.D. Similarly assaulted by the Chinese in the 11th Century were Burma and Java.

The second dimension is the refinement of the Chinese thrust south as envisaged by Mao Tse-tung. Dean Acheson, the former Secretary of State who is deeply experienced in the tactics of cold war diplomacy, has this to say about the new China:

> "The United States faces in Communist China an aggressive nation imbued with the same primitive Communist theology which the Soviet Union had twenty years ago and possessing, (as the Soviet Union did) military resources far greater than those of her neighbors. The area to the south, [of China] afflicted by foreign occupation and years of war, offers an invitation to aggression by means of the war of national liberation. Only the United States has the resources to make resistance possible."[1]

This is the doctrine of inundating the countryside in the process of surrounding the cities of the world. For Lin Piao, inundation in Southeast Asia meant the exporting of revolution. This involved aiding and abetting national liberation movements which could exploit the historic roots of nationalism, the divisive force of political strife, and the plight of the peasant class. What it involved for Mao was sending into each of the developing areas of Southeast Asia supplies of "do-it-yourself" revolutionary kits with which guerrillas could multiply many times over their impact in backward rural areas. It was this tactic which prompted President Marcos of the Philippines to warn that there could be no peace in Eastern Asia until China abandons and foreswears her policy of exporting violence and of fomenting disorder among her neighbors.

To understand the role of the National Liberation Front, it is well to remember that it was not a single invention of the North Vietnamese to be used against South Vietnam. The Front movement was a political and military tactic for expanding the influence of the Maoists into all of Southeast Asia. Even as they operated in the northern provinces of South Vietnam, they were mobilizing their own guerrilla cadres in the five northeastern provinces of Thailand. Others of them have turned up in Northern Burma. And in recent months even Prince Sihanouk of Cambodia has acknowledged that they are in his own border provinces.

Much of the confusion over the nature of the conflict in Vietnam seems to stem from the conflicting interpretations of what the National Liberation Front is all about. If indeed, as some critics assert, it is simply an endemic, local revolutionary society seeking a better life for its children in South Vietnam, that is one thing. But if it can be established to be a part of a rather substantial assault on local populations in many parts of Southeast Asia, then it becomes something else again.

What do we know about the National Liberation Front?

In seeking to understand the national liberation front movement, not only do we have the advantage of placing it in its proper order among the shifting tactics of the world revolutionaries, but we also have the additional advantage of an operational preview of its methods.

First, we have to position it in the evolution of world revolutionary tactics. Immediately following World War II, the tactic was that of occupying the Eastern European countries adjacent to the frontiers of the Soviet Union. Communist regimes were set up under the umbrella of Soviet troops, and all political opposition was liquidated. For the time being, this sealed the fate of the small nations of Eastern Europe which became satellites of Moscow.

The second stage of Cold War tactics applied to those countries left in confusion by the War but not directly occupied by Soviet troops. Here, internal subversion with external supplies and leadership from Russia were provided by the Communists. The newly activated Communist Parties of Italy and France utilized this tactic in Western Europe, while the assaults upon Greece and Eastern Turkey illustrated the point in the Balkans.

The third stage was to resort to the threat of war, thereby seeking to isolate the position of the United States from the Allies. The Berlin Blockade was the first instance and perhaps the most dramatic. No less significant, however, were the second Berlin crisis of 1961 and the Cuban missile crisis of 1962.

The fourth stage of world Communist tactics was the encouragement of peripheral wars waged by other nationals, not by troops of the Soviet Union. The Korean War was the first notable case. North

Koreans, pressed into crossing the 38th Parallel, were openly supplied and directed by the Soviets. The later entrance of a million Chinese into the conflict only played further into the hands of the Russians who sought to achieve military victory with the blood of other nationals.

In three of these first four stages, it should be noted, the tactic was met and thwarted by successive policies of the United States. The obvious exception is the first stage in which Eastern Europe was occupied by the Russians. The reason for the American acquiescence there was obvious. In the turmoil of the last months of World War II, the Soviet occupation of the countries of Eastern Europe had become a fact of international life rather than just a policy. What would have been required to force the Russians to withdraw, it was felt, was a massive military assault involving at least as many troops and as much material as the Soviets had available. This meant committing millions of men from both sides, at a price far greater than war-weary America and Western Europe were ready to risk.

The policymakers in Washington felt that a subsequent policy of firmness could erode the Soviet hold at a lesser price than an extension of World War II in the area. Events during the past twenty years bear out the wisdom of their decision.

The challenge of internal subversion, posed in stage two, was countered by the Marshall Plan, NATO, and the Truman Doctrine—all successful.

The threat of World War III, through direct confrontation between the Russians and the Americans, was countered by the unilateral diplomacy of the United States. The American airlift at Berlin, the Kennedy firmness toward Khrushchev in August of 1961, and President Kennedy's challenge to "put up or get out" over the Russian missiles in Cuba forced a Russian backdown in each instance. The successful waging of the war in Korea, reestablishing intact the prestige of the 38th Parallel, was the measure of success of the fourth stage.

What this indicated is that, while the world revolutionaries are capable of changing and shifting their tactics, their strategy remains constant. They seek to exploit to their advantage weakness and chaos, fatigue and indifference. Thwarted by American policy in each of their thrusts, they fashioned the fifth and current stage of Communist tactics—the wars of national liberation in Southeast Asia.

With this shift in tactics there also occurred a shift in the center of control—from the USSR to China. Reflected in this change was the constantly widening gap between the two chief centers of world communist movement: Moscow and Peking.

The new tactic of liberation fronts involved disguising the outside thrust in a cloak of internal insurrection and civil war.

It became a subtle endeavor in exporting revolutionary leadership and training to those who could be mobilized into carrying out the tactic. Aided and abetted further by direct military invasion from bases outside the Chinese mainland, it was more difficult to restrain or to block it.

Just as the Soviets in Korea sought to wage the war with other countries' armies, so the newest tactic of liberation fronts sought to wage the battles with non-Chinese cadres. This was to become the chief, though often confusing, dimension of the conflicts fomented by the National Liberation Front.

The preview of its operations and capabilities occurred in Malaysia in the 1950's. There, guerrilla cadres, running into the thousands, set up their bases of operation in the more remote areas of what used to be the Malay States.

To begin with, they used small bands to peck away at settlements and villages in the outlying areas. Their most effective weapon was terrorism to force village cooperation with their own needs, which meant supplying food, labor, and sometimes manpower. The British, who were still in control but preparing for their own phaseout, nonetheless came to grips with this new warfare tactic under the leadership of Sir Gerald Templer. The "strategic village concept" was instituted to create sectors of security against the guerrilla predators.

It was a long and protracted struggle at best. The difficulty was coping with an enemy whose chief tactic was "hit and run" rather than "stand and fight." The British estimated that manpower strength in the ratio of 10 or 12 to one was necessary to achieve success. Success, indeed, was the result in Malaysia but only after a high price was extracted from the defenders.

This becomes an interesting parallel case study some years in advance of the crisis in Vietnam. Because we now have access to a good bit of information about the guerrilla operations in Malaysia, we have the opportunity to understand better the dimensions of this new and frustrating type of warfare. That study should convince us of the shrewdness of the Chinese in mobilizing this new tactic of peripheral warfare. The difficulties it posed for conventional methods of war increased its advantages. Given the advance view, then, we are in a better position to evaluate the tactics and strategies as well as the scope of the National Liberation Front in those small nations which lie more directly under the shadow of China.

This should not be construed as an isolated factor in American self interest. Its implications were by no means lost on the Asians who lived closest to China and who were directly involved in the area. Even now the newly independent countries of Southeast Asia have a deep sense of restlessness in regard to the intentions of China.

As far back as 1962, when I was in Manila, a leading member of the Philippine Congress told me, "We don't like the Chinese. We don't want any part of them. But there is nothing we can do about them alone." He went on to say, "The Chinese claim to be the 'wave of the future' and, in my country, we have no reason to doubt it. None of us is strong enough to stop them. Therefore, it means that we're going to have to come under their domination because we lack alternatives."

In Kuala Lumpur, the Tunku, shortly after the above incident, noted that for many years most of the new leaders in Asia thought there was nothing they dared to do about China.

Many of the leaders of Southeast Asia who had taken a more sympathetic view of China, and who saw in the Chinese only the attributes of peaceful revolution, soon began to have a change of heart. Typical of those who began to change was another member of the Philippine legislature, a Congresswoman. During her Peking visit in 1962 she was so shocked by the constancy of the litany of hate she encountered there that, upon returning to Manila, her first order of business was to propose to President Marcos an increase in Philippine troops in Vietnam.

In India, Dr. C. Rajagopalachari, a Gandhi companion and leader in India's struggle for independence who became Governor General, wrote the following in June, 1965:

"There is not the slightest doubt that if America withdraws and leaves Southeast Asia to itself, Communist China will advance and seize the continent. All the people of Asia will soon be intimidated to pay homage to the Communist parties in each of the regions of Asia. . . . There is no hope for freedom of thought in Asia if the hegemony, if not the empire, of China is established."[2]

In my own conversations with Asian leaders, their expressions of fear of China were invariably coupled by their fear of a large-scale war between the United States and China. The result is that their expressions of misgivings about a big war in Asia have been interpreted by the American press to mean that they were critical of the American position in Vietnam. In my travels through India, Nepal, and Burma, I found this not to be the case. As reflected in the dialogue with my friend in the Philippine legislature, they were afraid of China but very uncertain about the readiness of the United States to stand firmly in Southeast Asia—a fact that would not be made known to them until the American build-up began in February, 1965.

It is important, then, to keep the apprehensive statements of the early 1960's in their proper context if we are to piece together an accurate assessment of the minds of the leaders in the Far East. Those attitudes may be summarized in this way: (1) Their distrust and fear of China dates back many hundreds of years. (2) The China of Mao Tse-tung is so overwhelming in its disproportionate size and its aggressive actions, in contrast to these tiny countries who have only recently won their independence, that the leaders in Eastern Asia believed that they would have to yield to Chinese domination rather than be destroyed. Apparently the presence of the American Fleet in the Formosan Straits and the American stance in the Korean War were not the guarantees that they were waiting to receive. They wanted to know where the United States stood in Southeast Asia.

At that moment there was no combination of South Asian countries capable of checking the outward expansion of China. The solution in Laos had been the closest to a measure which might have been taken, but the results there were so inconclusive that new doubts were raised in the minds of the Asians.

This, then, was why the American decision to build up rapidly its military presence in Vietnam was so much more important than some people realized at the time. It was this move that removed the question mark about American intentions which had hovered so long over the capitals of the governments of Southeast Asia.

Of one thing there could be no doubt. Since my first trip to the countries on the rim of China in 1959, I had noted a decided shift of outlook toward Mainland China both during travels there in 1962 and again in 1965. By this latter date, they had closed ranks.

President Marcos of the Philippines, on a visit to the United States in 1966, told a Joint Session of the Congress that the American position in Vietnam had already made a difference in Asia. It had given the small governments there a reason to hope that they had a future other than domination by China. The American commitment, Marcos was careful to explain, should not end in Southeast Asia but should be aimed at containing an expansionist China wherever necessary. The Philippine President made this observation:

> "With this 'cordon sanitaire' effectively established around the eastern and southern flanks of Communist China, the latter might then realize that it could more usefully harness its energies to the enormous task of satisfying the needs and improving the livelihood of its 700 million people."[3]

On the same occasion, Marcos was careful to make another significant point. He said to the American Congress:

> "No Asian country or government desires the destruction of Communist China. We who are its neighbors realize that we must coexist with China and the Chinese people ... But, equally, Communist China must accept the obligation to coexist peacefully with its neighbors. This means that it must abandon and forswear its policy of exporting violence and fomenting disorder amongst its neighbors."[4]

Similar sentiments have been expressed recently by the government leaders in Malaysia and Indonesia. The External Affairs Minister in Australia put it best when he said that the new areas of Asia are not strong enough to resist the pressures of China. He went on to add that the Europeans ought not to be so blind but to see that what happens in Southeast Asia jeopardizes their own security as well.

The American decision to stand firmly in Vietnam has coincided with a decline in Peking's fortunes overseas. But this should not cause us to lose sight of the cocky confidence of the Chinese Government until very recently.

By 1960 the Chinese were speaking of themselves as the "wave of the future." And indeed if we blot out the last three years of events in Vietnam, it is easy to reconstruct the atmosphere of confidence which pervaded the capital of Red China. They were openly challenging the Russians in the realm of Communist ideology. They were directing assaults upon the new frontiers of Africa. Their cause was articulately represented by a dozen or more nations in the United Nations. And in Eastern Asia, who could stop them? Mao and his Red Guards seemed to be an ominous portent of the future. As late as February 6, 1965, Mao was proclaiming that Thailand would be next after Vietnam.

The Minister of Defense in Peking, Mr. Lin Piao, was equally militant in his predictions. He spoke of the kind of tactics which would be successful in Asia:

> "Many countries and peoples in Asia, Africa, and Latin America are now being subjected to aggression and enslavement on a serious scale by the imperialists headed by the United States and their lackeys. The basic political and economic conditions in many of these countries have many similarities to those that prevailed in old China. As in China, the peasant question is extremely important in these regions. The peasants constitute the main force of the national-democratic revolution against the imperialists and their lackeys. In committing aggression against these countries, the imperialists usually begin by seizing the big cities and the main lines of communication, but they are unable to bring the vast countryside completely under their control. The countryside, and the countryside alone, can provide the broad areas in which the revolutionaries can maneuver freely. The countryside, and the countryside alone, can provide the revolutionary bases from which the revolutionaries can go forward to final victory.

Precisely for this reason, Comrade Mao Tse-tung's theory
of establishing revolutionary base areas in the rural
districts and encircling the cities from the countryside is
attracting more and more attention among the people in
these regions."[5]

Lin Piao proclaimed that the assault from Peking would be like
the successful assault of the Chinese Communists who surrounded
the cities even as they inundated the countryside. And in his
parlance, the United States and Western Europe were the "cities,"
and the rest of the developing world—including Southeast Asia—was
the "countryside."

For China, the takeover of Southeast Asia would achieve several
goals at once. It would supply badly needed surpluses of food and
raw materials for her overburdened industrial machine. At the same
time, Chinese penetration of Southeast Asia would at once outflank
India, confront the offshore Philippine Islands, and carry the
Communists close to the jumping-off point to Malaysia and to
Indonesia.

This is not to say that the Chinese were inventing some new bit of
skulduggery in regard to Southeast Asia. The interest of the Chinese
had long gravitated in that direction—just as the interest of other
nations of the world had focused on the riches of the East. No less
than seven times through the centuries had Chinese invaders
jeopardized the people who lived in Indochina. From the Portuguese
and Spanish in the 16th Century through the Dutch, French, British,
and Germans in the 19th Century, Eastern Asia had represented the
number-one goal of the white man as well. Even Japan, herself an
Asian power, made Southeast Asia her prime target at the beginning
of World War II.

From the local guerrilla cadres it seems now in hindsight but a
short jump to the terrorist bands aimed at destroying local
government and disrupting local economic and social programs. The
technique when skillfully applied exploited local unrest and unhappiness. The purpose, however, remained a constant factor; namely,
that of disrupting and eroding stability and orderliness.

In the light of our experiences of the last few years, it is now possible to establish more clearly what at the outset was a matter of some
speculation—that is, the ties of the NLF in Vietnam with a central

control headquarters in a foreign location. In this particular instance that central control reposes in Hanoi.

To understand how this could happen—or better, that it was intended to happen—it is important to take a closer look at the evolution of the Southeast Asian National Liberation Front movement.

The Vietnamese National Liberation Front itself was created by Hanoi, and it remains down to the present under the control of Hanoi. Douglas Pike has rightfully concluded in his definitive work entitled *Viet Cong* that "the management of the NLF was in the hands of the Hanoi-trained and indoctrinated Communists."

As the late Professor Bernard Fall was very careful to note, the Viet Cong operated in the South until December, 1960 as "the extension of the then existing Communist underground apparatus."

In September, 1960 the Third National Congress of the Lao Dong, the Communist Party in Hanoi, adopted a simple resolution urging the creation of a front group to achieve unity in all of Vietnam. That resolution passed by the Communist Party in Hanoi said that "our people (meaning the North Vietnamese in the Lao Dong Party) must strive to establish a united block of workers, peasants, and soldiers and to bring into being a broad, national, united front . . ."

Let it be noted that this resolution was not drawn up in the Viet Cong areas of South Vietnam, nor was it even drafted by South Vietnamese Communists. It was a simple resolution adopted by the government in Hanoi to reflect a policy for Hanoi. Allegations by some critics that the NLF had its origins south of the 17th Parallel have no substance in fact. Efforts to trace other roots of the NLF to native origins in South Vietnam have been unrewarding. Assertions continue to be made to this effect, but there seems to be no evidence to support them.

Not only does the evidence support the fact that the September statements in Hanoi contain no reference whatsoever to any rice roots developments in South Vietnam, but the group in Hanoi went so far as to remind themselves that they had better move quickly and inject such a front group in the South to provide the "cover" for a rallying point for their cause.

The resolution coming out of Hanoi at the instigation of the Lao Dong Party meeting is not the only substantive factor describing the origins of the NLF. That group is clearly identifiable as well through its leadership.

Until as late as April of 1962, as Professor Fall has reminded us, the National Liberation Front had not revealed the names of its alleged leaders. That was nearly two years after its invention. And when the names of a few leaders were finally disclosed, it was impossible to find among them the identities of any individual who had ever occupied a significant position in South Vietnamese political life either before or since 1954 (the year of the Geneva Conference). Those few southerners who later appeared as leaders were, according to Douglas Pike, "responsible to the wishes of the leaders of the DRV (The Democratic Republic of North Vietnam)."

The first Secretary General of the NLF, for example, was Mr. Van Hieu. He had been an active Communist Party member, a known promoter of Communist causes, and self-identified in that role ever since 1945. There is no record of his having held a position of political responsibility in Vietnam either before or after the French were there.

Or look at the so-called Chairman of the NLF, Nguyan Huu Tho. He was another self-styled member of the Lao Dong in the North. The leadership, therefore, of the early National Liberation Front organization was confined to North Vietnam.

What this adds up to is the rather obvious conclusion that the NLF was a concoction invented for psychological warfare purposes to conceal the role of Hanoi in the affairs south of the 17th Parallel. It was this Front which was to enable the North to exploit the genuine attributes of civil war in the South to her own (North's) advantage.

The role of the Hanoi Communist Party in the National Liberation Front is beyond question. It is a role that has been certified in detail by the International Control Commission which had been established by the Geneva Agreements of 1954 to inspect conditions along the Demilitarized Zone which separated North and South Vietnam.

That Commission, which is composed of a Canadian, an Indian, and a Pole, released an intercepted circular dated December 8, 1961, which had been drawn up by the NLF. In it the National Liberation Front advised its members that:

> "The Vietnamese People's Revolutionary party has only
> the *appearance* of being an endemic group within South
> Vietnam . . . We need this group in our efforts to take
> over the South in the interests of the North.

And then follows a noteworthy, cautionary warning to the Front
members to whom this circular was sent,

> "However, during any explanations, you must take care
> to keep this intent strictly secret, especially in South
> Vietnam, so that the enemy does not perceive our
> purpose."

How the role of the NLF could have been described more clearly
or its purposes put more bluntly would be difficult to imagine. But
this is not all.

The National Liberation Front has never claimed that it was *the*
government or even *a* government. It has never asserted that it had
governmental status. The term "professional government" does not
appear in its releases. Nowhere does one find reference to a
government in exile.

These elements help to strip the phrase "National Liberation
Front" bare of the pretentions critics ascribe to it when they talk
about it loosely as a mobilized group in the South engaged in a civil
war against Saigon. The Front itself has no resemblance to genuine
nationalist rebel organizations that have operated in other countries
at similar times. The fact that there may be within its membership
some genuine South Vietnamese nationalists who are latecomers and
who are looking for a political roosting place should not obscure the
central truth that, in origin, in leadership, and in purposes, the NLF
is simply a front group to serve the ends of the government in Hanoi.

Other confirmation of the nature of the National Liberation
Front has come from neutral observers in the two Vietnams. George
Chaffard of *L'Express*, for example, who after visiting NLF groups
and roaming around parts of South Vietnam and conversing with
some of their spokesmen, concluded that the aims of the National
Liberation Front are classically those of a national front preceding a
Communist takeover. The North Vietnamese Lao Dong Party
coordinates the whole operation, Chaffard concluded. And as the
years have passed, the leaders of the NLF make less and less effort to
conceal their disguise.

If more evidence is needed, it is to be found in the captured documents falling into the hands of both Vietnamese and American intelligence groups on the field of battle.

In January, 1966, a captured document recovered from the body of a North Vietnamese officer made it clear that the men in the field should not be alarmed if negotiations should be agreed to by Hanoi. Just know, it was explained, that the Party (Lao Dong) would be using negotiations only to gain an opening for building up their military capabilities in the South.

Later on in September, 1967 another document was found on a captured enemy soldier. The document consisted of lecture notes taken down in September by a member of a Viet Cong unit subordinate to the Viet Cong Military Regime IV. The notes revealed a candid definition of what the leaders in the North mean by "coalition government"—the type of government they say they would form if they could win the war in South Vietnam.

In a coalition government, the notes explain,

> "Our People's Revolutionary Party will exercise overall control of the government.
> "The coalition government may include a non-revolutionary element as President. But he basically must follow the line of action of the Front's political program.
> "The Front will be the core element ... To all appearances it will be a coalition government but the real power will lie in our hands and we will follow the Front's political program, the revolutionary line."

Two months later another captured document disclosed still more about the enemy's mentality. These instructions said (November, 1967),

> "Uncle [Ho Chi Minh] has decreed that this is what you do [infiltrate, work for coalition government, even negotiated settlement] . But don't admit that this directive is from Uncle Ho. Say only that the National Liberation Front will do these things."

Before there can be any clearing of the air on the issue in Vietnam, it is necessary to separate the loose talk about National

Liberation Front from the genuine Viet Cong elements in the South who may have their own real grievances within their own national state. There can be no doubt that the NLF is Hanoi. Its direction, purposes, and timing become matters determined by those around Ho Chi Minh.

Having made the point that the NLF is the creature of Hanoi, we should not deny ourselves any opportunity to exploit cleavages between the command at the top of the NLF and its peasant operators at the other end of the line in the rice paddies and the villages. As those openings occur, I would hope that our position would be flexible enough to take advantage of the opening.

But it is the monolithic structure of the NLF which dominates the present, and it is that kind of a NLF which concerns us right now. It would seem fair to assume that this examination of how the NLF has in fact operated out of Hanoi into South Vietnam tells us something about how it is likely to be operating in the surrounding countries where it has already made its appearance.

In Laos, for example, the continuing presence of thousands of Hanoi-trained militia of one sort or another antedate the stepped-up invasion into South Vietnam by many months. Under terms of negotiated talks in Laos in 1962, all foreign troops were to be withdrawn. The only flagrant violation of that agreement has been practiced by Hanoi. The current North Vietnamese military presence in Laos is enough in itself to call into question the integrity of the proclaimed intentions of Ho Chi Minh to seek only legitimate self-government for his people in Asia.

In Cambodia, adjacent to the Ho Chi Minh Trail through Laos into South Vietnam, Prince Sihanouk—hardly a friendly partisan—confesses that he has become alarmed at the incidents of infiltration into his northeastern provinces along the supply lines kept open by Hanoi.

The activities of the National Liberation Front organization in northeastern Thailand have been mentioned previously.

In Burma, where the remoteness of the northern provinces has always represented a problem of control and stability from Rangoon's point of view, affairs have begun to take a sharper turn. That turn is a classic case of the technique of infiltration and penetration from the outside by the NLF movement. As in the other neighboring countries, the original impact was disguised as local protest against a domineering national regime. But during the last few years, it has flowered into a more sinister movement obviously directed from the outside. In recent months in particular the details of the techniques of infiltration have begun to filter through the isolation imposed upon the area by both terrain and remoteness.

Not only has it been established that the local revolutionaries were indeed trained and often supplied from points outside Burma, but the heavy hand of Red China finally was exposed. The exposure resulted from a simple news story from Rangoon describing local riots against the Chinese and acts of violence committed against members of the Chinese diplomatic delegation. Behind it all the outside world has learned to its chagrin—and surely to the special chagrin of Mr. U Thant, whose country it happens to be—that several hundred Chinese "technicians" had all the time been skillfully subverting the Burmese political infrastructure.

It was as recent as 1961 that the Red Chinese announced a program of aid for Burma. The program envisaged technological cooperation from Peking in constructing textile and sugar mills, plywood factories and other projects aimed at strengthening Burma's economy.

Suspicions about the dimensions of the Chinese aid were aroused first by the failure of the Chinese to "get with it." The only evidence of new construction was along the border with the longest frontiers of Burma with China and Thailand where the men from Peking were busily building bridges.

The Thais were the first to protest. They were suspicious of the construction of all-weather highways and new bridges which conceivably could open the way for a Chinese invasion of either Thailand or Burma—or both. Amid the flurry of these protests from Bangkok, the Burmese—whose history is filled with border disputes with the Thais—experienced the next stage of Chinese aid.

Peking began to demand that the Burmese accept millions of dollars worth of Chinese production—for a price, that is. These were not gifts but sales. When the goods arrived, the Burmese were shocked at the shoddy condition of the products. The automobile and truck tires, for example, were rejects. Most of the other goods were seconds or thirds. The government of Burma finally complained, and the undelivered shipments were canceled.

The first two stages of penetration into Burma, thus, were the negotiation of an economic assistance program and the default on most of the commitments except construction in areas of strategic importance to the Chinese.

The third stage in the relations between the two countries then began to unfold.

It took the form of a considerable and obviously planned effort at subversion and sabotage. The rioting by Chinese students began. Trains were blown up. Propaganda broadsides attacked the Burmese Government. From Peking came a mounting crescendo of threats against the government in Rangoon. In Peking the usual technique of harassing and molesting Burmese diplomats was under way.

The upshot of it all was the withdrawal from Burma of several hundred Chinese technicians. What it all adds up to is that a carefully calculated plan of overt penetration through economic assistance was quickly subverted by covert operations to overthrow a government and to seize control of a neighboring country. What has been taking place almost unnoticed in Burma is a meaningful part of the "Why" of Vietnam.

The fact that the government of President Ne Win could successfully force the Chinese out of his country reflects in part the presence of the United States in that part of the world. It must be obvious to any student of the area that Burma would be helpless against the will or intent of the Chinese were it not for the presence of another powerful force capable of at least restraining or containing the pressures from Peking. Ne Win, who only a very few years ago was bitterly critical of the Americans and often militantly anti-USA, has now been able to capitalize on the consequences of a strong American presence in Southeast Asia.

And the many facets of Chinese policy which sometimes appear to be unrelated turn out in hindsight to be a part of a synchronized whole.

As we have already seen, the legacy of the guerrilla warfare in Malaya was a successful repudiation of the tactic. It nonetheless reflects the pattern of persistent efforts to penetrate the treasure troves of Southeast Asia. And in its wake the hill bands of surviving Communist guerrillas still constitute a restless and uncertain political factor in the jungle areas in the southernmost territories of Thailand where the long and narrow wisp of land represents the unknown frontier between Thailand and Malaysia.

The tentacles of the new Chinese octopus reached still further into the South Seas.

Indonesia is a dramatic—indeed, a bloody—case in point. Here again, the local roots of discontent were the familiar ones—native populations exploited by unresponsive politicians in faraway Djakarta, long overdue reforms delayed or even thwarted by self-serving politicians in or out of uniform. The Partai Komunis Indonesia (PKI) quickly became the focus for the chance of millions of Indonesians all the way from Borneo to Western Sumatra to Mali and the aborigines of Western New Guinea to achieve their frustrated hopes and dreams of a better life.

It was not long, however, before the PKI became identified not only as a Communist party, which is less important, but as a close ally—even instrumentality—of the Chinese Communist Party of Mao Tse-tung. Here was an instance of the "wave of the future" proclaimed earlier by Mao not only washing the shores of those countries contiguous to China, but even rolling on across the China Sea to lands hundreds of miles removed from the Chinese mainland.

By 1965, in fact, it was regarded by many astute observers of the area as almost certain that a Chinese-oriented, and perhaps dominated, regime was emerging in Djakarta. Sukarno, if not the architect, seemed at least to be a willing collaborator of the new alignment.

The prize which Indonesia represented was obvious. The fifth most populous nation in the world and rich with natural resources, it would be an obvious plus for whatever new Chinese sphere of influence might emerge. The abortive coups of September and October, 1965 shattered whatever dreams its promoters may have had. The fact of its failure, however, should not be permitted to obscure the glowing prospects of Chinese domination which immediately preceded it.

In the wake of the utter collapse of the Communist efforts in Indonesia, the man-in-the-street is inclined to forget the ominous forebodings of the Chinese specter of the mid-1960's.

The real point of all these events is to reveal the scope—indeed, the sheer massiveness—of the Chinese psychological and diplomatic offensive of just a few years ago.

That grand American soldier, General Omar Bradley, said after his recent visit to Vietnam:

> "Vietnam is an historical necessity, not because we said so but because the Communists want it that way. On September 2, 1965, the Red Chinese Defense Minister Lin Piao declared in Peking that Vietnam was the 'testing ground' for the worldwide application of Mao Tse-tung's military-revolutionary strategy. This strategy, used by Mao in China and by Ho Chi Minh in Southeast Asia, starts with a peasant base and gradually encircles, throttles and captures the cities. Marshall Lin likened underdeveloped countries such as South Vietnam to the peasants and described the capitalist countries as the 'cities of the world.' We are on notice then that this is the challenge."[6]

This is but another way of saying that the countries of Southeast Asia have long been the grand prize in the competition for balance of power in the world. This area lies astride the principal seaways to the East. It possesses a quarter of a billion people capable of great material production. It has all of the sinews of strategic power and, thus, who controls Southeast Asia and in what form makes a difference to the new balance of power in the East.

As our former Ambassador to Thailand, Mr. Kenneth Young, has put it,

> "Asian fear of engulfment by China, to use an Asian phrase, has stalked Southeast Asia since 1950. . . . Asians see the destiny of the nationalist half of Asia directly tied to the *judicious* exercise of American diplomacy and power in Asia . . . [in their view] Vietnam is the hinge of Southeast Asia. In turn, the outcome in Southeast Asia will swing the direction of forces throughout Asia."[7]

That places a great deal of stress on the importance of a very tiny segment of the surface of the earth—South Vietnam. For a country of only a few million people with a total area less than that of my own state of Wyoming, it is a microcosm of world politics. Or as Ambassador Young has better described it, "Vietnam is an uninsulated crossway of high density and huge voltage." The outcome of events there can be more explosive, and certainly more significant, than any similar spot on the globe today.

Yet, for one to try to see in Vietnam the full meaning of all it portends for the chances of a more peaceful world in our time would be an elusive exercise in confusion. To understand the issues at all, one has to see Vietnam in terms of all her neighbors, all of Eastern Asia, and the capitals of the great and the powerful—Washington and Moscow.

This becomes the "Why" of Vietnam. These are the elements which inspired General Omar Bradley to write after his recent trip to Southeast Asia, "after tramping throughout the length and width of South Vietnam . . . I am convinced that this is a war at the right place, at the right time and with the right enemy."[8]

Recasting Vietnam against the backdrop of the larger events of the Far East, therefore, places it in its correct relationship to the events elsewhere in the world. Only in understanding it in those terms does American policy in Southeast Asia acquire its deepest meaning. Placed in this context, the development of events in Southeast Asia during the past ten years begin to make sense. Only when one retreats from a world setting to the local geography of Indochina is the true dimension lost.

That is why I contend that to understand Vietnam, it is important to understand that the issue is not Vietnam but the chance for stability and orderly change in all of Eastern Asia. Failure to grasp this fact has evoked questions about the credibility of American policy in Asia. It is the root of the problem of dissent and criticism among Americans which has become so intense and emotional as to raise doubts among some observers about the stability of the Administration to survive election-year politics.

It may help to recast dissent in the perspective of our other wars.

Chapter VIII

Dissent in Perspective

Never was it more important that we have a great debate on American foreign policy than in these years when we examine the question of the purpose of the American role in Asia. It is so important, in fact, that we can ill-afford the unrelated and emotional side issues that are thrown into the cauldron of public dissent by some of the critics. This is another way of saying that there are hard, basic premises relating to the United States position in the Far East that need to be scrutinized from every angle. Hot-headedness and self-serving diatribes do not aid us in arriving at the wisest answers.

What are the legitimate areas for dialogue on Vietnam? One obviously is whether the United States ought to have any political, military, and diplomatic role in the Far East. Would we better serve our national interest to concentrate our endeavors in the citadels of western civilization rather than venture forth into the Orient?

How serious is the threat of China? Is this threat Communist China or just China? What are the signs that should alert us to Chinese intentions? What are the signs which might ease our apprehensions about Mainland China? Do we tend to overreact to the fear of Chinese aggressiveness against her neighbors?

Another necessary area of discussion must focus on whether or not Southeast Asia is in fact all that important to the security of the Orient as well as to ourselves. Could that part of the world be forfeited to a "Chinese sphere of influence" without weakening the prospect of overall security in the world structure? Is the United States over-extended because of Vietnam?

A fourth disturbing question worthy of soul-searching debate is, Is the price being paid in Southeast Asia worth the costs to the South Vietnamese themselves in terms of the destruction of their country inherent in the waging of a larger war and inevitable disruption of their historical and cultural traditions? Has the American dominance in the war become so pronounced that the Vietnamese people may be obliterated in the process? Where along the scale of priorities in the conflict should be placed the internal consequences in Vietnam?

A fifth area of needful dialogue is in the realm of Chinese intentions. It is important to thrash out the difference in estimates between those who advocate almost unlimited military action against the North regardless of China and those who overreact the other way in the fear of provoking a war with China. What the Chinese do or fail to do is a matter of great importance. How close we come to an accurate estimate could well make the difference between a successful policy and a disastrous one.

Still another necessary area of responsible dialogue is the impact of all of this on Soviet-American relations. What limitations have to be observed to avoid worsening East-West relations elsewhere? What calculated risks have to be undertaken even with the Soviet presence in North Vietnam?

Yet another area of debate should carefully weigh the importance of world opinion in regard to what we hope to achieve and how we hope to achieve it in Eastern Asia. Is there a point at which hostile world opinion might make the price of success too high? Is there a time when the consequences of hostility could destroy the success of a limited action? Where on the scale of evaluations should the attitude and state of mind of the Asian governments immediately involved in the area be placed?

Another necessary question concerns the effect this war in Southeast Asia has had on the role of the Executive and the Congress in spelling out American policy around the world. Has the Senate suffered irretrievable damage? Has the President abused or otherwise exceeded his proper authority? Should there be a formal declaration of war? Is a restructuring of the Constitutional separation of those responsibilities called for in the light of the facts of international life today?

Searching inquiry is needed on the question of where we go from here. Have we kept in the proper order the question of negotiations and with whom in relation to the stated limited objectives which we seek? What should be our minimum terms for settlement? What have we a right to include in our maximum hopes? Is there a conceivable future point at which the Asians themselves could better assume this responsibility? Which Asians? Does the "containment" of China into the indefinite future constitute a realistic objective for Asian policy? Does a policy in Asia which seeks to keep China isolated offer the best chance for a peaceful Asia, or should the reinvolvement of China in all international undertakings become the goal? At what point does military policy threaten to overbalance political and diplomatic ends? How wide should be the range of American economic cooperation in Asia? Should this include China, North Vietnam, North Korea?

These are areas where it is necessary—even desperately urgent—that we come up with unimpassioned answers. The trouble is those right answers will not be found in absolute or definitive terms. As in so many problems in a nuclear age, the ultimate decisions will be made up of the lesser of evil alternatives or the compromise between extremes. More often than not, policy decisions will be composed of a combination of 51 percent "good" and 49 percent "bad."

The gap between the rational and the irrational begins to widen at this point. Unfortunately, the times do not allow us the luxury of some subsequent hindsight to see what we should have done. We have to take a chance, and take it now, when the decision has to be made. The decision no longer can reflect either the blacks or whites but will end up in some shade of gray. It is increasingly easy to theorize on what might be done or what should have been done. It is obviously more difficult to determine with finality what can be done.

In the war in Southeast Asia we find the policy of the United States under constant attack by its critics at home. The attacks often are unrestrained. The attackers are virtually unlimited by a sense of responsibility. And the areas of disagreement and dissent have become boundless in scope. Perhaps at no time in our history has dissent been as relentless or as intense.

By the same token, if we are to arrive at the wisest possible policy conclusions, it can only be within the narrowest range of responsible dissent and disagreement.

That dissent has gotten out of hand seems somewhat obvious. What its real dimensions have become and what price is being paid for it are questions which only future historians can fairly assess. The most that we can do at this moment perhaps is to measure both the dissent and the dissenters in the context of the present.

Lest there be those today who think that the intensity of modern dissent on Vietnam is unique to the 1960's or, more particularly, that it has been aggravated by the policies of President Johnson, it is well to remember that every war in our history has provoked bitter dissent.

The War of 1812 was openly referred to as "Mr. Madison's War," just as some United States Senators refer to Vietnam as "Mr. McNamara's War." From the floor of the Congress, John Randolph of Virginia not only warned that the American people "will not submit to be taxed for this war of conquest and dominion," but he also dubbed two of the war's chief advocates as "war hawks." He called into question their patriotism and referred to their "aggrarian cupidity." In the struggle Randolph thought he saw a crude conspiracy on the part of the United States Government to conquer Canada.

Elsewhere in the country, manifestoes were issued, urging dissenters to "organize a peace party." Three New England governors (Massachusetts, Rhode Island, and Connecticut) refused to send their state militias into national service.

The ultimate step taken by the dissenters in the War of 1812 was the calling of the Hartford Convention to be convened in New England for the purpose of either amending the Constitution to prevent future commitments to war or actually seceding from the Union, or both. As this war neared its close, it appeared to many that only President James Madison and General Andrew Jackson still stood firmly. (Like President Johnson and General Westmoreland?)

Three decades later, President James K. Polk faced the prospect of war with Mexico. The ensuing conflict was called Polk's "unconstitutional" war. A former President of the United States,

John Quincy Adams, denounced the struggle as one instigated by slave hunters solely for the extension of slave territory. A contemporary, James Russell Lowell, castigated the conflict with his sharpened pen. Another man of letters, Henry Thoreau, refused to pay his private taxes as a protest against the war. He sought to justify his opposition in his "Essay on the Duty of Civil Disobedience."

From Virginia came the caustic assessment of Alexander Stephens. "Never did I expect to see the day," he declared, "when the Executive of this country should announce that our honor was such a loathsome beastly thing that it could not be satisfied with any achievements in arms but must feed on earth—gross, vile dirt."

At the start of the war, the Whig Party had proclaimed that "doubt, division and reproach will be unknown." But as the war with Mexico continued, the Whig Party Congressmen voted "to declare that the war with Mexico was unnecessarily and unconstitutionally commenced by the President." That vote was ardently defended by a freshman Congressman from Illinois, Abraham Lincoln. Lincoln said, "I more than suspect that he (the President) is deeply conscious of being in the wrong—that he feels the blood of this war, like the blood of Abel, is crying to heaven against him." Lincoln in turn was christened by his hostile press back home as "a second Benedict Arnold."

The American Civil War naturally triggered more emotionalism and sharper epithets than any other conflict in the early history of our country. President Lincoln was accused of waging a war which was, in the judgment of Congressman Vallandigham of Ohio, "a most bloody and costly failure." (A contemporary Ohio solon, Senator Steve Young, said as recently as February 1, 1968, that "Vietnam is the worst mistake ever made by any administration in our Nation's history."[1] This is the same Steve Young who, as a Congressman in the 77th Congress speaking on the lend-lease bill said, "I am determined to do my utmost to keep war 3,000 miles distant from our shores. Let us strengthen, not weaken the hands of the Commander-in-Chief of our Army and Navy so that no dictators will dare attack us."[2]) By December of 1862 a House Resolution demanding a "negotiated settlement" was tabled by a surprisingly close vote.

Harper's Weekly, perhaps the most prestigious magazine in the country in those days, questioned in sarcastic meter:

> "You saw the mighty legions, Abe,
> And heard their manly tread.
> You counted hosts of living men,
> Pray—can you count the dead?"

(Today's more militant critics have updated the *Harper's* poetry to a more "hip" query: "Hey, hey, LBJ—How many kids have you killed today?")

From New England again a suggestion was advanced by a prominent newspaper to throw out Lincoln and the Constitution and adopt a conference form of government.

Within the ranks of the military itself, there were some 200 desertions a day by 1863. Modern-day historians estimate that over 117,000 deserted from Lincoln's armies during the war. (As of January 31, 1968, there was a total of 21 known American deserters in Sweden, and unconfirmed estimates from deserters themselves that there are 100 in France and others in Switzerland.) An entire Illinois regiment was arrested and put under guard as mutineers. Draft-dodging became a national sport (not too dissimilar to today's draft card burners and self-exiled draft refugees in Canada). In New York City alone draft riots left more than 1,000 people killed or wounded.

Perhaps the most powerful newspaper of the time, the *New York World,* had already said that trusting the country to "two ignorant, boorish, third-rate backwoods lawyers (Lincoln and Johnson)" was an insult to the common sense of the people. Other leading papers, including the *New York Daily News,* the *New York Tribune,* the *New York Evening Post,* the *Chicago Times,* and the *Detroit Free Press* were also among the "doves." And a few weeks before the fall of Atlanta the *New York Times* advocated a national "peace commission" to negotiate an end to the war with the South.

The Spanish-American War opened the doors to America's new role in the world. It also introduced the naive in the land to the strange new vernacular of power politics. "Imperialists" and "Expansionists of 1898" and "Remember the Maine" were cliches which conveniently substituted for thinking among the litigants over the war. The war with Spain was conveniently short and more conveniently cheap. But these factors did not clarify the issues of the war in the minds of the dissenters.

Eighteen thousand miles distant in Manila Bay, hostilities broke out. Troops under the command of General Arthur MacArthur, whose son would wage war in the same arena in a later generation, soon scattered the resisting remnants of the Philippine Army. The surviving rebels, however, shifted to a new tactic of combat called "guerrilla warfare" which pinned down the Americans for several years and required some 60,000 troops to restore order. In Congress, moreover, dialogue over the war approached violence. The Republican Speaker of the House of Representatives, Thomas B. Reed, resigned in disgust. President McKinley was called "a contemptible rascal" by Carl Schurz, a noted liberal in the Republican camp.

The industrialist, Andrew Carnegie, criticized a friend in the government by writing to him, "you seem to have about finished your work of civilizing the Filipinos; it is thought that about 8,000 of them have been completely civilized and sent to heaven; I hope you like it."

Intellectuals and academics joined in forming an "Anti-imperialist League" to try to stop the war. Supporting this group were men of the stature of William James, the Harvard psychologist; John Dewey, regarded by some as the father of modern education; writers William Dean Howell and Mark Twain. They urged American troops to rebel against their commanders, to lay down their arms and refuse to fight.

From the U.S. Senate, leadership in the movement was epitomized in the voice and actions of Senator George Hoar of Massachusetts. He rose on the floor to condemn the President and to predict that the Philippines would never surrender and that the United States could never win the war. The struggle, he said, would last 300 years.

Another critic of the war, John Foreman, described by contemporaries as a leading authority on the Philippine Islands, said America could never hope to stay in the Philippines without a large standing army; and the only option left to the government now was to "extricate herself with honor."

One of the interesting consequences of the vocalized dissent at home was that the Philippines became convinced that an overwhelming portion of the people in the United States sympathized with them. The record further reveals that the Filipinos, even while they were paying an unbearable price for holding out, gambled on a Democratic Party victory in the United States in the election of 1900 to bail them out of defeat. (Not, it is argued, unlike the hopes of Hanoi in 1968.)

The wars of the 20th Century which have engaged the Americans afford no significant changes in the bitterness of dissent. In World War I even the Kaiser's predatory activities on the high seas failed to unite the people in the United States. Fifty Members of the House of Representatives actually voted against the Declaration of War. Six Members of the United States Senate also voted "no." The I.W.W. called it a "Businessman's war, and we don't see why we should go out and get shot." Before the armistice was signed the Congress was fighting President Wilson demanding that the Chief Executive surrender control on military affairs.

World War II, on the other hand, was preceded by a protracted period of bitterness, emotionalism, and back-biting. The sharp exchanges between the "isolationists" and the "interventionists" were only the surface indicators of a very deep cleavage within the country as a whole. Many Americans today tend to forget the bitterness of 1939 and 1940, largely because the shock of the Japanese assault on Pearl Harbor tended to close the ranks overnight.

President Roosevelt was very sensitive on this matter. His biographers tell us that, as far back as 1937, he faced up to the prospect of eventually having to join the European effort to stop Adolph Hitler. Apparently as late as 1940, however, he still entertained the hope that somehow the British would be able to hold the line. It was that assumption which likely prompted him to make his famous utterance in New England during the Presidential campaign in October, 1940, when he said. "To you mothers and fathers, I give one more assurance. I have said this before, but I shall say it again and again and again: Your boys are not going to be sent into any foreign wars." (The circumstances are not dissimilar to those prevailing when President Johnson, in October, 1964, made the statement that American boys would not be sent to fight a land war in Asia—made with the hope at that time that South Vietnam, with the aid of advisers, would be able to contain the pressures from the North.) During World War II, moreover, juvenile delinquency jumped

56 percent while high school enrollment dropped 56 percent. Racist tensions flared. Detroit and other cities experienced bloodshed and violence. Black marketing and inflation threatened the cost of living.

Congressional critics pre-Pearl Harbor were not lacking. In the House, the Honorable Frank C. Osmers, Jr. of New Jersey said on July 9, 1941, in discussing the dispatching of Marines to Iceland,

> "The only freedom we have left here is to answer 'Ja' to the President's proclamations."[3]

In further arguing against European involvement, Representative Robert F. Rich of Pennsylvania proclaimed in July, 1941,

> "We have enough to do if we stay in the Western Hemisphere and attend to our own business, as we like good Americans should."[4]

Much of the ire in Congress prior to December 7, 1941, was directed at the Lend-Lease proposals. Montana Senator Burton K. Wheeler in January declared,

> "Never before has the Congress of the United States been asked by any President to violate international law. Never before has this nation resorted to duplicity in the conduct of its foreign affairs . . . The lend-lease give-away program is the New Deal's triple A foreign policy; it will plow under every fourth American boy."[5]

Representative Dewey Short of Missouri was even less temperate. He said,

> "You can dress this measure up all you please, you can sprinkle it with perfume and pour powder on it, masquerade it in any form you please with these innocuous and meaningless amendments that have been offered, but it is still foul and it stinks to high heaven. It does not need a doctor, it needs an undertaker. . . . This bill is a war bill, it is a dictatorship bill, and it is a bankruptcy bill."[6]

The Korean War was the first major test of the Americans in their new role as a great power leading the rest of the "non-Communist" world or the Free World. Because it was unlike the total war concept of the immediate past and was, instead, waged under very limiting circumstances, many people in the United States strongly objected to the new struggle in Asia. It was difficult for the average citizen to adjust to the restraints of world power and the responsible use of that power.

The war in Korea was led by General Douglas MacArthur, who had established his brilliant credentials in fighting *big* wars rather than *limited* ones. His admittedly great military acumen probably saved the American position in South Korea from disaster in the early fighting. The near miracle of this early success may have had an unfortunate fringe consequence. As the distinguished American historian, Samuel Elliott Morrison, has pointed out, "It made MacArthur infallible in his own opinion."

The subsequent showdown during the war between President Truman and General MacArthur unloosed perhaps the most heated of dissents present in any American war in the 20th Century. The war was soon to be described by the new critics as "Mr. Truman's War." Secretary of State Dean Acheson was singled out by Republicans in Congress as an "appeaser."

Senator Joseph McCarthy resorted to the floor of the United States Senate and to the nationwide forums of private meetings and banquets to unleash a steady drumfire of attack on the President's conduct of the war in Asia.

At the start of the conflict the people backed President Truman by 81 percent to 13 percent. But by the time General MacArthur was fired, the President's popularity dropped to 29 percent, according to pollster George Gallup. And a year later it had dropped to 26 percent.

It would be difficult to exaggerate the dimensions of the uproar which swept across the land when Truman dismissed MacArthur. Senator McCarthy sneered that Truman was "an SOB who decided when drunk to remove MacArthur." Senator Richard Nixon insisted that the General be restored to his command. Still other Senators called for the impeachment of the President.

Again in the Nation's Capitol, the dismissed General coined a new phrase which came to capsulize the Korean conflict in simple terms. He told a Joint Session of the Congress that "in war there is no substitute for victory." The MacArthur phrase quickly became, however, a substitute for thinking. News columnist William S. White later reported that one United States Senator (unnamed) told him that, if MacArthur's speech had gone on much longer, there might have been a march on the White House.

While emotions were running rampant, eight members of the Senate Foreign Relations and the Armed Services Committees issued a joint statement in August, 1951, attacking the Administration for having "squandered military victory." They pronounced the war "a catastrophic failure." By the war's end, President Truman and the troops in Korea seemed to be the only ones still standing. Later on, committees of the Congress did back Truman on the MacArthur issue and contributed to restoring a sense of calm and intelligence in the Capitol. A combined hearing by the Senate Foreign Relations and Armed Services Committees, chaired by Senator Richard Russell of Georgia, undertook a study of the MacArthur demise. In their conclusions, they pointed up the correct significance of the whole fracas; namely, that the issue at stake was whether the military ran the government or whether this was to remain a civilian responsibility. The Committee concluded unanimously that the structure of the American system must always be such that control was kept in the hands of its civilian leaders—that the President of the United States in truth was Commander-in-Chief of all of our military forces.

This brief recap of dissent and dissenters in other wars in our history hopefully serves the purpose of casting in proper perspective current dissent over Vietnam. The record shows that many of the things now being said about the struggle in Asia have been said over and over again by similar persons at other times; it should suggest that this is neither new nor unique nor particularly triggered by the exceptional or unusual events which have accompanied our policy and commitments in Southeast Asia. This makes no pretense of saying either that one side or the other is right or wrong. But it does indicate clearly that this generation of Americans is not alone in experiencing the torture and the travail of doubts and uncertainties in regard to major policies involving the national interest.

To leave the reader with the impression that dissent and the war in Vietnam can be explained in the malaise of other wars would be an injustice to current dissent. That the present generation of dissenters is caught in the midst of great change is a commonplace observation. Because those changes are more violent and more sweeping than any which have gone before make our times, or these days, distinctly different from other eras.

Change at any time is chaotic. Never has there been a time in recent history at least when the chaos of change so completely dominated our daily thoughts or deeds. Never has it hung so heavily over our continuing efforts to peer into a future dimly seen.

In this current time of "instant communications," moreover, when events ten thousand miles away are minutely reported on a TV screen within a matter of minutes, or hours at most, we find ourselves, as mere bystanders or viewers, more deeply involved, more emotionally disturbed, and more politically aroused than any other generation could have been in its own time.

Quite literally, we hang breathlessly on the brink of each day's crisis in the midst of a war, the larger dimensions of which we have long since lost sight—a war which is peculiarly over-reported and then almost exclusively on one side since the other side neither tolerates freedom of the press nor accessibility to their battlefronts save as it may serve their own mysterious purposes.

So profusely have the words rolled out of Vietnam in an attempt to "cover" the war there that they have tended to drown out the warnings of those who have dared to remind that the key issue is *all* of Eastern Asia—not just a part of Vietnam. Or they blur the view of the "big picture" as they overfocus on the minutia of day-to-day combat. The war news by its very nature has tended to focus more and more on the violence of change, obscuring the meaning of that change.

Battle scenes, casualty lists, and the atrocities of combat tend to displace the narratives of significance on the front page. "Who done it?" has become the news collector's obsession far more often than his searching inquiry into "What did it?" If any attention at all is devoted to the "big picture," it is often relegated to the more obscure sections of that day's newspaper.

When one adds to the plethora of communications media the limitations of any conflict in a nuclear age, he has captured the new dimension of modern warfare that sets today's conflict apart from all other wars. But this accentuates the ever-present issue of credibility.

Chapter IX

The Credibility Gap

Is there a Credibility Gap about what is happening in Vietnam? If there is, what is it? If not, why has it become such an important and controversial theme in our everyday life?

Complicated as those questions may be, the substance of them remains—that as long as people think there is a gap, we have to address ourselves to their doubts. This involves a constant searching for the truth.

Truth, while a war is going on, is not easy to determine. Ask any historian or good reporter. There are honest differences of opinion and sometimes a haunting divide between what one hopes and what one ends up having to write about.

In the most popular sense, the Credibility Gap issue means to the man-in-the-street that he believes someone has "slickered" him into the war in Vietnam. Or to put it another way, others with the same doubts about credibility contend that we have stumbled into our present commitment in Asia through a succession of mistaken decisions which have been compounded by rigidly imposed secrecy to conceal the mistakes.

The more common citations alluded to as the bench marks of public doubts would include the following:

First, the optimistic assessments coming from American spokes-men in Saigon in the early 1960's proclaiming that the Diem regime was on top of the problems within; that there were no guerrillas or

115

Viet Cong within many miles of Saigon; and that the government's land reform program was making enough headway to forestall the prospect of serious internal violence.

Yet, by 1963, the Diem Government was down the drain; confusion and chaos were everywhere in evidence in South Vietnam. The "strategic hamlet" concept, which had been represented as the hope for security, appeared to be less than successful.

A second, well-remembered statement was that by Secretary of Defense Robert S. McNamara delivered in October of 1963 when he and General Maxwell Taylor reported to the President on the outlook of our commitment in Asia. The Secretary observed that it appeared the American military commitment in Vietnam was over the hump (25,000 advisers) and that a cutback of American troops could begin by Christmas, 1965.

Yet, by October, 1965, the 25,000 advisers had been increased to 150,000 regular United States troops.

Third was the campaign statement made in September, 1964 by President Lyndon B. Johnson that, "We don't want our American boys to do the fighting for Asian boys."

Yet, in less than three months after the election, the President was ordering American bombing raids into North Vietnam; and several hundred thousand American boys were being sent to the Far East.

A fourth case involved the optimistic predictions by General Westmoreland, while in Washington to address the Congress in April, 1965, when he spoke in interviews of the possibility of cutting back American manpower in Southeast Asia perhaps in another year.

Yet, within a very few months, the demands on American manpower were heavier than ever, the casualties higher, and the prospects of a longer and more intensified conflict greater.

In each of the above particulars, as we now know in hindsight, there was a reasonable basis for the educated guesses. All of those guesses appear more ridiculous in hindsight than at the time— primarily for one reason, that the enemy for his own purposes sharply escalated his own participation in the conflict in South Vietnam.

In Chapter Sixteen an effort is made to evaluate the above events.

The conclusion reached is that, at the very most, they were bad guesses and, at the very least, in some instances were not without considerable supporting evidence but that, in any event, they did not reflect any kind of a conspiracy to deceive or to mislead.

Credibility at best remains a relative term. Every time we have had a significant national crisis in world affairs—at least since Woodrow Wilson and World War I—the Credibility Gap question always rears its head. Wilson had his gaps as did Franklin D. Roosevelt in World War II. The question is, why?

In quest of the explanations it would seem fair to suggest that the American people by their very nature would prefer to rationalize out of or around war. Thus, the man-in-the-street tries desperately to pretend in the final analysis that there are some other alternatives open to him "short of war."

Public leaders, on the other hand, often have a propensity for optimism—or sometimes strive to put the best face on a situation, the outcome of which is not yet determined. No one, for example, can fault Woodrow Wilson or his original intentions in striving to keep the United States out of World War I. He successfully won re-election to a second term, moreover, with a simple campaign slogan, "He kept us out of war."

Wilson was hardly sworn in for the second term, however, when the German Government made its fateful decision to resume unlimited submarine warfare and to force the President's hand.

President Wilson was confronted, thus, by a new circumstance (unlimited sub warfare) *not* present during the Presidential campaign of 1916. As Chief Executive, he had to act in the face of the *new* facts which arose *after* the election rather than pursue a policy which fit only the facts before the election. To have done other than that would have betrayed his responsibilities as Commander-in-Chief presiding over the national interest of the country.

This Credibility Gap in Wilson's policies was sharply obscured in the public mind by the abruptness of the German decision on the high seas. The German decision tended to defer most popular explosions over the "gap" until near the end of the War when it was resurrected by Wilson's political opponents in an effort to discredit him.

The case of Franklin D. Roosevelt and World War II is far more apropos to the circumstance of Credibility Gaps than the earlier case of Woodrow Wilson. As early as 1937, we are told, FDR made up his mind that the United States had to mobilize its national efforts in some way to stop Hitler. The problem which bothered him, however, was how to bring public opinion around to support such a policy.

Remembering that the mid-1930's were the peak of so-called isolationism, of anti-World War I-ism, we should allow for the bitterness of the debates in the country over the approach of World War II and the depth of the cleavages between the "interventionalists" and the "isolationists."

Along the way, Roosevelt was less than candid—or so it appeared to his critics. He talked about measures "short of war;" of transferring overage American destroyers to the British; of extending the frontiers of the Monroe Doctrine across the Atlantic to distant lands. And during the Presidential campaign of 1940, FDR declared in Boston, "Your boys are not going to be sent into any foreign wars."

Before Pearl Harbor some of the press were openly challenging the Roosevelt statements and calling into question his "credibility."

The upshot of FDR's Credibility Gaps has been a succession of monographs and books, both during and after the War, accusing him of a massive conspiracy to plunge the United States into a foreign war.

Even as scholarly and stable an historian as Samuel Flagg Bemis of Yale prefers the conclusion that Roosevelt "tricked us into war for our own good."

Why, then, did not Franklin Roosevelt suffer more from the consequences of credibility gap than he did? A portion of the answer would have to rest with the specific way in which the war began; namely, the Japanese attack on Pearl Harbor. Quite literally overnight, a questioning and doubtful America—until then badly split over the question of involvement—suddenly closed ranks in the wake of the assault which was to "live in infamy."

It would be difficult to exaggerate the extent to which Pearl Harbor closed the Credibility Gap.

From these earlier cases of Credibility Gaps in our time, one then is entitled to ask, why has Credibility Gap remained such a constant issue in the public arena? I believe there are several explanations.

The most obvious is that in Vietnam there has been no single galvanizing incident commensurate with Pearl Harbor or even the

German submarine. A single incident of the dimension of those which preceded other wars would almost certainly make a great difference today.

A second explanation lies in the nature of the war in Southeast Asia. It is undeclared. It is prosecuted without the strictures of a grave national emergency and all of the limitations of censorship, total mobilization, rationing, and other curbs characteristic of "total war." Limited objectives, the effort to isolate a conflict to avoid its spread to neighboring areas, all contribute to a public sense of frustration and futility the longer the conflict goes on. Cliches about a "no-win" policy, "get in or get out," or "no substitute for victory" only add fuel to the flames and, again, become poor substitutes for thinking.

A third reason stems from the lack of public sophistication in understanding the connection between waging peace or probing for a pause simultaneously with the vigorous prosecution of a war.

A fourth—the modern phenomenon of "instant communications." For the first time, the general public not only witnesses the details of day-to-day warfare on a screen in the living room, it also experiences the emotions, the shock, the horror that unavoidably warp rational judgments.

The nature of the news-gathering in itself tends to do violence to one's sense of perspective. The competition among news gatherers to file a story first often tortures truth. The facts have a way of becoming the first casualty. Sensational assertions made by a reporter have a way of surviving longer in public opinion than any corrections to those assertions which may be supplied later from the advantage of hindsight as well as of more hard information.

Vietnam must be the most over-reported war in all history. For example, many of us can recall the television shots of street fighting in Saigon during the Tet assaults of 1968 in which there appeared to be more newsmen than soldiers surrounding some of the targets.

If facts become the first casualty, then perspective becomes the second. News reporting from the battlefronts often reflects a high stress account from one front. Rarely do newsmen, even editors, have the advantage of collating the reports from *all* fronts or assessing them in a situation room—evaluating them in the context of the "big picture." A newsman witnesses a South Vietnamese military unit fighting only from dawn to dark. From it, the conclusion quickly spreads across our own country that the ARVN are only daylight soldiers.

Or in another instance, one ARVN Unit "caved in" under enemy attack. Quickly the generalization is spread via news accounts that the ARVN can't fight.

Both of these actual cases in point do violence to the record of the regular army of South Vietnam. To General Westmoreland, who has in front of him a situation map of the military activity in the whole country, it means one thing. To the reporter on the scene, it means quite something else. And to the reader, what the reporter saw will create greater shock than what the General in charge may see. Thus, credibility once again becomes an issue.

Fifth, closely related to the demand for unlimited reporting remains the need to withhold—even from the "free American press"—vital information which could prove of value to the enemy. Many illustrations come to mind which make this point.

An obvious one was the preoccupation in the press over American aircraft losses. There are occasions when the precise number of aircraft destroyed in combat should have been withheld for the reason that the other side needed to know as badly as we did. Even the running totals of aircraft losses must aid and abet the enemy's efforts to keep their own accurate books.

When we add to battle losses the numbers of aircraft lost through accidents or other non-enemy actions, we have exposed another sensitive nerve as far as the press is concerned. In some of this matter of accurate information, moreover, it is impossible to win with the press.

When casualties were once estimated in round numbers, like 100 or 2,000, the criticism was often made that round numbers were most unlikely. Therefore, somebody was withholding the facts. Yet, recently when casualty figures were listed as 727 or totaling 2,209, some press accounts carried critical comments that it would be impossible for anyone to know casualty figures with such preciseness.

The specifics of the reference were called into question by the same press that had challenged the generalities of the round numbers estimates used earlier!

Another favorite gimmick which aggravates credibility involves the "leaked" speculation that the government is weighing some sinister policy alternative which in itself carries frightening implications. At different times in the course of events in the war in Vietnam, scare headlines about gas warfare required denials and explanation. To the man-in-the-street, "gas" meant mustard gas of World War I fame or some more lethal type of gas. When the gas used in Vietnam turned out to be riot gasses or tear gas, the impact of the corrections was not sufficient to overcome the near panic of the first assertions.

Similar reactions greeted the rumor that bacteriological warfare was about to be launched against the North. Even the prospect of a "preventive war" against Peking received a major play in some headlines.

More recently, some Senators have had "fun and games" over the horrifying prospect of the United States using nuclear weapons against North Vietnam.

It is not that these possible extremes should be viewed complacently by *anyone*. But there is no case for responsible people—especially Senators—employing them on "fishing expeditions" or as trial balloons either to gain a headline for themselves or to cause embarrassment to a government which they oppose.

Seventh, credibility is further strained through the play on words. A favorite one is "escalation." At issue is whether the build-up of American troops in Vietnam should be a matter subject to the principles of "freedom of the press;" or conversely, does the withholding of troop information sustain the criticism of "managed news?" Is it not conceivable that the mere announcement of troop arrivals is of some benefit to the enemy?

Each time another 3,000 men have landed in Vietnam or a new air squadron arrives, the press tends to label it as the latest "escalation." Because the word "escalation" is usually construed as meaning the widening of the war or the lessening of the efforts to keep it a limited conflict, it is unfortunate that the communications media couldn't have chosen another word to describe the steady build-up of the limited forces necessary for insuring success in a limited and restrained operation.

The increase in the number of troops does not *ipso facto* change either the scope of the war or its purposes. It only intensifies the power available to achieve the original goals.

Eighth, credibility has been confused by some of the terminology used in explaining the American commitments in Southeast Asia. Such phrases as "special advisers" or "free elections" or "democracy" or "will of the people" have been employed interchangeably in the dialogue on Vietnam. So also have the phrases "containment of China" or "balance of power" or "stopping aggression." The point is that critics or some Administration spokesmen have tended in the past to dwell on the more noble of the explanations—sometimes in an apparent attempt to avoid the blunt and the unpleasant.

In rereading the public declarations on why we are in Vietnam, I have been struck with the steady reference to which the President and the Secretary of State have resorted in explaining the issue as one involving all of Eastern Asia; as being much bigger than just a single country. It is possible, however, for a writer to lift any one of these phrases out of context and make what he will out of it. Unfortunately, this has been done at the sacrifice of perspective.

It is in this context that one's memory goes back again to the "gap" which concerned Franklin D. Roosevelt and the lag in American public opinion in the 1930's. While it is entirely possible that a case can be made to show that FDR had to "plant" stories or to contrive incidents in order to move public opinion along with him toward a confrontation against Hitler, that is not necessarily a valid parallel for the present. I say that because the American people unquestionably learned a great deal about the harsh facts of international life during World War II. What's more, they learned a great deal more about the dimensions of limited war during the conflict in Korea. I rather believe that the sophistication of the American public in the ways of world politics today, after three wars in Asia in less than a generation, is one that demands bluntness, candor, and straight-forwardness.

Politicians, in particular, should be loathe to cater to what *they think* the public might prefer to hear and should cater more to what their public *ought* to hear. The time for spoon-feeding the people with a lot of international pablum is long gone. The man-in-the-street is not afraid of the bad or the ugly or even the bloody if only he believes it to be genuine and needful.

The public dialogues of the future on American foreign policy must be dominated by forthrightness, clarity, and conducted without pulling punches.

But to assess the issue of credibility fairly, it is necessary to examine the policies of North Vietnam in recent years. So much of the dialogue on American policy in Asia has focused upon the details and daily crises in South Vietnam and, at the same time, has ignored Hanoi almost entirely.

This final exercise remains to be run through in order to evaluate the substance of the Credibility Gap controversy: With the advantage of some hindsight, what has been the truth about the operations of the North Vietnamese in South Vietnam? Lurking behind many of the credibility charges has always been an assumption among some people that the need for the American presence in Southeast Asia was a fake—that there was no cause—that it was without reason. Assertions that the conflict is only a civil war at worst, or a case of latent nationalism finally asserting itself, have been common during the debates on Vietnam. The heart of the matter usually comes down to the widely held belief that there has been no forceful intervention into the South by Hanoi.

What evidence is there that the North in fact is trying to overthrow South Vietnam by force? During the course of the Vietnamese conflict, an increasing number of captured documents from the bodies of enemy dead or on the person of those captives who have since been interrogated make for more than interesting reading. They tend to confirm in cold terms the substance of the Administration's case for Vietnam.

There has become available an increasing number of the actual texts of enemy documents captured in operations against both the North Vietnamese and the NLF headquarters and bases in South Vietnam during the past two years.

While the insurgency has been in part South Vietnamese from the start, the *North Vietnamese involvement has been a determining factor at every stage.* The scope of this Northern involvement is all-encompassing. It extends from the power of decision to make war, which the Lao Dong Party Politburo exercised in 1959, to the power of making peace, which the Politburo has so far chosen not to exert. It includes the definition of strategy and the provision of the indispensable means—human as well as material. In both the political and the military sphere, the authority of Hanoi is final.

Among the most interesting documents captured was a notebook containing a 10,000-word review of the "Experiences of the South Viet-Nam Revolutionary Movement" during the years 1954-1963. According to this document, the most interesting development of this period was a far-reaching policy decision taken by the Second Party Central Committee at its 15th Conference in early 1959. The resolution of this conference clearly spelled out the revolutionary task in South Viet-Nam and at the same time outlined "the path which the South Viet-Nam revolution should take."

Throughout these documents, it should be made clear, the party organs referred to are those of the *Lao Dong,* or Vietnamese Worker's Party, as the Communist Party of Vietnam has been called since 1951. In 1959 as before and since, it was a single party throughout Vietnam with a unified central command headquartered in the North where its main strength lay. First formed in 1930 as the Indochina Communist Party (ICP), it then included sections in Laos and Cambodia as well as Vietnam and still is a force in those countries.

If one studies these documents, there are several key themes that are summarized under the following headings:

North Vietnamese Policy: 1954-59

The nature of the policy directives from North Vietnam to its southern agents in the immediate aftermath of Geneva has been documented from many sources, including captured party papers, defectors, interrogation of prisoners, and Hanoi's own public statements. In essence, Hanoi's policy was two-fold; on the one hand, to create the impression that it was living up to the Geneva Agreements; on the other, to build up its southern apparatus and to carry on a "political struggle," by all means legal and illegal, short of open violence, against the South Vietnamese Government.

1959: The Decision for War

Captured documents illustrate revealingly the extent of northern control over the insurgent apparatus in the South. By 1958, according to the author quoted above, "the majority of the party members and cadres felt that it was necessary to immediately launch armed struggle in order to preserve the movement and protect the forces. In several areas the party members on their own initiative had organized armed struggle against the enemy.

"Since the end of 1958 . . . the situation truly ripened for an armed movement against the enemy. But the leadership of the Nam Bo Regional Committee at that time still hesitated, for many reasons, but the principal reason was the fear of violating the party line." Not until the Central Committee and Politburo in Hanoi had given the order was the new phase of violence launched.

Why the North Vietnamese regime waited so long before intervening in force in the South is uncertain. There were serious problems at home, however; and Hanoi was providing substantial assistance in troops and supplies to the Pathet Lao rebels in Laos—another basic violation of its commitments at Geneva.

However, the critical decision of the 15th Conference, (1959) to which I referred earlier, was taken. Thus, the struggle took the form of revolutionary warfare in the South. Secret briefings for the party cadre made this still more explicit: With North Vietnamese help, the scattered Viet Cong units were to be built into a major fighting force—a "liberation army."

In late 1959 the real upsurge of terror began. By the end of the year, more than 580 civilians had been murdered. Armed attacks had increased significantly in size with company-strength Viet Cong units appearing in assaults on army outposts and patrols.

As a matter of record, it should be noted that, at the time of the decisive 15th Central Committee Conference, the number of American military personnel helping to train the South Vietnamese Army was still very small, in compliance with the Geneva armistice terms. It was not until after 1961, more than two years after North Vietnam had decided to mount a broad military effort to overthrow the government in Saigon, that the build-up of this body of military instructors and advisers began. No United States combat unit was sent to South Vietnam until 1965.

1964: Commitment of North Vietnamese Resources
(excluding order of battle [or] date)

By 1964, the Communists had reason to believe they were well on their way to victory in South Vietnam. Under the pressure of political subversion and armed attack, the Diem Government had become increasingly dictatorial; in November, 1963 it fell to a coup, after a violent confrontation with dissident Buddhists. Political instability in Saigon deepened, army effectiveness declined, and the strategic hamlet program started by Diem disintegrated. To capitalize on this trend, Hanoi decided to commit its army and resources on a still broader scale in a drive for final success.

As a result of the massive infiltration, the ratio of North Vietnamese regular army to Viet Cong battalions in the south rose considerably during 1966 and 1967.

With the eastern portions of the Laotian panhandle securely under Communist control, Hanoi had begun as early as 1964 to develop its infiltration trails into an army-scale supply route, capable of handling continuous heavy truck traffic to South Vietnam. Motorable roads from the Laos-North Vietnam border, at the Mu Gia Pass, were extended south almost 500 miles.

At some point in this review, it is important to emphasize what captured documents reveal about North Vietnamese control and political direction of the war in the South.

The National Liberation Front

In 1960, Party Secretary Le Duan stated at the Third Party Congress that "a broad national united front" must be organized in South Vietnam. This stemmed from the 1959 Assembly resolution that the "struggle plan" should be composed of a liberation army supported by a national liberation front.

Several captured documents describe in detail the Communist role in organizing and directing the "Liberation Army"—supposedly the creature of the Front.

Control of the Liberation Front

Communist control of the National Liberation Front in its political aspect is equally comprehensive as many documents and statements of party members testify. The testimony of a party functionary who played a role in the Western Region Front Committee before his capture in 1962 is representative. In all departments, he said, the Front committee leadership included Lao Dong Party agents who directed the work. While in theory the Front committee in his area assumed responsibility for the insurgents' military, political, economic, and cultural affairs, in reality it had little authority. Its principal function was to conduct overt propaganda campaigns.

The People's Revolutionary Party

In addition to forming the National Liberation Front, Hanoi decided on another measure to conceal the North Vietnamese hand in the affairs of the South. This was to give the appearance of separating the Communist elements in South Vietnam from the party in the North by giving them a different party identity. In January, 1962, accordingly, Hanoi Radio announced that a conference of "Marxist-Leninist" delegates in South Vietnam had organized a new party—a "People's Revolutionary Party" (PRP), to serve "workers, peasants, and laborers" in South Vietnam as a "vanguard group." The new party, according to the broadcast, had immediately "volunteered" to join the Liberation Front. This tactic is exposed in a number of documents, perhaps nowhere more succinctly than in this quotation from a party committee report in Ba Xuyen Province:

> "The People's Revolutionary Party has only the appearance of an independent existence; actually, our party is nothing but the Lao Dong Party of Viet-Nam, unified from North to South, under the direction of the Central Executive Committee of the Party, the chief of which is President Ho."

The Central Office for South Vietnam (COSVN)

From a considerable number of confirmed prisoner statements and authenticated documents, the organizational machinery by which North Vietnam controls the insurgent movement can be reconstructed. The apparatus is complex and includes both a party control channel and direct military control over certain units in each case from Hanoi.

The primary control link, and the one to which all others are ultimately subordinate, runs from the policy-making Central Committee and Politburo of the Lao Dong Party at Hanoi to its top echelon in the South—the Central Committee of the People's

Revolutionary Party. According to a former staff member who defected in 1966, the PRP's Central Committee is made up of 30 to 40 high-ranking Communists. Although the size and the composition of the committee varies, the real decision-making power resides in a select group of its highest ranking members. This standing committee is known as the *Trung Dong Cuc Mien Nam,* the Central Office for South Vietnam (COSVN).

As the overall military and political command body, COSVN has two major arms—a Military Affairs Committee and a (political) Current Affairs Committee. The Military Affairs Committee in turn directs the Communist military effort through two subordinate organizations—a Chief of the General Staff and a Political Department of the Army. Since 1965 and perhaps earlier, COSVN and its military committee have been heavily weighted with prominent North Vietnamese general officers.

The Choice of War or Peace

Documents captured during the past year have provided fresh evidence to show that the Central Committee and the Politburo in Hanoi are setting the pace and direction of the war. Among the most revealing of these documents is a 17-page letter signed by the First Secretary of the Lao Dong Party, Le Duan, then transmitted to the southern command and reproduced in early 1966 for lower echelons.

As the party's chief executive under Ho Chi Minh, Le Duan was explaining to the field commanders the newest strategic decisions for the conduct of the war. These had just been taken in secret at the Twelfth Conference of the Third Central Committee in December, 1965 and expressed in an important "Resolution 12."

As Le Duan's letter notes, before the introduction of U.S. combat units in South Vietnam, "We were winning" and were "about to defeat the enemy." But by the time of the Twelfth Conference, American troops had begun to inflict heavy losses on the communist forces.

The Central Committee had also fixed the Party position on another topic of importance—"the problem of war and negotiation," as Le Duan's letter puts it. Le Duan described the Committee decision:

"There are those who hold the view that the political struggle is of major importance, but such a view is different from ours as to degree and time to use this strategy. At present the U.S. imperialists . . . are trying to force us to the negotiation table for some concessions . . . [but] our strategy on negotiation must serve in a practical manner our concrete political aims."

Other documents give more details. One is a record of a briefing on Resolution 12 by "Comrade Vinh," undoubtedly Lieutenant General Nguyen Van Vinh, a deputy chief of staff of the army and chief of the Central Committee's National Reunification Commission. The Central Committee judged, according to this source, that "the situation is not yet ripe for negotiations . . . as long as we have not yet acquired adequate strength a situation where fighting and negotiations are conducted simultaneously does not exist."

I cannot believe that any citizen who takes the time to read these statements—and they are authentic*—can have any question about the necessity for our stand in South Vietnam. Let me give you two final quotations from the captured documents:

"The future situation may lead to negotiations . . . While negotiating, we will continue fighting the enemy more vigorously . . . "

And finally, whatever the future,

"the Party Central Committee entrusts the Politburo with the task of deciding on the time for negotiations."

The latter is the clearest statement I have seen on North Vietnamese responsibility for the war in South Vietnam. How else can you put it? It is the Lao Dong Politburo in Hanoi which will decide when to negotiate for peace.

Lest there be those who would say the enemy documents may be phonies, so how can we be sure? We can never be absolutely sure. Nor could it be established beyond doubt that some of the documents are deliberately planted by the other side for the purpose of deceiving or misleading. The pace of events in Asia denies us the luxury of biding our time until "certainty" can be determined. This

*Arrangements are being made to make the texts, and summaries of them, available for study at the State Department and at various academic centers around the country.

is not unique to the current struggle in Southeast Asia. The uncertainties in Europe in 1939, or in Korea in 1950, haunted most of us who recall those crisis years.

In sorting through the mass of intelligence materials, however, responsibility requires that we fit the useful pieces together in as wise a way as reason among mortals permits. Some would call that an "educated guess." Whatever else, the educated guess appears to me to come closer to the larger developments which have dominated the landscape in Eastern Asia since World War II than do the absence of materials or credentials hinted at, speculated about, but never discovered by the Critical Establishment. In other words, the burden of proof falls heavily upon those who doubt.

This brings us back to the beginning of this chapter which set out to be an exploration of credibility and the war in Vietnam. The role of the government may often appear to be contradictory or complex. There is no substantive evidence, however, that the government is deliberately deceptive; nor is it involved in a conscious conspiracy to keep the public in the dark.

The government does not lie. It could not, even if it chose. Constantly under the scrutiny of the press as it is, and much as it must remain ever at the mercy of searching inquiries from the Members of Congress, it couldn't get away with it even if it so designed.   It is important, therefore, that we carefully separate judgment from conspiracy—mistakes from plots—and allow for the hairline difference between the total weights of the pluses and the minuses which have to be thrown on the scales of judgment in arriving at policy decisions.

A "Credibility Gap" in Vietnam? It depends to some extent on whether the measuring stick is the maze of daily minutia with which we are deluged or whether it is the hard basis for an American presence in Eastern Asia—a presence which four Presidents in succession have reaffirmed.

In retrospect, the constancy of an American policy which has said that what happens in Southeast Asia makes a difference to the United States, that its shape and form affect our national interest, and constitutes a credible basis for our Vietnam policy.

A "Credibility Gap" in Vietnam? On balance, it would seem to be the accusation itself that tends to strain one's credibility. The extremes of the straining become, in fact, incredible.

CHAPTER X

The Incredibility Gap

The national anguish over what is meant by credibility on the part of the government is only one side of the coin. The doubts about credibility should not blind us to the "incredibility" gaps which have also appeared during the dialogues on Vietnam. Whatever one chooses to believe about the credibility of policy statements on the part of the government establishment, it would be at least fair to say that this group is disciplined by having to take the consequences for its decisions and thus is restricted in its options by a large measure of responsibility.

Among the dissenters and the critics, the opposite has been true. The Critical Establishment enjoys the luxury of irresponsibility. It can afford to speculate, to theorize, even to contradict itself in the quest for attacks against Administration policy. It is this circumstance which lends itself to the incredibility gap.

Because too little attention has been paid to some of the more incredible assertions by even the prestigious members of the Critical Establishment, it is in order to note the extremes to which they have gone in their criticisms. This is done not to discredit the sincerity of these men, but rather to question the validity of their judgments.

When the Vietnam dialogue began on the floor of the Senate soon after President Johnson's decision to bomb the North (February, 1965), the shifting sands of dissent quickly appeared. One of the most common arguments made by the critics at that time was that a tougher American policy would drive the Russian Communists and the Chinese Communists closer together. This was a warning repeated many times in that first year of heated debate. (One still hears its echoes in the wings today.)

However, as the war continued, the opposite seemed to be the case; and the Critical Establishment blithely shifted to new ground for debate. This was that, regardless of the Russians, American policy in Vietnam was headed toward a land war with China. They ignored the fact that the American air attacks were severely curbed by deliberate efforts to avoid incidents along the Chinese border; and that policies, which in other ways might incite the Chinese to war, were specifically rejected (such as committing Nationalist Chinese troops from Taiwan to the field in Vietnam). The critics took solace in the advice from somebody, sometime, about never fighting a land war in Asia. *What kind* of a land war, and *with whom,* did not seem to bother those who retreated to this argument.

The dean of the American political pundits is Mr. Walter Lippmann. Almost from the outset, he has been out front on the firing line in behalf of the Critical Establishment. Mr. Lippmann, who contended from the very first after World War II (in *The Cold War,* 1947) that a policy of containment of Russia was both unrealistic and reckless, has carried the same disproven thesis all the way to the China Sea. He has published a little essay proposing that the United States get out of Asia in fact and put our forward base in Australia instead.

To reach that conclusion, he travels by way of the Asian mainland. He writes,

> "It always has been axiomatic that we must exert our power offshore and must never allow ourselves to get pulled deeply onto the mainland."[1]

If he had only said stay out of Asia, one could at least come to grips with his assertion on that basis. But he says instead it had always been "axiomatic" which suggests that somehow there was a deeply written and invaluable bit of wisdom which has accumulated in our country's history advising us of this fact.

History now tells us that the late entry of the United States into World War II probably tipped the scales in favor of the Allies. But there is no record in that War that more than 2 million American troops stayed in boats offshore. The problem that threatened the security of the world lay on the mainland of Europe, and that's where the soldiers were sent.

Again, in the assault upon Hitler's fortress Europe, what was required was the smashing of the Wehrmacht on land—not of Hitler's power on the sea. There is no record of the millions of American troops having remained offshore of the mainland of the European continent.

In the Cold War the Greeks were not emboldened to resist the Communists from across their frontier because of American loud-speakers which broadcast messages of encouragement to them from the safe waters of the Mediterranean.

Nor did the South Koreans succeed in maintaining their own independence below the 38th Parallel because of a flotilla of American ships that remained in the Sea of Japan.

By the same token, the American Navy poised off the seacoast of Thailand and Burma, to assure them that we were backing them against their Chinese neighbors to the north, would hardly inspire either government to rejoice in a new sense of security.

In each case American fighting men were committed to the mainland because that is where the problem was. If there is any axiom at all in the history of the last fifty years, it is that the United States has rarely settled its final differences on the high seas. In every case the ultimate outcome was slugged out on somebody's mainland somewhere.

This is why it remains incredible for a philosopher of Mr. Lippmann's credentials to take the record of history as lightly as he has.

Subsequently, the man generally credited with being the author of that statement (no land war in Asia), General Omar Bradley, has made it clear that, in the days of Korea when he talked about avoiding a land war in Asia, he was talking about waging campaigns on Chinese territory, under Chinese terms. At no time, Bradley has explained, did he have in mind excluding the need for conflicts around the rim of China. General Bradley has taken great care, in fact, to explain that, in his opinion, Vietnam is the right place at the right time.

Soon thereafter the critics again shifted their focus—this time to the conditions inside Vietnam, excluding from their dialogue any reference to the larger context of the crisis in Asia. Their debate was immersed in the internal politics of Saigon—in corruption and the misery of noncombatants. It was a "shotgun" attack, apparently reflecting the hope that a few of the pellets might strike some kind of target.

But the pellet which seemed to strike home was that which had to do with the mechanism of democracy inside Vietnam. This was selected, perhaps, because it struck a familiar chord here in the United States; it evoked in the minds of the average American parallel thoughts about his own appreciation of democratic processes.

The tactic on the part of the critics was to dare policymakers in Washington to do the impossible in South Vietnam, (never bothering in the process to challenge Ho Chi Minh to achieve similarly hopeless deeds in the North).

First the dissenters demanded the calling of a Constituent Assembly in Vietnam for the "impossible" task of drafting a constitution—all to be achieved in a country that had known no democracy, that had not experienced the processes of self-government, and that was caught in the throes of all-out war for its very survival. It must have hit the critics with some surprise when the Constituent Assembly was indeed called and a national constitution was in fact drafted and ratified.

One might have expected the critics now to acknowledge these "near miracles" and to concede that some progress had been made. Instead, they argued almost as one voice that it was all a hoax anyway—that neither the Assembly nor the constitution meant anything unless free elections could be held under them.

When the plans for those elections were finally announced, Senatorial critics rushed to the floor to pronounce them "phony" or "rigged" or to assess them as a "hoax." Senator Javits said the election should be postponed because "the whole election process has been gravely compromised by actions direct and indirect, of the present military authorities."[2] Senator Clark predicted the election would be "meaningless in terms of representing the will of the people of South Vietnam . . ."[3] Senator Robert Kennedy declared

"There is mounting and distressing evidence of efforts to interfere with the free choice of the people . . ."[4] Senator Clark predicted the election "will be close to a fraud."[5] Senator Steve Young said "It is hard to imagine any more complete rigging of an election than this . . ."[6] Senator Frank Church asserted that "the upcoming elections in South Vietnam are little more than charade."[7] All these comments before a single vote had been cast!

The elections themselves came off surprisingly well. Inspection teams, not only from the United States but from many other countries, discovered few flagrant cases of corruption and ballot-box stuffing. To be sure, the voting exercise was not perfect. As one veteran of South Vietnamese politics put it, "Of course the elections weren't totally free, but they were the freest ever held in Vietnam." He might well have added that they were also staged under the most trying of circumstances—in the midst of a war in which many of the voters were threatened with their lives if they dared to go to the polls. The important thing is that the elections worked.

Once again, it would not have been unreasonable to expect the critics to acknowledge that another "near miracle" had taken place in the South; but they were already scattering in other directions, out of reach of the facts of this newest bit of progress. Immediately they zeroed in on the new government elected at the polls, castigating its minority dimensions and its military overtones. Senator Charles Percy, in a Senate speech, decried the validity of the elected government because "the winning candidate received only 34.8 percent of the vote."[8]

It is difficult to escape the conclusion at this point that the critics of American policy in Vietnam were not looking for light on that policy any more than they were in quest of a genuine solution to the problem of Southeast Asia other than the abandonment of the region. Apparently they felt they dared not directly advocate withdrawal but rather had to sneak up gradually on that proposition. Very few of the dissenters, in fact, were forthright enough to say that the Americans didn't belong there in the first place and that the sooner we withdrew from Asia the better.

There began also, by the late spring of 1965, the first of the demands for a bombing pause over the North to try to induce Hanoi to sit down at the negotiating table. When this was first tried in May,

(May 13-17) 1965 and failed, the critics immediately raised the cry that it had not been long enough. As if to call their hand, President Johnson initiated a bombing pause at the end of the year which was extended for thirty-seven days. Again, no response. In all, there have been nine bombing pauses. In each case the response seemed only to be an escalation of the epithets hurled by Hanoi at the United States and its intentions, along with a behind-the-lines build-up of supplies and men for the prosecution of the war.

When a limited bombing pause was ordered by President Johnson shortly after his March 31 address to the nation, the Critical Establishment at once began to nit-pick the terms of the pause. One critic called the President dishonest in the charge. Others apparently chose to ignore that the pause had been ordered only above the 20th Parallel. All of them, moreover, temporarily caught short by the pause, then asserted that the feelers for a negotiation site proved they had been right all along!

The hard fact is that the pressures maintained by the bombing produced the feelers. The critics once again were guilty of reasoning backwards from effect to cause.

So much, then, for the shifting tactics of the Critical Establishment. The critics were caught up in their own incredibility. They were soon bent upon a new tactic, however, aimed at extricating themselves from the shifting positions which spelled out their successive lines of retreat. The new approach was to invent their own arguments against American policy in Asia, erect them as "strawmen" in their *own* dialogues with each other, and then proceed to knock them down.

The most sensational—and most incredible—attack on American policy in Asia has been the dissenters' charge that the *Administration was changing its reasons for the war in Vietnam and retreating behind the specter of the Yellow Peril.*

Ever since the beginning of the dissent on Vietnam, there has been a rhythmic beat among the critics reflecting this charge, both from the Senate floor and from spokesmen for the intellectual community. It exploded in the public forum when Senator Eugene McCarthy made it the principal thrust of a Senate speech, obviously in preparation of his announcement to run for President. James Reston of the *New York Times* had already carefully detailed the charge shortly in advance of the McCarthy address.

The point of the charge is two-fold; first, that Secretary Rusk in a statement on October 12, 1967, had referred to a billion Chinese constituting the real threat at this time. This, it was asserted, was stooping to a new low in cheap propaganda tactics by reviving the old "Yellow Peril" fear characteristic of the wave of imperialism which swept the world at the turn of the 20th Century.

The second point of the charge was that this tactic was a basic change by the Administration of its excuses for the "why" of Vietnam. The critics argued that the President and the Secretary of State had, until then, rested the justification for the American presence in Vietnam on Saigon's need for help in winning democracy, freedom, and national independence, and that never before had the reasons for American policy been put in terms of the containment of China.

The critics went on to assert that, not only had President Johnson changed his own purposes in the war, but that his predecessor, President Kennedy, would have done it all quite differently.

Both of these assertions are incredible, as an examination of each will prove.

At no time did the President or Secretary Rusk or anyone else mention Yellow Peril or cast the crisis in Asia in racial terms of any shape or form. This was invented by newspaper columnists and Senators.

What Secretary of State Dean Rusk *did* say was,

> "Within the next decade or two, there will be a billion Chinese on the Mainland, armed with nuclear weapons, with no certainty about what their attitude toward the rest of Asia will be."

Only an inventor resorting to "incredible" insinuations could read into that declaration what the critics claimed. The suggestion that one billion Chinese posed a potential problem in Asia was balanced by his reminder that there would soon be another billion non-Chinese (also yellow?) who had as much right as Peking to determine the future of Asia.

It was simply the Secretary's way of reminding us, as American scholars and Asian statesmen have been doing for many years, that the central problem in Asia is China—the color is irrelevant. That it is an overwhelming factor in terms of power *is* relevant to the billion Asians who have to live in the shadow of China. It is also relevant to the United States whose destiny seems to be linked irretrievably to the course of events in the Pacific. Anyone who expresses shock at the mention of China as an Asian problem related to our presence in Vietnam has closed his mind to the power politics of his own time.

From the beginning of the postwar quest for peace, American policy committed itself to the restructuring of some sense of stability in Eastern Asia. It was epitomized by President Truman's Administration and his Secretary of State, Dean Acheson. It was characteristic of both of the Eisenhower Administrations and the diplomacy of Secretary of State John Foster Dulles in the decade of the 1950's. Whether the issue was Quemoy and Matsu, "unleashing Chiang," restoring the 38th Parallel in northeastern Asia, rushing aid to India in 1961, or dispatching the Marines to the border of Laos and Thailand in 1962, it all stemmed from the same basic concern—the threat posed by Mainland China to the chances for stability and orderly change in the Far East.

Even in non-military terms it could be seen that the major chunks of the American economic system under the AID program were reserved for South Korea, Formosa, and South Vietnam. The United States national interest already lay in keeping those strategically important areas out of the hands of the Red Chinese. The AID programs, the efforts to inspire a SEATO collective security organization, the intensity of American diplomatic missions along the eastern front of Asia, all were surface manifestations stemming from a deep conviction that what might happen in that part of the world made a great difference to the United States.

When Secretary Rusk was upbraided by a questioner for having "invented" the China threat so late in the game, his reply was sharp and to the point. He said, "Who do you think we have been preparing these defenses against in all of Asia—the Eskimos?"

In sum, the main thrust of the American policy in Vietnam from the very beginning was that it was to the advantage of the United States to prevent the loss of Southeast Asia either to China directly, or through liberation fronts and "suitcase revolutions" indirectly.

In regard to the second charge made by the Critical Establish-ment—*that President Johnson has changed his purposes in the war*—the record itself lays bare another falsehood. In most of his public statements, the President has repeated the importance of containing China. There is no quarrel with the fact that the intensity of the fighting in Vietnam has changed very much, but there has been no change in the basic premises as to *why* we are there.

Yet the Senator from New York, Robert F. Kennedy, contended otherwise. He asserted not only that his brother, the President, would have acted differently (more on this below), but also that the John-son Administration has switched its purposes. That switch, he con-tended, was from helping the Vietnamese to decide their own future to fighting for the American national interest.

In the same vein, Senator Fulbright said he was puzzled by the interchangeable references to the self-determination of the South Vietnamese people and the excuse that we are restraining Chinese expansion. "These don't seem to me to be consistent," he concluded.

What the Chairman of the Foreign Relations Committee sees as irrelevant is the fact that our purposes in Southeast Asia are multiple. The public record, moreover, is emphatic on one point—that the President of the United States has constantly repeated the same and rationale for Vietnam, specifically, that the right of the South to determine her own future must not be allowed to be foreclosed by force from the North because to do so would encourage similar thrusts of Chinese pressures elsewhere in Asia.

In January, 1965, for example, President Johnson declared in his State of the Union message that "In Asia communism wears a more aggressive face . . . our own security is tied to the peace of Asia . . . to ignore aggression now would only increase the danger of a much larger war."

Three months later, in his famous Johns Hopkins speech of April, 1965, he not only referred to the narrow base of "a promise to keep" to the Vietnamese Government, but also offered the stronger argument that if the United States were to abandon Vietnam it would "shake the confidence of all of these people [in Asia] in the value of an American commitment and in the value of America's word."

We have a strong responsibility to Asia, he went on to emphasize, "for the same reason that we have a responsibility for the defense of Europe."

By mid-year 1965 (July 28), during the rapid build-up of American forces, the President declared that the war "is guided by North Vietnam and it's spurred by Communist China." He also referred to the Chinese threat by saying that "if we are driven from the field in Vietnam, then no nation can ever again have the same confidence in American promise or in American protection."

But what would President John F. Kennedy have done?

Some of the critics profess to know with certainty. They continually suggest that, whatever it was, it would have been different from what President Johnson has done. The argument goes like this. Eisenhower and Kennedy avoided a big war in Vietnam, and it was LBJ who got us into it. That is like saying that Coolidge and Hoover kept us out of World War II, but FDR plunged us into it.

The simple truth is that no one can know for sure what JFK's response would have been to the commitment of North Vietnamese main forces to the struggle in the South by late 1964. Even those closest to the late President cannot know what he would have done had the total collapse of the Saigon Government been imminent. What we do know, however, is what President Kennedy *said for the record* when he was the Commander-in-Chief.

On August 3, 1961, while there were yet only a few hundred American advisers in Vietnam and the struggle there was still a Vietnamese struggle, he said, "The United States is determined that the Republic of Vietnam shall not be lost to the Communists for lack of any support which the United States can render."

Within two years, President Kennedy made another interesting declaration which reveals his concept of what Southeast Asia meant to the United States. By that time, thousands of American military advisers were engaged in the actual fighting. As President Kennedy spoke of the threat of Communist China by the 1970's, he described China's overwhelming power as measurable in these terms: She was surrounded on her borders by small countries so weak that they could not hope to restrain her. In addition, Kennedy said, China's other worrisome attributes are "700 million people, a Stalinist internal regime, and nuclear powers, and a government determined on war as a means of bringing about its ultimate success." This was "potentially a more dangerous situation than any we faced since the end of the Second War ... [by contrast] the Russians pursued in most cases their ambitions with some caution. Even in the case of the most overt aggression, which was the North Korean invasion of South Korea, other forces were used and not the Russians."[9]

Those comments sound strangely like the utterances of Secretary of State Dean Rusk about "a billion Chinese" to which the critics have responded with such bitter attacks. When President Kennedy was asked whether the United States should withdraw from Vietnam, he replied, "that would be a great mistake. . . . We made this effort to defend Europe and now Europe is quite secure. We also have to participate—and may not like it—in the defense of Asia."

At no time, however, was President Kennedy more explicit in his analysis of the problem in Southeast Asia then during an NBC televised interview on September 9, 1963—scarcely more than two months before his death. On that occasion, he was asked if he had any reason to doubt the "domino theory"—that a defeat at the hands of the Communists in one key Asian country would cause the others to topple. He responded:

> "No. I believe it. I believe it. I think the struggle is close enough. China is so large, looms so high just beyond the frontiers, that if South Viet-Nam went, it would not only give them an improved geographic position for a guerrilla assault on Malaya, but would also give the impression that the wave of the future in southeast Asia was China and the Communists. So I believe it."[10]

Whatever misgivings John F. Kennedy may have had about the internal weaknesses of the Saigon Government, he always seemed to be at pains to urge patience and, invariably, to dismiss the idea that the United States should get out. All of this from the open, public records says that, for seven years, Presidents Kennedy and Johnson pursued an unbroken and unfaltering policy of commitment in Southeast Asia—a policy rooted deeply in the actions of Eisenhower and Truman before them.

Another Straw Man

Among the critics the charge is leveled that *American policy is rigidly dominated by the concept that a monolithic world-Communist structure is our enemy.*

In the intellectual world, Professor Henry Steele Commager has asserted,

> "The trouble with our foreign policy has been our assumption that communism was monolithic and universal . . . this we have come to in the face of the fact that communism is as varied as any other 'ism.' "

Professor Hans Morgenthau has constantly belabored the same point.

From the Senate Chamber in Washington the issue has been echoed repeatedly. Senator George Aiken of Vermont said on January 19, 1968,

> "We have for far too long now duped the American people with the invention of a monolithic enemy called communism in order to justify our often quite inadvertent foreign policy initiatives. . . . Having designated the [Vietnam] war as a war against 'world communism' we must now produce a victory over an elusive and almost indefinable enemy."[11]

Senate Majority Leader Mansfield in January, 1968 told the Foreign Policy Association that post-World War II voters will,

> " . . . frankly question policies which were designed two decades ago for two decades ago and largely for jousting with what was then assumed to be the indivisible monolith of Communism."[12]

The Junior Senator from Illinois, Charles Percy, echoed this view from the same platform, asserting, "we cannot afford the extravagance of simplistic dogmatism. We cannot wage holy wars of anti-Communism."[13]

Not only is this assertion utterly false, but the record compiled under the careful scrutiny of all of these gentlemen—and sometimes even under their direction—exposes their forgetfulness. Surely they would acknowledge the importance of distinguishing between the two periods of modern, aggressive communism; the one, when indeed the movement did appear to be coordinated and monolithic in its structure; the other, when the first cracks began to appear in the Kremlin Wall soon after the death of Stalin.

One's memory does not have to go back very far in our history to recall those frightening days when the facade of the world Communist movement was yet unbroken. Whatever weaknesses were suspected of being at the heart of its inner workings in those days, its strength obviously lay in the seeming unity of the Communists everywhere. Whatever the crisis, they always managed to march in cadence to the tune played in Moscow. Even at that time, however, American policy—while addressing itself to the fact of world communism—was pointed in selective thrusts at piercing the Iron Curtain and in fostering the defiant independence of Tito in Yugoslavia.

No American administration has ever regarded world communism as a monolithic phenomenon. Tito's successful defiance of the Kremlin in fact was fostered and kept alive during very bleak days largely by direct aid from the Truman Administration. Poland and Yugoslavia, then Czechoslovakia, experienced a further loosening of their ties with the Soviet Union by help from the Eisenhower Administration. Presidents Kennedy and Johnson have attempted to build additional bridges between East and West.

Eastern Asia has been no exception. While the American stance in Korea was triggered by the need to protect South Korea from being seized by force from North Korea, the continued presence of United States troops there ever since has served also to prevent the South from trying to seize the North by force.

Witness also the Seventh Fleet in the Formosan Straits, originally positioned here to save Chiang Kai-shek and the Nationalists from being captured by Mao Tse-tung. The Fleet has remained ever since that crisis in 1949 also for the purpose of "containing" General Chiang Kai-shek, making certain that his army did not launch reckless attacks on the Mainland, which in themselves would open up new crises that might be impossible to isolate and to prevent from spreading into larger wars.

Likewise Vietnam. The American presence along the 17th Parallel was not only intended to cut off the North from its invasion of the South, but also to prevent the South from moving north by force of arms. The character of the Far Eastern Policy of the United States has been more to achieve stability and less to be narrowly anti-Communist than the critics have ever acknowledged.

At the very moment that the United States has stood firmly in Southeast Asia, moreover, the Johnson Administration has pushed the bridge-building efforts to the East and has pursued negotiations toward controlling nuclear arms. Other measures have been undertaken to ease the tensions between Moscow and Washington at the same time as firm positions in Eastern Asia have been reenforced.

It is a curious flaw, both among American scholars and among scholarly American politicians, that they are so expert in judging the events in the safe past; but in the spotlight of current affairs, they tend to blot out that past and to disintegrate in the face of the passions and prejudices of the moment.

Even the respected ranks of the Fourth Estate have been infiltrated by these emotions. One could reasonably expect a diversity among newspapermen to place them along every segment of this spectrum of opinion and interpretation. But newspaper readers are surely entitled to a better performance in news credibility than has occurred during the Vietnam dialogues. The incredibility has surely been aided and abetted by the total lack of censorship. Vietnam must be the first of the modern wars in which the press has had a free hand. In some respects, they have failed to live up to the opportunity which that "freedom of the press" gave them. For purposes of illustration only, I select a few conspicuous cases in which the more prestigious part of the Fourth Estate has been involved.

One as distinguished as Harry Ashmore, for example, could hardly have been expected to tell us that Uncle Ho really wants peace and is ready for more talks, but the United States refuses to permit him that indulgence. Due to the fact that American bombing raids in the North are so frustrating in Hanoi, Ho's naturally conciliatory instincts have been perverted.

How one as astute as Harry Ashmore can omit from his evaluation the almost weekly initiatives for peace talks coming from some source initiated by the United States and then excuse a man like Ho Chi Minh who has not yet abandoned the hard line which seems to imprison his outlook toward negotiations is difficult to understand. Ho's newspaper *Hoc Tap* continues to say, "The liberation of South Vietnam can be settled only by force. . . ." It remains incredible for an American newspaper figure, held in such high esteem, to couch his criticism of American policy in that context.

Nor is it easy to forget the television spectacle of two other notable newspaper types—Harrison Salisbury of the *New York Times* and David Schoenbrun of Columbia Broadcasting System. After both had visited North Vietnam, they verified each other's view about Ho Chi Minh's fine intentions.

When they got to the question of Ho's statement that there were no North Vietnamese troops south of the 17th Parallel, both men treated it with obviously enjoyable levity. The same two, on the other hand, have taken a very dim view whenever the President of the United States withholds information for reasons of security.

In President Johnson's case, it constitutes a credibility gap in the vernacular of the press. But when Ho Chi Minh propounds a naked lie, it becomes clever.

This, too, is incredible.

Several months ago, a national television network program, "Meet the Press," carried a one-hour, joint interrogation of Secretary of State Dean Rusk and Secretary of Defense Robert McNamara. In the course of the show, the Secretaries were asked whether or not it was conceivable that at any time the intelligence ship USS *Pueblo* might have been within the territorial waters of North Korea. I watched the show closely and with a critical eye.

Secretary McNamara replied with candor and forthrightness. He said in effect that, as far as *he knew,* there had been no violation—that the real point of the American position was when the seizure of the vessel had occurred it was (1) not in hot pursuit, (2) on the high seas in international waters, and (3) thus the North Korean procedure was in direct violation to international law and constituted at least an act of piracy. He went on to explain in all honesty, however, that because he hadn't been aboard the ship and no one had been able to examine the ship's log or talk to the skipper, he couldn't vouch for where the ship had been when its communications system had been blacked-out for eleven days. The ship was not supposed to go into territorial waters, he explained, but he couldn't vouch for it without knowing the unknown. (And that which was on that afternoon unknowable.)

The next day's press and newscasts carried the sensational insinuation that McNamara had forfeited ground for the Administration and, in effect, had undercut Ambassador Goldberg at the United Nations. When I read those charges in the press the next morning, I could neither believe the headlines nor the substance of the charge as spelled out in the context of the articles. Somebody writing the "news" had to strain at the leash of credibility in order to glean that kind of an interpretation from the "Meet the Press" exchanges.

As the later records quickly substantiated, nothing in the McNamara response in any way contradicts Ambassador Goldberg's testimony at the UN. Yet, the popular newsline was that the question of the Administration's credibility had reared its ugly head again.

Another journalist in his report on what the two Secretaries had said characterized it as "having the shadings of a debate rather than a united defense of Administration policy."[14] Once again, meanings that were neither intended nor existed in fact were read into the responses of the two Cabinet Members.

In hindsight, it would seem fair to suggest that the principal credibility that was brought into doubt by the incident was the credibility of the news media. As someone noted at the time, it was much as though the President were asked if his chief adviser had ever robbed a bank, to which the President replied, certainly not—not to my knowledge. And then the news collector, pressing the question further, would say, how long have you known this aide, Mr. President? When he replied he had only known him since 1950, the press then queried, is it possible that he might have robbed a bank in the years before you knew him? When the President admitted that it might have been possible but most unlikely, the press rushed into headlines which read, "President concedes aide might have robbed bank before he knew him."

For the press to construe an honest declaration in the public forum of national televised questions and answers to mean what the press tried to make the answer mean becomes incredible.

On another occasion, a major television network—as a part of a 90-minute special on Vietnam—began it with a film clip highlighting how the United States got into Vietnam. The clip featured almost exclusively the extreme incidents that occurred, as the gory sight of the police chief in Saigon shooting a captured VC in the head, or the extreme statements that had been uttered, such as the famous prediction by the Secretary of Defense that American troops would start coming home by Christmas of 1965, and the optimistic statements by several Presidents about the course of events in Southeast Asia.

Nowhere in the film clip was there an attempt by the editors to capture the perspective of Vietnam. (1) How easy it would have been for them to have featured the Eisenhower-Dulles, Kennedy-Rusk, Johnson-Rusk statements again and again about the need to contain China or the importance of restraining acts of aggression and terror against all of Southeast Asia. (2) Why didn't the editors mention the assassination of several thousand North Vietnamese political leaders by which Ho Chi Minh seized control? (3) Why didn't they mention the bloody massacre of thousands of other North Vietnamese which caused a million to flee to South Vietnam to save their lives? (4) Why was there no mention that the Diem Government in South Vietnam conducted two elections and won both of them? (5) Why was there no mention that South Vietnam from the very first asked for U.S. aid? (6) Why didn't the editors mention that South Vietnam had been set up as a separate nation and was so regarded after the breakdown of the Geneva Agreements to the point of being invited to join the United Nations (which would have occurred except for the Soviet veto)? (7) Why no mention that the only American build-up was preceded in each instance by a North Vietnamese escalation? (8) Or if they were going to portray the violence of the Tet attacks, why couldn't they have at least balanced the police chief's inexcusable atrocity with the pictures of reputable families in Saigon who were deliberately annihilated by the attackers, women and children being struck down in cold blood without even the excuse of the accident of war to cover the crime?

In this day and age of instant communications, the media surely have a greater responsibility than they have sometimes exhibited for achieving balance on the war in Vietnam.

The ultimate in journalistic incredibility would have to be the question-and-answer exchange on whom to believe regarding news from Vietnam.

In Walter Scott's *Personality Parade* under which is the question, "Want the facts?," a reader asked, "Whom should the average U.S. citizen believe on the war—the government or the press?" The answer by Mr. Scott:

> "On the war in Vietnam, it is preferable to believe the Press. Its record for accuracy, honesty, and foresight is far better than the Administration's. The government believes it is defensible on occasion to lie to the people, and it has. The press is dedicated to reporting the truth. More important yet, the press is not running for re-election."[15]

One finds it difficult to believe that this response was printed in all seriousness in this modern age of enlightenment. Imagine what would happen to the whole process of responsibility for law and order and policy if we were to tell the citizenry not to follow its government, just to follow its newspaper reporters. The consequence could only bring down governments and encourage anarchy.

In a sense it tends to reinforce the contention of some of the members of the Fourth Estate that the credibility gap is largely an invention of the news media and that, in any case, it is dwarfed into insignificance by the incredibility gap created by some of the members of the Fourth Estate.

As Betty Beale of the *Washington Star* put it so well,

> "In my opinion, if the press publicly ever applied the 'credibility gap' test to some of its own members, the readers would get quite a shock."[16]

Even members of the press have experienced such a shock. One of these—the esteemed columnist and television commentator—Howard K. Smith, frankly describes the phrase "credibility gap" as "one of the most distorting oversimplifications of the time." The gap, according to Smith, has been largely invented by the press. He has described the news coverage of Vietnam as being full of one-sided journalism.

On the question of credibility, Smith writes that the President is compelled to make decisions even when all of the subsequent facts may not be readily available.

"We tend to call it calculated deception if he does not instantly provide conclusive facts and admit failure. If he does not keep a frozen consistency he is held to be lying. No government ever has been run that way and none ever will."[17]

Howard K. Smith, whose liberal credentials remain unimpeachable, has decided to give up the ghost, because the former "exhilarating feeling" he once had of being a tiny part in a great age of journalism has disappeared, largely because of what the press has done to the news on Vietnam.

Amid this potpourri of arguments mustered against the policy of the United States in Eastern Asia, a few of the critics have taxed their own credibility still further. Some of the liberals, for example, who most deplored the meddling by the United States in the internal affairs of Vietnam, place themselves out in front of those who demand American intervention in Rhodesia or in the Union of South Africa. So many intellectuals who say they are appalled at our military interference in Southeast Asia would applaud an American expeditionary force sent all the way to Capetown to overthrow apartheid, even though South Africa offers no imaginable threat to American security. It bothers them not at all that they contradict themselves in the process.

Still others among them, including distinguished scholars, who deplored the risk of spreading war among the great powers of Asia, were quick to voice their shrill demands that the United States intervene on the side of Israel in the Middle East war in June, 1967. As Anthony Hartley shrewdly observed, "If they applaud the Israeli victory over the Arabs, they cannot then use pacifist arguments to condemn American policy in Vietnam. Napalm is indivisible."

The fact that American intervention in behalf of Israel might well have triggered a major confrontation with the Soviet Union did not seem to bother them. They were certain that the Russians would not respond with guns. Yet they seem to be completely certain that China will! Again, their inconsistency does not deter them.

One academic critic of American policy in Asia, Arthur Schlesinger, was at least forthright enough to say of those who demanded unilateral action in behalf of Israel but who condemn it in

Vietnam, "I think it is inconsistent to favor unilateral intervention in one part of the world while opposing it in another part of the world."

In general, the critics, who for the sake of simplicity blame President Johnson for everything that goes wrong in foreign policy, have no hesitation in repeating falsehoods and fabrications which happen to support their side. They are quick to pick up allegations fired from Hanoi or Peking or Moscow and to hurl them back at the President. Yet, they rose in self-righteous anger when General Westmoreland appeared before the Congress to protest flag-burning and draft-dodging. The General and the President alike were accused of intimidating the dissenters and abridging the very right to dissent.

As though it was not enough for the critics to blame the President for everything that goes wrong and even to ascribe to him propaganda inventions concocted in Hanoi, they also claim for themselves whatever successes the President seems to score.

For example, President Lyndon Johnson has contended from the first that, if the hard military pressures are kept on Hanoi, they will force the North to the conference table. Now that the North Vietnamese Government has reflected an interest in talking, the critics are quick to take credit for it—even though it came as a consequence of the unrelenting pressures which the President kept on the enemy.

The obvious case in point is the claim by Presidential contender Eugene McCarthy. When the Paris talks were announced, candidate McCarthy was quick to assert that this was the result of his attacks on America's policy of firmness and of his forcing the President out of the political race. Both assertions strain fact and truth.

Three and one-half years of steady American military pressure on the armies of the North have taken a very severe toll of the enemy. The Tet offensive, moreover, collapsed at mid-point and cost Hanoi still more.

It is much more plausible to believe that the combination of the long-range pressure and the short-range debacle of Tet required that Hanoi test the conference waters before continuing along Ho Chi Minh's prescribed dictum of "fighting forever if necessary." Had the McCarthy suggestion been followed, there would have been no reason for North Vietnam to want to talk. Why talk when by waiting it out they could get it all for nothing?

If it is fair and constructive for the Critical Establishment to charge that the President's policies cannot bring peace, it is at the very least dishonest of them (not to mention opportunistic) to deny to the President the credits when his policies pay off.

Political and intellectual critics, in short, have set up for themselves a would-be standard. If the war happens to inflame their emotions, they do not concern themselves much with moral behavior. If the war is far away, however, it more readily becomes an intellectual exercise and a moral problem. As novelist Constantine FitzGibbon has noted, "The less he [the run-of-the-mill intellectual] knows about a complex issue far away, the stronger his moral judgments."

It should not be surprising that, in the wake of this kind of irresponsibility, hatred and violence have appeared as new attributes of the war protest movement here at home. The net result has been to remove dissent from the public market place of ideas and to replace it with overt actions.

One is forced to do a double-take, moreover, when listening to the dissenters assert that the President is not telling the people the truth. And yet, in the very next breath, they declare before nationwide audiences that, in the words of one Senator, "We are killing innocent people in Vietnam," or that "the South Vietnamese Army has really pulled out of the war," or that "the whole moral position of the United States is being undermined."

This reckless language in itself hardly contributes to public confidence. It is couched in the most slovenly of innuendos, hardly measuring up to the kind of integrity which the dissenters profess to demand from the Nation's leaders. It does not clear the air or define the issues to allege, as Professor Hans Morgenthau did with me on a University of Chicago Roundtable telecast, that we have a President of the United States who finds "a kind of sporting pleasure in not telling the truth."

One has to pinch himself to make sure this was not the echo of a bad dream rather than the straight-out assertions of an otherwise creditable academic on the American scene. Somewhere along the line even our scholars seem to have forgotten the disciplines of scholarship and reason and to have surrendered themselves to the hysteria of the moment.

Enough, however, for the role of politicians in dissent as well as the intellectuals and those of their compatriots who designate themselves as liberal spokesmen. There remains one other class of dissenters. This is a class which is perhaps the most important of all because its members ranked highest in the hierarchy of administration and, in many cases, actually participated in the development of American policy in Vietnam.

The class members possess another common attribute. They are no longer associated in any meaningful way with the Administration. I refer, of course, to some of the decision-makers under the late President John F. Kennedy and even some who served in positions of responsibility during the early tenure of President Lyndon B. Johnson. This group is of particular significance not only because its membership is well-educated—sometimes brilliant—but it has to be presumed that they are both experienced and sophisticated in the power-politics of world diplomacy. These are experts, moreover, who said one thing when they were in charge and had to take the consequences for their decisions, but who later said something else after they were no longer connected with a position of policy responsibility.

Let their statements speak for them.

President Kennedy's closest confidante and counselor was his brother, Attorney General Robert Kennedy. At the request of President Kennedy, Attorney General Robert Kennedy delivered to the German Government a speech spelling out the American foreign policy position around the world. In that speech the young President had his brother say that Vietnam was as vital a commitment by the United States as was our earlier commitment in Berlin.

On the 18th of February, 1962, at an airport stop in Saigon, Robert Kennedy was asked by a British correspondent, "Do the American people understand and approve of what is going on [in Vietnam]?" The Attorney General's reply, as reported by the *New York Times,* was,

> "I think the American people understand and fully
> support this struggle. Americans have great affection for
> the people of Vietnam. I think the United States will do
> what is necessary to help a country that is trying to repel
> aggression with its own blood, tears, and sweat . . . "

Robert Kennedy went on to explain:

> "This is a new kind of war, but war it is in a very real
> sense of the word. It is war fought not by massive
> divisions, but secretly by terror, assassination, ambush,
> and infiltration."

The Attorney General then turned to Hanoi's role in the conflict by saying,

> "Hanoi may deny its responsibility but the guilt is clear.
> In a flagrant violation of its signed pledge at Geneva in
> 1954, the North Vietnamese regime has launched on a
> course to destroy Vietnam."

Neither President Johnson nor Secretary of State Dean Rusk put it any blunter than that. But what about the people back home, Robert Kennedy was asked. Will they support such a policy? He replied that, not only will the people support it but,

> "We are going to win in Vietnam. We will remain here
> until we do win."[18]

No terminal date was affixed to the predictions of how long the struggle would last in Southeast Asia. Nor did he raise the question of moral judgment.

Later, as a Senator outside the Administration, however, Robert Kennedy spoke a different language. He described American motivations in Vietnam as being "fouled by the fact that we are acting there in our self-interest." Other contridictions in language to that used by Attorney General Kennedy and that contained in his many speeches as Senator Kennedy criticizing our Vietnam policy were conspicuous.

For instance, as recently as February 8, 1968, Senator Kennedy made the following statements in Chicago:

> "The third illusion [about U.S. policy] is that the
> unswerving pursuit of military victory, whatever its cost,
> is in the interest of either ourselves or the people of
> Vietnam."

And further, he said,

> "Unable to defeat our enemy or break his will—at least
> without a huge, long and ever more costly effort—we

must actively seek a peaceful settlement. We can no longer harden our terms every time Hanoi indicates it may be prepared to negotiate; and we must be willing to foresee a settlement which will give the Vietcong a chance to participate in the political life of the country."[19]

The inconsistency of the Attorney General's statement that "We will remain here until we do win . . . " and the Senator's statement in Chicago speaks for itself.

In all fairness, Senator Robert Kennedy said that he had changed his mind about Vietnam. This was an honorable and forthright declaration. His switch after leaving the Administration, however, entitles us to ask, "Which Kennedy judgment comes closest to the facts of life in Southeast Asia?"—the one made when the consequences for deciding rested heavily upon his *own* shoulders, or the one made later when he was free from direct responsibility for making policy?

Another of the advisers close to John F. Kennedy was Arthur Schlesinger, a distinguished historian in his own right and sometimes regarded as the President's "intellectual-in-residence." When he was serving as Special Assistant to the President, Schlesinger viewed Southeast Asia in a noticeably different light than he seems to regard it today.

Under JFK, Schlesinger noted in regard to the crisis in Laos,

"If the Communists gained possession of the Mekong Valley they could materially intensify their pressure against South Vietnam and Thailand. If Laos was not precisely a dagger pointed at the heart of Kansas, it was very plainly a gateway to Southeast Asia . . . the United States had no choice but to stiffen its position, whether in preparation for negotiation or for resistance."[20]

On another occasion, Special Assistant Schlesinger spoke of,

" . . . military necessities that at times have rendered an enlarged American role [in Southeast Asia] impera-tive. . . . Negotiation gestures out of Hanoi can be exercises in political warfare, too. . . . "[21]

This is presumably the same Arthur Schlesinger who, now out from under the umbrella of Administration responsibility, is saying,

"There is no evidence that Asian Communism is a
unified movement run out of Peking. . . . The Vietnam
War simply does not offer evidence of any threat of
global aggression comparable to that which confronted
Roosevelt 25 years ago . . . we are over-reacting to a
local war. . . . If any expectation is clearly futile, it is
that the armed intervention of white men will determine
the ultimate course of history on the mainland of Asia."

Yet another of the late President Kennedy's confidants was the
Harvard economist, John Kenneth Galbraith. Under the aegis of the
New Frontier, Ken Galbraith served a distinguished tour of duty as
Ambassador to India. It was during his tenure in New Delhi that the
Indian crisis with China broke out. The tensions along their mutual
frontier of more than 2,000 miles reached the critical stages in 1961
and 1962. It was the pressure of the Chinese through Tibet and
along the Himalayan frontiers that prompted the Indian Government
to request the help of the United States in thwarting this new threat.

Galbraith, as Ambassador, was strong in urging the President of
the United States to dispatch both warplanes and material to back
the Indians against China. In essence, he became a militant
Himalayan hawk when the responsibilities for policy advice were
his.

Later, however, Chairman Galbraith of the Americans for Democratic Action has replaced his talons of the hawk with a coo of a
dove.

As a critic of President Johnson, he has come to assess China very
differently than when he was Ambassador. As Ambassador, he had
stressed the importance of containing China as Peking pressed its
encroachments upon the borders of India. But now he regards the
role of China far differently.

Divested of his official responsibilities, the former Ambassador
now contends that internal dissension in China is making it impotent
and "not even the most ardent defender of the war can now believe
that Hanoi wants to be part of a Chinese-led empire."

No longer, according to Galbraith, is there need for concern over
"containment."

Elsewhere in the State Department, the Assistant Secretary of
State for Far Eastern Affairs under President Kennedy, Roger

Hilsman, can be said to have been a principal architect of the Kennedy policies in Southeast Asia referred to earlier.

Now free from the responsibilities of policy-making and back in the classroom as a Professor of Political Science at Columbia University, Dr. Hilsman not only tells us what President Kennedy would have done in Vietnam had he lived, but he goes on to contradict what must have been his own advice as the Assistant Secretary of State to his President.

The same Hilsman who had urged troop build-ups in Vietnam in Congressional hearings in March, 1965, told another Committee in 1966 as a Columbia Professor that war between the United States and Communist China with Vietnam as the opening chapter was almost inevitable. He said the two countries ". . . are on a collision course. . . . The outcome can only be war." By 1967, Mr. Hilsman was telling a CBS television panel the Vietnam War was not politically "winable," that we should halt bombing in the North and that even if the United States were able to defeat the Communists militarily, the political result "will not be viable."

Another of the current dissenters who was brought in under President Kennedy as a consultant to the State Department and a some-time lecturer at the National War College was Professor Hans J. Morgenthau of the University of Chicago. In an article written at that time (June 12, 1962) entitled "Vietnam: Another Korea?" policy-consultant Morgenthau wrote,

> "As far as Communist China was concerned, the war [in Vietnam] is an attempt to extend the areas of influence and communism."

This is the same Professor Morgenthau who now says that we can count on the present government in Peking to let China's neighbors live peacefully in China's shadow because this was the lesson taught by all of China's history.

As a critic, Professor Morgenthau seems to have forgotten the significant history of Chinese predatory activities in Southeast Asia. Perhaps it made a difference when he had to supply a sober position paper for the Department of State and when he could give vent to his choice of irresponsibility in merely proving wrong the President, whom he had come to dislike.

The central point of these suggestions is that men serving under the discipline of responsibility for the consequences of their decisions were advocating different policies from those they advocate outside the echelons of government.

Either they owed the government a greater sense of integrity in their advocacy while they served it, or they owe the people a greater sense of personal integrity in regard to what they say as critics in private life now.

If their position has not switched, they should have been honest enough to leave the government sooner than they did. If their position has changed, they at least owe it to the country at large not to pontificate in the guise of having been in government.

Some might equate this shift of ground with an attitude of arrogance. The line between the incredible and the arrogant may be a fine one indeed. But such an attitude should not be assigned alone to those who have previously served in government. It is a mantle that is worn by many in the Critical Establishment.

CHAPTER XI

Arrogance of Dissent

The right of dissent is not equal at all levels. How much this is true has been underscored by the issue of Vietnam. If a fault must be assigned in this syndrome of dissent, it should fall upon the politicians rather than the academicians. On the campus, criticism is accompanied by the luxury of irresponsibility—that is, the professor can afford less concern over the consequences of being wrong than can the Member of Congress. (To put it in personal terms, Professor McGee had many more solutions to the problems of the world than has Senator McGee.)

Even Senator McGee, however, has more rights of dissent than do Chairman Fulbright of the Committee on Foreign Relations, or Chairman Russell of the Armed Services Committee, or Chairman Hayden of the Appropriations Committee. The chairmen of those powerful committees gave up some "freedoms" when they became the heads of powerful Senate groups. No longer could they speak as freely as individuals without weighing the consequences of their words.

Yet, all of these chairmen are freer from responsibility in comparison with the President of the United States. Senator Lyndon B. Johnson, even as Majority Leader, could speak out much more freely than President Lyndon B. Johnson. If the rest of us make a mistake, we may be given yet another chance to correct it. But the President has to be right the *first* time.

This has not always been the case. For most of our country's history, our concern was largely national in scope. And the impact of whatever decisions we made rarely reverberated beyond our shoreline. Under the conditions of the "good old days," it was possible to survive demagogues, prima donnas, and flamboyant orators in the United States Senate. What they might choose to say to appease their constituency back home had little impact on the rest of the world. But no longer is this true.

Particularly since World War II the United States has been thrust by circumstances into a role of frightening responsibility in influencing the direction of world events. Not only what the President says or what the Secretary of State says, but even what a United States Senator says may make a difference in Capetown, in Taipei, Katmandu, or Hanoi. Whether the issue is civil rights, nuclear disarmament, or Vietnam, the whole world is tuned-in on our wave length. The day has long since passed when a United States Senator could carelessly expound his views on the great questions of our time without first measuring the consequences of their impact on the rest of the human race.

The late Prime Minister of India, Jawaharlal Nehru, put it vividly when he likened the United States to a modern Atlas with the world on his shoulders. "If you stumble," he said, "the rest of us in the world fall with you."

No issue has made it more difficult for men in public life (or in private life either, for that matter) to rise to the higher levels demanded by modern leadership than that of Vietnam. This is due in part to the kind of war it is. Never before has our Nation assumed the responsibilities of warfare under such difficult conditions circumscribed by the limitations of peripheral conflict.

With the exception of Korea, no other American war even came close to these frustrating restraints. In addition, the man-in-the-street is, for the first time, watching a war on television. The ugliness and the horrors of all wars have suddenly been compressed onto a 21-inch screen in the living room. This in itself has made the individual citizen more vulnerable to the harangues of those politicians who would exploit the heart rather than appeal to the head.

But aggravating the problem even more has been the introduction of the television camera into the Senate hearing room. Great as television has been in educating vast public audiences about some of the facts of international life, it has also raised new problems. One of these is the almost mesmerizing effect it has on politicos.

During my tenure on the Foreign Relations Committee, there were numerous occasions for noting the difference in the manner in which witnesses were interrogated in the privacy of the Committee's Executive Sessions on the one hand and while under the glare of TV lights on the other. More often than one would like to have seen in a Senate hearing room where the proceedings were being televised, individual Senators tended to become showmen rather than statesmen. On occasion, Senate inquisitors seemed to be in quest of higher Neilsen ratings rather than the facts.

Unfortunately, too, personal invective, cutting epithets, and political vengeance had a way of intruding onto the screen. Techniques and tactics, cliches and irate tones of voice, all better described on the pages of *Variety* than the *Congressional Record*, crept into the dialogue. In that kind of atmosphere it is understandable that statesmanship becomes the casualty of showmanship. But it still remains not only unforgivable, but, in these times, unaffordable.

During the dialogues on Vietnam, some of the critics expressed their fear of an American "arrogance of power." Whatever the substance of this particular charge, it suggests to me a parallel application to the abuses by the critics of the realm of legitimate and constructive criticism—a form of arrogance in itself, *an arrogance of dissent.*

At times some of the Congressional dissenters seemed to assume a privileged insight on truth and a self-appointed monopoly on wisdom, leaving no room for doubt that there could hardly be another fragment of truth floating around which had escaped them. This arrogant assault on the United States position in Eastern Asia tended to ascribe mostly good motives to Hanoi and to the National Liberation Front or, at least not to prejudge their motivation, while at the same time viewed the decisions and the tactics flowing out of Washington as a massive conspiratorial operation or an infamous plot hatched by evil men in the Administration.

Secretary of State Rusk and Secretary of Defense McNamara were the most popular victims of this form of arrogance. As principal architects of American policy in Asia, along with the President, they were understandably on the firing line. Not only did they have the thankless task of making decisions of the greatest importance, they had the even more sobering responsibility of taking the consequences for whatever they might decide. To expect them to defend their decisions, to justify their policies, and to explain daily developments was within reason. At times, however, while under Committee scrutiny, they were abused, harried, and insulted. Their loyalty to their country was impugned. Their integrity was called into question. Their patriotism was placed in doubt. And perhaps most significantly of all, the deep trust and respectability of high public office in a free society was demeaned in a very public way under the bright lights of the televised hearing.

The price paid for this kind of conduct in the name of a committee of Congress was much more than personal injury to the individual men involved. At the moment when the United States was holding out its form of government as a model for the rest of the world to study and perhaps to emulate, the attacks on Rusk and McNamara had the effect of downgrading the American system.

The process also reflects a curious contradiction of an American legal tradition—that of being innocent until proven guilty. At times it was difficult to avoid feeling that the Senators bombarding the two Secretaries with questions started with the assumption of their guilt of some heinous crime unless they could come up with a good alibi.

What prompts me to label this conduct as "arrogant" is the 180-degree shift of attitude whenever the questioning was in the quiet of the Committee's Executive Sessions. Behind the closed doors of the Committee on Foreign Relations, the confrontations between Senators and Cabinet Members seemed to be less noisy, the charges less flagrant, and the invectives almost nonexistent. In fact, the questions put by the members on these occasions were tough ones, but at least they were the right ones. Both the questioners and the questioned learned a great deal during the exchange. The give-and-take between Executive and Legislative spokesmen stood in sharp contrast to the public spectacles.

Televised hearings caused increased attendance by Committee members. It is difficult to avoid the conclusion that the prospect of national exposure took precedence over possibilities of learning substantive things about the problems of American policies in the Far East. The drop-off in Committee Executive Session was sharp indeed. Also, the questions from several of the Senators in public tended to be accompanied by lengthy speeches in search of an audience rather than in search of information—again, a contrast to the private session.

It is within this context of difference between public and closed hearings that one may find a partial explanation for the reluctance of the Secretary of State, for example, to appear publicly before the Foreign Relations Committee.

This segment of the broader issue of Congressional dissent might well underscore that the right to dissent for which we have properly shown so much concern, must be accompanied by the observation and guarantees of an equal right; and that is the right to be reasonable—or, to phrase it differently, the right to be right. As the late Adlai Stevenson once declared, "I do not impugn the good faith of those who hold different views than mine. I would only ask them in the name of courtesies and decencies of a free society that they should refrain from impugning mine."

Senatorial arrogance showed itself in another way when on April 28, 1967, General Westmoreland addressed a Joint Session on the Congress. Congressional dissenters at once charged the Administration with "intimidation" and with "steam roller" tactics. In their arrogance they would deny the right of the advocates even as they exploited the rights of dissent.

Again, Senatorial impatience and Presidential-candidate opportunism asserted themselves. At the time that President Johnson withdrew his candidacy and announced a bombing halt in Vietnam, the restlessness of the critics became conspicuous.

First of all, they had lost their prime target—the President of the United States. As if groping for something to say, they began by charging the President with misleading the nation and the world in regard to the bombing pause. One influential Senator even went so far as to charge that the President's reckless disregard of his own bombing pause now made it unlikely that the North would agree to talk.

Another Senatorial line condemned the President for attaching strings to the location of the talk site. The cries were loud and clear from the halls of Congress that LBJ really had not meant it when he said he would go "anywhere, any time." Strong demands were forthcoming from the legislators that the proposal from Hanoi to meet in Warsaw be accepted. The Administration persevered, however, knowing that Warsaw was a propaganda ploy by the other side rather than a serious suggestion. Hanoi seemed to agree. Although American candidates for the Presidency sounded either naive or exploitive in their eagerness to go to Warsaw, the men in Hanoi seemed to understand that it was only a form of diplomatic "fun and games."

Representatives in the government of North Vietnam continued to dicker seriously with American spokesmen for an acceptable site. When a few days later Paris was agreed upon, it served to underscore the irresponsibility of those Senators who had condemned the President's bombing policy and candidates who had advocated going to Warsaw.

The luxury of irresponsibility was illustrated again.

The political dissenters have no monopoly on arrogance. Intellectual critics of American foreign policy are at least the equal in attitude of some of the Congressional dissenters; and in their own private view, probably, they are superior to their political compatriots in protest.

To understand the arrogance of the intellectuals, it is important to measure from whence they have come. The scholar, whatever his discipline, has often been accused of being unrealistic. It is a Main Street cliche to allude to intellectuals as long hairs, day-dreamers, and impractical. In our country's history, the intellectuals and the academics have enjoyed the luxury of isolation, unchallenged by the forces of power and violence prevailing in the world at large. This was due, in part, to the fact that Great Britain in the preceding century had assumed the responsibilities for maintaining a balance of forces around the world. It was a role pursued so effectively that intellectuals in the United States, behind the protective shield of the British Fleet and the broad expanse of the Pacific Ocean, could play with the intriguing questions of domestic liberalism without risk to their base of operations.

At the beginning of the 20th Century, however, the "fun and games" of the 19th Century were called to task by the new power politics. Thus, it is no accident in American history that the intellectuals—the "New Freedom" crusaders—were militantly opposed to World War I. The liberal academics, moreover, were quick to identify with the social programs of FDR's New Deal in the 1930's, only to part company with him over the war against Hitler.

Nor was it a new development when the intellectuals and political liberals at home became conspicuous isolationists abroad. Inspired by Theodore Roosevelt, and ultimately captured by the Progressive Movement, were the antiwar spokesmen of both World Wars in this Century. The Hiram Johnsons and Burton K. Wheelers, the Bob LaFollettes and George Norrises; these are the great liberal leaders of the first third of the 20th Century. But, with the exception of Nebraska's George Norris, they became militant isolationists at the onset of the Hitler threat.

It is against this backdrop that we must evaluate the qualifications of the intellectual-academics for making political judgments or resolving complicated political problems. On the hopeful side, the propensity of intellectuals for comitting themselves in public ways to political matters is commendable. It has brought them out of the Ivory Tower down to Main Street. The shortcoming of this latter day development, however, is that it is often accompanied by a simultaneous assumption of omniscience—that the mere fact of intellectualism at once connotes a monopoly of wisdom.

Former Assistant Secretary of State Charles Frankel, himself a distinguished intellectual, has warned his colleagues that "international affairs are peculiarly susceptible to galloping abstractions." Some members of the intellectual community have forcefully underscored the truth of that statement.

Basic Books editor and *Foreign Affairs* contributor Irving Kristol has defined an intellectual as a "man who speaks with general authority about a subject on which he has no particular competence." A more precise definition than that would probably be denied by those who have appointed themselves to this elite group.

The arrogance of liberal dissenters is reflected in several ways. First is their conviction, or at least their assumption, that they are right and all others are wrong. To refine the assessment of this attitude, they not only believe that their arguments are right but that *they* are right because of who they are and what their backgrounds represent. As one American scholar put it, "The intellectual often lays claim to a moral authority over the intentions and actions of political leaders." The intellectual community is prone to villify and to denounce ineptness in high political places as though this was some low crime beneath the capabilities of their own intellect.

The intolerance of the intellectuals toward those who may think otherwise on Vietnam has become one of the more sordid sides of the current dispute over American policy. Whereas it was once popular to associate narrow-mindedness, extremism, and arrogance with the so-called right-wingers, many of today's spokesmen for the New Left protest groups have conducted themselves in such extreme ways that it is difficult to distinguish between the extremism of the right and the extremism of the left.

Arrogance in the ranks of the Critical Establishment is reflected in other ways. In a self-assumed air of being above emotions or above response to popular feelings, they try to look upon themselves as ones who view the war in Vietnam with a sort of clinical dispassion. For them, the war becomes an intellectual exercise or a problem in intellectualism, a moral riddle or a political exploitation. They regard themselves as those high-level, high-minded men and women who have made history's final assessment of the events of our time and are now delivering the ultimate judgment. It is this air of supreme confidence that they—and they alone—are right and all others are ignorantly or innocently or unwittingly wrong that illustrates their attitude of arrogance. Theirs become cruel voices indeed for those among our citizens who have already experienced great personal losses in the war in Southeast Asia. Because these arrogant dissenters have drained all of the blood out of the veins of human compassion in reaching their cold diagnosis of the "why" or the "why not" of Vietnam, they have contributed to the embittered feelings of people who still strive to understand the issues.

In a sense, then, the consequence of what they do and how they rationalize it opens wide a gap in their credibility—a cardinal sin which they previously reserved for the government alone.

Their arrogance finds its expression through still another position which they have assumed. This is that they alone speak for the liberal intellectuals in the land.

The role of intellectuals in foreign policy has come under a succession of public and private assessments. Whatever the conclusions, they should be kept in correct perspective. It is necessary to understand whom we are talking about in referring to intellectuals as much as it is important to understand who are the liberals.

Vietnam has unleashed emotional shock waves which have tended to obscure both. Earlier in our country's history, for example, it might have been accurate to equate intellectualism with college professors. In these current times, however, one should be entitled to challenge that description. The proliferation of both colleges and students has produced an explosion in the sheer numbers of college teachers. One result has been to shove all college teachers under the tent of intellectualism. Thus to conclude that the long lists of professors who sign increasing numbers of newspaper ads and petitions, in fact represent the intellectual community is incorrect.

Many bona fide intellectuals on campuses are tuned-in to the Vietnam protest movement. It must also be acknowledged, however, that very large numbers of nonintellectuals who merely fill the employment gaps on rapidly expanding campuses have likewise become linked to the Critical Establishment. This may account in part for the disparity both in numbers and in quality between those academics whose professional background is not the field of international politics and related areas and those who have found their academic roosts in other fields far removed from the centers of the politics of peace and war around the world.

Two assumptions entrap the critics within these ranks. One is their apparent assumption that all intellectuals are on the outside looking in on the decision-making process in the Administration today. The other is that they alone also speak for the liberals in the land. Both assumptions are not only wrong, but even ridiculously so. Let us look at the first of those assumptions.

Intimately involved in decision-making at the executive level are obvious intellectual and academic individuals. Dean Rusk was a professor of political science at Mills College; Robert McNamara, an M.B.A. at Harvard; Walt Rostow, who received his Ph.D at Yale and was a Rhodes Scholar, subsequently taught American history at Cambridge and economic history at MIT; John Roche, the current "intellectual-in-residence" at the White House, before joining the Johnson Administration was a professor of political science at Brandeis University.

Others who were and are the principal architects of the policies now being deplored by the academic-intellectual community as devoid of the wisdom of the mental giants are: Arthur Schlesinger, Jr., A.B., Harvard, Doctor of Letters, Muhlenburg, Doctor Civil Law, New Brunswick; Kenneth Galbraith, B.S., M.S., Ph.D; Roger Hilsman, M.A., Yale, Ph.D, Yale; Zbigniew Brzezinski, Ph.D, Harvard.

Aside from those in the Government making the decisions, the support of significant and influential academics outside the government should be noted—like the fourteen Asian scholars who essentially endorsed the basic Southeast Asian policy assumptions of the Government; and the efforts of still other intellectual-academic types collected under the aegis of the Peace With Freedom organization directed by former Senator Paul Douglas—himself a creditable academic. Unfortunately, the play given these latter groups by the communication media at no time equals that given the Critical Establishment.

The second of the very questionable assumptions, that the Critical Establishment speaks for the liberals of the land, is open to serious challenge. The weakness of this contention was pointed up in the early days of the liberal peace crusade by Senator Eugene McCarthy.

By asserting that he spoke for the liberal establishment, McCarthy was guilty of gross overstatement. He, in fact, spoke for only some of the liberals; and it was never quite clear at any one time which liberals were with him. It is clear, on the other hand, that there are many sincere and proven liberals whose credentials are at least as impeccable as McCarthy's and Galbraith's and Schlesinger's who stand firmly behind American policy in Southeast Asia.

This writer is a case in point. (For example, the Americans for Constitutional Action—ACA—the antithesis of the Americans for Democratic Action (ADA)—rates McCarthy 8 percent whereas McGee's rating with them is still "0" percent.

As a matter of interest and comparison, the conservative association handed out the following "grades" for Senators' percentages of support for pro-conservative causes during the first six months of the Second Session of the 89th Congress:

	Percent
Fulbright	64
Church	55
Morse	50
Gore	46
Clark	40
McGovern	31
Gruening	22

Sharing honors for a "0" rating along with the author were Senators Mondale, Metcalf, McIntyre, Jackson, Ribicoff, and Brewster, none of whom can be numbered among the bitterest critics on Vietnam.

Another current misconception that many would like to see accepted as fact is the charge that there is a serious absence of support for Administration policy by well-known liberals outside the government establishment. How then, does one explain Paul Douglas, Dean Acheson, Thurman Arnold, Morris Ernst, George Meany, Paul Porter, Professor Robert A. Scalapino, Joseph Beirne, Dr. Harry Gideonse, or Frank Trager?

Even among the ultimate of all liberal organizations, Americans for Democratic Action, the ranks have been split over the question of Vietnam. Already mentioned was John Roche, a former chairman of ADA. Others include Robert Nathan, Gus Tyler, Governor Endicott Peabody, Milton Sachs, Sidney Dean, James Loeb, Reg Zalles, Ed Rovner, Emile Benoit, and Leon Kyserling.

Not only do the McCarthyites do violence to their own "liberal" principles by pretending to speak for the liberal community, in their position they do violence also to the very deep meanings of liberalism itself. This can be illustrated readily in Vietnam.

If the protest against our policy in Asia is indeed to be couched in liberal terms, what kind of liberalism is it that would have had the United States step aside following the Geneva Conference and permit the bloodbath which likely would have followed had not the rival forces of North and South Vietnam been separated by the arbitrary dividing line at the 17th Parallel?

What kind of liberal is it that would have had the United States withdraw from Southeast Asia in the wake of the political chaos and confusion which the American-Allied victory in World War II had created?

What kind of liberal is it who would equate the deliberate and coldly calculated actions of terrorism and murder with the accidental, though equally tragic, casualties of warfare aimed at thwarting terrorism? Even in the narrowest sense of moralism, there has to be a difference.

What kind of liberalism is it that would have us look the other way when one side to a dispute deliberately violates a "negotiated settlement" by invading the territory of the other side by military force?

What kind of liberal is it who gives lip-service to the United Nations or to economic and political cooperation without sustaining both with military sanction? The most far-out liberal surely understands the inability of the United Nations, as it is now structured, to enforce a policy of non-violence and stability in Southeast Asia.

How honest is the liberal who would forfeit somebody else's real estate (South Vietnam, Northeast Thailand, and Eastern Laos) to the aggressiveness of those outside forces who employ the subtle tactics of guerrilla warfare and terrorist teams to bring down established governments?

The liberal critic assures us that, had the United States not stood firmly in Vietnam, peace and good will rather than violence would have swept through most of Southeast Asia after World War II. Dare we believe this? History has a way of not permitting us to look at the consequences if we had acted differently. But can the liberals be certain that the casualties would have been less had the United States acted otherwise? I believe not.

The problem, therefore, becomes one of distinguishing between theoretical liberalism and responsible liberalism. The latter has to take into account the consequences of the decisions that are made before we can stand on the theoretical niceties which seem so attractive. Therefore, it is important that the voices of the responsible liberals now be heard and that they articulate the rationale of war in Eastern Asia and integrate it with the chances for some measure of peace in our time.

CHAPTER XII

Brickbats from the Campus

The academic domain has traditionally been a source of ferment. Rarely has the college campus, however, become such a center of protest and demonstration in regard to foreign policy as it has in the last few years. The interest of students may sometimes have been obscured by conflicting motivations (desire to avoid the draft or desire for public attention).

My own experience leads me to conclude, however, that the majority of students on campus are genuinely and deeply concerned about the shape and the form of the world around them. After addressing nearly 200 campus groups in more than 40 states over a period of 4 years on the subject of Vietnam, I have been struck with the fact that they are asking the right questions; and they only ask for forthrightness and candor in the dialogue.

Some wag has suggested that the "generation gap" stems from the difference between the primary concerns of the present governing generation and the present college generation. The oldsters worry about a world run by the younger generation. The youngsters worry about having a world left to run at all—by anybody. In short, they are disturbed by the prospects of nuclear war. It is the difference in the priorities established by each of these groups that may tell us a great deal about why the one generation seems to misunderstand the other and vice versa.

The hippies, nuts, kooks, and extreme protesters and demon-strators are not a representative cross section of the young people of this country. Most of the students want to know in unvarnished terms where we are heading and why. They believe they have a right to have a hand in determining those directions and the conditions which will influence them. With more than one-half of the population of this country under the age of twenty-five, it would be foolish to pretend that the way in which we come to grips with this gap does not matter.

Among the developments on campus which seemed to make a constructive contribution toward closing that gap was a succession of debates in which the close issues of Vietnam were discussed.

In my own case, those debates made a special kind of contribution on the campus when Senator George McGovern of South Dakota and Senator Gale McGee of Wyoming were debating them. It had nothing to do with whether either of the two Senators had more knowledge than somebody else or was more articulate. Rather, it had very much to do with the similarity of the background of McGovern and McGee.

Both men are Ph.D's in American History. Both were professors of history for many years. Both are liberal Democrats from Western states. Yet, on Vietnam the two men come out at opposite ends.

What this seemed to say to the many student bodies before which we appeared was that nearly identical individuals could split on the question of American policy in Southeast Asia. It seemed to say that the issues themselves were difficult to break down into "right" and "wrong" or "true" or "false"—that the lines of judgment were so finely drawn as to make soul-satisfying or clean-cut conclusions impossible to reach.

In short, the debates tended to inject into an atmosphere where absolutes were commonplace a note of caution and tolerance for another point of view.

In the pages which follow, I have sought to glean from the past four years of campus appearances the more typical questions raised.

(1) Why can't the most powerful nation in the world win a war against one of the weakest nations in the world?

The answer is, of course, that our limited objective is only to stop the other side from doing what it is doing. The issue is not all-out war between North Vietnam and the United States. And in a nuclear age, it is safe to say that you no longer "win" wars; but you could lose them.

The goal of the two sides makes the difference. In order to win, North Vietnam has only to disrupt and destroy. The great advantage in guerrilla warfare lies with the guerrillas. As the experience in Malaysia has shown, a handful of men can more than cope with ten times their number. It is easier to sustain a conflict of hit-and-run than it is to sustain a program of seize-and-hold, particularly when that holding requires stability and reform.

To put it another way, the advantage of a great power lies in the weaponry of total wars rather than of the limited weaponry of peripheral conflicts in remote areas.

(2) How do we justify a no-win policy?

The crux of the answer lies in winning what? The rules of war have changed because of the nuclear bomb. No longer can wars be won or lost like basketball games. In Korea, for example, the war was won not after the North Koreans were destroyed or after they gave up their territories, but only when they pulled back behind the 38th Parallel. Victory, in other words, occurred when the status quo in territorial boundaries was reestablished.

The same is true in Vietnam. Winning simply means stopping an aggressor from doing what he has set out to do to his neighbors.

(3) Why save a people who refuse to save themselves?

The ability of an immature, new country to withstand the impact of terrorist raids and teams equipped with do-it-yourself revolutionary kits is very limited at best. The advantage is heavily weighted in favor of the troublemakers. The will to resist is not enough. The capability of resisting in physical and material terms is what counts.

The Vietnamese have been at war for twenty years. Most young Vietnamese have never known anything but war. They have a remarkable record of striving to achieve some kind of independent identification. It is wrong to equate their efforts in our terms.

In addition, what happens to Vietnam—whatever the attitude of the Vietnamese people may or may not be—makes a difference to all of the surrounding countries in Southeast Asia. Therefore, the question is a larger one than just the spirit of the Vietnamese people. Hinged to it also is the national interest of our own country in achieving some relative degree of stability in Asia. As a large nation, we have found that what happens even in a small country like Vietnam has a way of determining what is going to happen to us.

(4) Why do we meddle in a civil war? Shouldn't we let it run its course?

The attributes of civil war are very much present in nearly all of the developing areas of the world. They were present in Greece in 1946, and Iran, Korea, China, and certainly now in Vietnam. It is safe to say that in virtually every country on the rim of China, and especially in that cluster of independent nations in Southeast Asia, the elements of civil war are serious and active.

There is a factor which looms larger, however, and that is the opportunity which the conditions of civil strife offer to outside predators who seek to exploit divided populations and to fish in troubled waters. Civil war in itself is serious enough. When aggravated by outside intervention, it becomes even more explosive.

In South Vietnam the general conditions of civil strife have been skillfully exploited by the National Liberation Front. It is important, therefore, to keep first things first. Civil conflict can weaken the foundations of an area, but not nearly so much as the efforts of outside groups like liberation fronts to move into weakened areas in order to seize them. Therefore, it is necessary to stop the outside intercession first before the civil issues can be resolved. What became critical in Vietnam was that the new government had its hands full simply maintaining law and order and providing for orderly change without the artificial pressures and disruptions introduced from the North.

American policy should not address itself to putting down civil wars but has a responsibility for addressing itself to the expansion of control by force and terror.

(5) If our cause is so great, why don't we get more help from our Allies?

The first thing we have to determine is, our Allies for what? For stopping Russia in Eastern Europe, or for achieving some other goal someplace else? It is a mistake to assume that because we had strong NATO Allies in Europe that those same governments would find it in their national interest to carry the alignment to the Far East.

We need to bear in mind, too, that the relative intensity of the crisis in Asia is influenced by the degree of stability in Europe—that, therefore, the mere presence of NATO and the emergence of a new stability in Europe has made it easier to hold in check the spread of the wars in Asia. After all, the world is round and remains quite inseparable as between regions and East versus West.

(6) Well, then, if it's Asia that's at stake, where are the Asians in this conflict?

The answer is that many of them are committed alongside us in Vietnam. The Koreans, with two divisions there, have more troops committed in Vietnam in proportion to their population than have we. Thailand has now committed a division. The Thais, moreover, have been a very considerable source of strength by cooperating in the building of bases covering the vulnerable flanks of the Allies in Vietnam. Australia in recent months has doubled her manpower commitment to nearly 7,000. The Philippine Government has committed several thousand combat engineers. And even tiny Laos—a so-called "neutral"—is losing more troops each year in the conflict than are the rest of the Allies combined in proportion to population.

If American troops were being killed at the same rate as Laotian troops, our losses would be 100,000 KIA's each year. Israel has small troop commitments in Vietnam. Other Asian countries whose internal political conditions remain fragile not only lack the trained manpower capabilities of sending troops to foreign lands but also lack assurance of maintaining stability even at home.

Yet in several cases, these Asian countries are lending economic assistance or dispatching nonmilitary teams at various levels of development in Vietnam. In sum, there are more non-American, non-Vietnamese soldiers committed in Vietnam than were committed in the Korean War.

(7) Why don't we turn Vietnam over to the United Nations?

The basic reason is that the kind of question Vietnam poses would destroy the United Nations. The United Nations was never initially structured to wage peace in an area as critical as Vietnam. It has no machinery, no troops, not even any resolutions which could be meaningful in enforcing a settlement in Vietnam. The world organization has enough problems at the present moment without dumping the issues of Southeast Asia into its lap. The role which the United Nations might fill, and has to some extent, is to provide opportunities for contacts through third parties between belligerent powers.

The trouble with the United Nations Resolutions passed by the United States Senate is that they tend to foster false hopes among our people without any chance of being implemented by significant actions. They remain exercises in politics rather than substantive explorations for peace.

(8) Why has the Administration changed its reasons for involvement in Vietnam?

The reasons for our Vietnam policy have not been changed. The shift that has occurred is in the awareness of the critics that perhaps the key issue among many is the containment of China. The heavy American commitments in economic assistance, in military assistance, in all of Southeast Asia as well as our efforts to promote collective security treaties among the Asian nations has consistently shown the basic strategic importance of that area to American security. Any critic surely understood that these substantive measures were not aimed at the Eskimos, as Secretary Rusk has said, but at China.

Nor has the need for our presence there been altered in any way. From the very first, the President, the Secretary of State, and the two preceding Administrations have described the Vietnamese issue as one involving the national interest of our country. These same spokesmen have described it further as a key to the balance of Asia, as a holding action to enable the smaller nations to put their own houses in order, as the preservation of the right to be independent, as a winning of the chance for democracy and freedom.

In a sense, it is all of these things. The critics have tended to select some among them—one or two—as the object of their own attacks, leaving out the full sweep of the factors that require an American presence in Eastern Asia.

(9) American boys are being killed. Isn't this morally wrong?

Any killing is morally wrong. One life lost in war is too many. But the harsh fact of life in our time is that man has not been smart enough to outlaw war. Until we achieve a world under law, boys will be killed on battlefields.

The real issue is not how many American men have been killed but rather how many lives will be spared because we have stood firmly in Vietnam. How many lives did we spare by letting the Japanese get away with their early aggressions in the 1930's? How many people were spared because the world refused to stop Hitler at the Rhineland in 1936? Because aggressors were not stopped when they started, some 12 to 15 million people were killed in World War II. The difficult thing about casualties in Vietnam is that history doesn't permit us the luxury of counting the cost if we had failed to stand in Vietnam.

(10) Why not declare war?

In a nuclear age, no nation can ever again risk a declaration of war. Even limited wars, while they must be waged, can rarely be declared. A war declaration by the United States would so freeze our options and escalate our requirements as to make it impossible to isolate the conflict or in other ways keep it from spreading.

(11) Why not destroy China now while she is relatively weak? Isn't war with her inevitable?

There are many reasons "why not." The first is that there is no such thing as an inevitable war. Who dares to pronounce inevitability? The pages of history are filled with "inevitable wars" which were talked about but never fought.

By the same token, you don't prevent a war by starting one. There is no such thing as a "preventive war."

Lastly, a deliberate attack by the United States—for whatever reasons—is not in the American character nor in our country's tradition of international responsibility.

(12) Why does the United States continue to escalate the war?

The United States does not continue to escalate the war. From our point of view, we would have preferred that nothing be done from the very beginning. It was the other side which escalated. As they stepped up their efforts, it became necessary to match those efforts in order to contain them or stop them. This was not of our choosing but of theirs.

Escalation, moreover, is a relative term. I regard "escalation" as a term which adds a new dimension to the war. Rather, since the rapid build-up which began in the winter of 1965, the United States has only intensified its participation in a limited conflict. It has not escalated the conflict. Escalating it would mean deciding to cross the Chinese frontier, or invading the North with an Inchon-type landing, or obliterating the cities of North Vietnam as we did the German industrial complexes, or blockading the China Sea. One of the most misleading phrases of the Vietnamese war has been the journalistic use of "escalation." Each time another 3,000 Marines arrive in the China Sea, it is described as an escalation. In fact, once the decision was made to stand firmly in Vietnam, the gradual increase in the number of troops to be committed there had nothing to do with escalating the war. It had only to do with implementing the tactics of achieving the limited objectives previously defined.

(13)   Isn't the United States simply replacing France as the colonial power in Vietnam?

No, she is not. The American purpose in Vietnam is to hold a line against the outside meddling in South Vietnamese affairs only until that time when the South Vietnamese are able to do it themselves. The President has made it clear that we do not intend to stay. This is no permanent American base. No colonial administrative machinery has been set up in any way. It is only a temporary holding action in order to win the time for Asians to do it themselves. American troops are still in Europe after twenty years. No one pretends to call that a colonial action. American troops are still in Korea after fifteen years. This is not regarded as an American colony.

We have already demonstrated our capabilities as a world power by gradually withdrawing from key areas that at one point were regarded as important to the security of the world balance of power. We assisted the Philippines in their independence. Bases in 50 places originally designed to contain the Soviet air threat have since been closed down in part because the tensions between the two countries have eased. In fact, no country in the postwar world has more vigorously encouraged independence movements than has the United States. The only exceptions were in the strategically important areas where the failure to have assumed a strong position would have weakened the balance of the world as well as the chances of that particular area to ever achieve its independence.

(14) Where did the United States get the right to play God or to act as policemen for the world?

The United States neither plays God nor polices the world. We do strive to shore-up the balance of power in the world to achieve stability—the only substitute for open violence and anarchy that there is in a lawless world. That is far different from policing.

One can think of any number of crises where the Americans did not meddle at all. As Secretary of State Rusk told the Senate Preparedness Investigating Committee in August, 1966:

"The last time I looked at such a list [of crises] out of the last 70 or so crises of one sort or another, we were directly involved in only about 6 of them. We did not, for example, rush with military force into the recent situation between India and Pakistan. We did not consider it our role to play a military role in the violence between Algeria and Morocco in recent years, or between Somalia and Ethiopia . . ."[1]

We did not meddle in the recent crisis in Nigeria, or the Israeli-Arab crisis of June, 1967, nor the Venezuelan-British Guianan border dispute in 1962, nor the United Arab Republic-Saudi Arabian intervention in Yemen during 1962-65. We have chosen to intervene only where it made a difference to the balance of the world security—like Berlin, Korea, Formosan Straits, missiles in Cuba, and Vietnam.

(15) Isn't it a mistake to promote a policy that is always anti-Communist? Doesn't Communism fit in some places?

The policy of the United States is not rigidly anti-Communist. It could more aptly be described as antiaggression.

In Asia, for example, the presence of American troops along the 38th Parallel is designed not only to protect South Korea from the so-called Communists in North Korea, but it is also to prevent the South from attacking or invading the Communists in the North.

The same can be said of the presence of the Seventh Fleet in the Formosan Straits. Not only is it designed to shield the Nationalist Chinese on Taiwan from the forces of Red China, it is also there to prevent the Nationalist Chinese from recklessly spreading war and conflict back to the Mainland.

In Vietnam, too, the purpose of guaranteeing a 17th Parallel is to try to minimize conflicts—not only to stop the Hanoi Communists from moving South but also to prevent the South from wiping out the North by force.

(16) But isn't communism different in different parts of the world?

Indeed it is. And so must our policy be toward it. Even as we seek to block a Communist aggression in Southeast Asia, we have worked simultaneously at building bridges of trade to the Eastern European Communist governments. At the same time that we pursue a policy of the containment of Red China, we pursue a policy of negotiating nuclear disarmament with the Soviet Union.

Throughout the Cold War we have had a policy of exploiting weaknesses along the communist front of the world—sometimes standing tough as in Berlin; other times, encouraging contacts, as in the case of Yugoslavia and Tito. This is the only wise basis for conducting a foreign policy; it best serves the national interest.

(17) Why don't we get out of Vietnam and let Ho Chi Minh become another Tito? After all, don't the North Vietnamese hate the Chinese, too?

History tells us how much the North Vietnamese hate the Chinese. But it also reminds us that Tito couldn't have lasted more than a few days without the presence of a counterforce in Europe to balance the Soviets. That counterforce was the United States. The best chance for a Tito to resist China in Southeast Asia is in the shadow of a strong American presence to counterbalance Peking.

(18) We have American spheres of influence in the Western Hemisphere. Why not agree to a Chinese sphere of influence in Asia? Isn't this only fair?

There is a difference. The so-called American influence in the Western Hemisphere is based upon the equality of the twenty republics—no domination or intimidation. The rest of the world has free access to the Hemisphere.

In the demonstrated Chinese concept of the sphere of influence, the covert and overt attempts to shape and to control not only the economies but the governments of the surrounding area is already a clear-cut pattern of Chinese policy. The same argument was used in the 1930's for allowing Japan a sphere of influence and allowing Hitler a sphere of influence. Those spheres were seized and exploited by aggressive governments to strengthen their capabilities of asserting their control of large sections of the globe.

The question of a Chinese sphere of influence also raises the moral question of what happens to the non-Chinese Asians. These non-Chinese who are as numerous as the Chinese themselves—nearly a billion of each group—don't want Chinese to control them. They resent the prospect of Chinese domination. They would like to control their own affairs.

For us, therefore, to seek to contain China is not only understandable and defensible but wise. It means that the potential power of any one nation in Asia is a bit more limited than if left unchecked. This factor in itself increases the chances for a more stable and even a more peaceful Asia.

(19) More and more people are saying that if President Kennedy had lived he would have kept us out of Southeast Asia. Is that true?

No, it is not true. One of the meanest tricks that the living play on the dead is to assert things in behalf of the dead which they never said or never did and possibly never even thought. The first victim of this little trick was President George Washington.

The best we can do in assessing the attitude of JFK is simply to go on what he said and did. It was President Kennedy who rapidly stepped-up the numbers of American advisers in Vietnam from 685 to 23,000. In March, 1963 he said,

> "I think that unless you want to withdraw from the field and decide that it is in the national interest to permit that area to collapse, I would think that it would be impossible to substantially change it particularly, as we

are in a very intensive struggle in those areas . . . So I
think that while we would all like to lighten the burden,
I don't see any real prospect of the burden being
lightened for the U.S. in Southeast Asia in the next year
if we are going to do the job and meet what I think are
very clear national needs."[2]

During an NBC television interview on September 9, 1963, in the
previously mentioned interview in which he affirmed his belief in the
"domino theory," (see p. 141) he also said:

"What I am concerned about is that Americans will get
impatient and say because they don't like events in
southeast Asia or they don't like the government in
Saigon, that we should withdraw. That only makes it
easy for the Communists. I think we should stay."

When all has been said, however, what really is germane is that
the living have to come to terms with the facts as they see them. The
dead are no longer here to know what the present circumstances
may be. Therefore, it is irrelevant in the final analysis to argue what
somebody might have done had he lived.

*(20) Secretary U Thant has likened the Vietnamese civil war to
our own American Revolution. Isn't this a fair comparison?*

It is not a fair comparison in most ways. First of all, the outcome
of the American Revolution did not carry with it the question of the
balance of power in the world. In Vietnam, on the other hand, the
issue is the security of all of Southeast Asia—not just of the rival
forces within Vietnam. It makes a difference.

Secondly, the bitterness and rivalry between the two Vietnams
had no clearly defined parallel in the American colonies. The early
centuries of history in Indochina as well as the 1954 Geneva
Conference reflected the complexities of those differences between the zones which lay on either side of the 17th Parallel.
In colonial America, on the other hand, the serious cleavages
which later contributed to the Civil War were not yet conspicuous
by 1776.

Also, U Thant's analogy would place the American Revolutionists
in the figure of the National Liberation Front which, I think, most
of our own people would reject as a comparable image.

(21) Didn't President Johnson lie to us when he promised in the 1964 campaign not to send American boys to fight in Asia?

What the President said in October, 1964 conformed with the best information that was available to all of our intelligence groups. It was not yet verified that North Vietnam had decided to step-up the tempo of the war by introducing regular troops and more sophisticated weapons. Thus, at the time the President referred to American boys in Asia, it appeared that Southeast Asia could be held with the existing manpower commitments.

(22) Well, then, at least Goldwater was proven to be right and Johnson wrong. Isn't that correct?

Hardly. Goldwater's advocacy of defoliation and stepping-up the bombing were too extreme, given what was known in October. The fact that in hindsight the Goldwater terminology seemed to fit subsequent developments should not obscure the fact that it was the wrong answer at the wrong time. The judgment to be made of a candidate and his decision-making has to be equated with the facts as he knows them at the time.

(23) Isn't the United States spreading itself too thin?

Not necessarily. Our capabilities for committing ourselves where it makes a difference have not yet been tested very heavily. A similar argument was used against waging two wars in 1941. The United States demonstrated a capability for mobilization which startled even the optimists.

What has to be determined is where are the critical areas being challenged in the balance of forces around the world. Korea, Southeast Asia, Germany? Whatever the determination, it is equally important that those pressures be met when they arise. At the same time, other areas with less impact on the world balance can be regarded with less critical consequences. (Nigeria, Rhodesia, Yeman).

(24) Well, at the very least—even if we're not overextended—can we afford it? It seems to me like we are being driven to national bankruptcy.

We can't afford not to. The price of abandoning the quest for security around the world would be many times higher than the costs of maintaining security forces capable of restraining major aggressions. We have not yet made a serious effort to mobilize our economic capabilities. Until now, it has been guns-and-butter, business-as-usual, even with the $25 to $30 billion outlay in Vietnam. Both the Gross National Product (GNP) and the standard of living continue to rise steadily.

(25) Doesn't Vietnam mean that we have to give up the war on poverty and the desperately important economic programs which are needed to help the cities? Think of what we could do with that $25 billion now going to the war.

If the war stopped tomorrow, it is not likely the Congress would convert those sums into the worthwhile programs you mentioned. The issue is not whether we can afford it but whether we have the will to allocate the priorities to these programs. There are still many members of the Congress unconvinced that some of the domestic programs are either necessary or worth the price.

(26) Why do we back a corrupt government in Saigon?

That is a loaded question. We back the government in Saigon as we back governments everywhere as the one available means of trying to stabilize the international community. The issue is one of preventing either aggression or anarchy in Southeast Asia. Corruption must remain a relative term. There are some things even worse than corruption in government, such as the surrender of all of the small countries in Asia to the tactics of terrorism.

(27) Isn't Senator Ted Kennedy correct in saying that, if the Saigon government doesn't eliminate corruption, the United States should pull out?

I strongly disagree with that analysis. It is more important to all of the countries in Southeast Asia that we stay and win for them the chance to improve and develop their own governments than to abandon them to force. It is a matter of putting first things first. Corruption has been a characteristic of governments in the Orient for many centuries. I doubt that it will be eliminated in your time or mine. The best way to control it or to cut it down is to help these countries retain their independence.

(28) Why not follow Professor Galbraith's suggestion to relegate Southeast Asia to the limbo which it deserves?

World War II and the events of the last twenty years have brought this part of the world to the forefront. It can never again be "relegated to limbo." What's more, this area of a third of a billion people—with rich critical resources, remains a grand prize for predatory forces interested in building power.

(29) Isn't the domino theory a phony?

I don't know about the theory; it is the domino *fact* that concerns me. We are prone to forget that scarcely three years ago all of the fabric of Southeast Asia seemed to be coming unraveled. Indochina, Burma, Cambodia, Laos. Since then, government after government has affirmed that, if Vietnam falls, they could not continue to resist the pressures of the liberal front tactics. As the late President Kennedy put it, if Vietnam goes, it is but a short jump to Malaysia.

(30) Why compromise the Vietnam issue like we compromised Laos a few years ago?

In hindsight Laos becomes a superb illustration of how not to do it. As a result of the so-called "negotiated truce," the territorial integrity of Laos has been continuously violated by the North Vietnamese. No less than 10,000 troops remained there in direct defiance of the compromise. And at the present moment, it is thought that several times that number of North Vietnamese troops are in Laos. In fact, Souvanna Phouma, the neutralist Premier of Laos, has now switched from his position of being critical of the United States to one in which he says without the Americans his government would have been totally destroyed by Hanoi.

(31) Why is it that the people of North Vietnam seem so orderly and dedicated while the people of South Vietnam seem so divided and indifferent?

This is an illusion generated by the communications media. Only the affairs in the South are minutely reported. There is rarely any uncensored, unplanned coverage of events in the North. Moreover, there are bound to be serious differences in public conduct between an area that is governed under a monolithic structure (dictatorship), as is North Vietnam, and one in which demands and efforts have required a much more fluid structure (democracy, freedom, etc.).

(32) Isn't it like President Eisenhower once said—that Ho Chi Minh had the support of 80 percent of the people? Why do we interfere in a political circumstance as overwhelming as that?

President Eisenhower made such a statement in 1954. It would be impossible to determine the percentage of support which Ho commanded at that time. Most of the Vietnamese people—North and South—rallied around the symbolism of Ho because he was anti-French—not because he was their own nationalist leader. George Gallup would have found it difficult to measure sentiment in the two Vietnams either then or now.

(33) A distinguished American journalist who interviewed Ho Chi Minh says that Ho would be a good guy if only the Americans would get out. Why not give him a chance?

It depends upon what you mean by "good guy." Ho destroyed some 30,000 or more of his political opponents. He abolished all political dissent. He drove nearly a million of his North Vietnamese out of the country. And he ordered the killing by terrorist squads of many thousands of local leaders in South Vietnam. While he has uttered some comforting platitudes, one is entitled to recall the old saying, "What you do speaks so loudly I cannot hear what you say."

(34) Weren't the 1967 elections in Vietnam a shock?

Far from it. They were held under extremely difficult conditions. Not only was there a war on, but in many areas individual voters went to the polls amid direct threats on their lives if they dared to do so. To be sure, it was a new experience for many of those who voted. But as the many observation teams from all parts of the world verified on the spot, the elections were reasonably orderly and reasonably fair. While far from perfect, they were the closest thing yet to free elections in South Vietnam. As you reach your own conclusions on the matter of elections, it might be well to ask again, when was the last election held in the North?

(35) You complain about the terrorism of the North. I don't see any difference between it and the bombing of innocent women and children by the United States. Aren't the people equally dead?

Let's not torture the meaning of words. The United States does not have a calculated policy of destroying civilians. To be sure, many innocent people become the victims of the violence of war. They remain tragedies. But this is far different from a cold-blooded destruction of pre-selected numbers of people. In terms of right and wrong or of morality (if one isn't torturing this phrase in the context of any war), there is a deep difference between deliberate civilian massacre and unintended accidental casualties.

(36) Wasn't the Tonkin Gulf Incident a put-up job in order to create an excuse to bomb North Vietnam?

The answer is no. Subsequent testimony has established that, indeed, there was an attack on the American naval vessels; that those vessels were in international waters; and that the response to the attack was a limited one. In the hindsight of four years, the original circumstances which evoked the American response have survived the tests of even the severest critics.

(37) But isn't it true that without the Tonkin Gulf Incident we would not have escalated the war in Vietnam?

That is not true. Tonkin becomes a symbol rather than a material factor in escalation. The build-up in American manpower commitments stemmed not from the Tonkin Gulf Incident but from the far more serious decision in Hanoi to commit their own regular army and new weapons system to the conflict south of the 17th Parallel. That decision, as we now know, was made by North Vietnam several months *before* the Tonkin affair—even though its existence was not verified until a few months after the incident. The point is that, if there never had been an attack on the *Maddox* and the *C. Turner Joy*, the United States would have had to act quickly on the question of its manpower commitments once the new dimension of the conflict was discovered in the late autumn of 1964.

(38) Isn't the Tonkin Resolution in the Senate a lame excuse for the President's actions in Vietnam?

Under the Constitution, the President of the United States doesn't need an "excuse." He is the Commander-in-Chief and is empowered to make the kind of decisions which he has been making. The Tonkin Gulf Resolution was simply a reaffirming of the

Congressional judgment of the urgency of the crisis to which he responded. At any time (even the next day) the Congress could repeal the Resolution. At this writing no repeal has been undertaken.

This remains a false refuge for critics of the war—most of whom themselves supported the Resolution at the time, some of whom now say they were wrong. But they remain unwilling to challenge the substance of the "wrong" by Congressional action. Even should some action be attempted, the fact that in nearly four years the critics failed to make a serious try at repealing the Tonkin Resolution must reveal something about the sincerity of their own misgivings.

(39) I am a conscientious objector. Don't I have a right to refuse to serve in this war?

You do indeed. If you can establish that, in your conscience, you oppose *all* wars and that you could not kill in war, you have recourse to a conscientious-objector designation.

(40) I conscientiously object to this *war—not to all wars. This war is wrong. Other wars might be right. The war against Hitler, for example, I could have supported. I would like to fight against the Nazis.*

You are guilty of making a *political* judgment rather than one of conscience.

Hitler is dead. World War II is past. You have to come to grips with this question in *your* time rather than in some bygone age. If you oppose only this war, you have no grounds to stand on. The whole fabric of government (as an alternative to anarchy) depends upon the participation by the citizen in policies which reflect the support of the majority.

Even if you choose to argue that a majority doesn't support our policy in Asia, under our system, you change this not by violence but by ballots. Were you to be permitted to pick and choose the laws which you would obey and those which you defy, you in effect revert to lawlessness and anarchy. You shred the fabric of orderly government and majority rule.

Every generation before you has passed through these identical misgivings about the wars of their time. And this is especially true when a young man is at first confronted by selective service. My generation was no less tortured by the prospect of being drafted than is yours. This becomes personal and political more than a matter of conscience.

CHAPTER XIII

Dissent: From the Campus to the Capitol

Vietnam has triggered an explosion, the fallout from which is striking the campuses of the colleges and universities of the land. I refer to new attempts on the part of some groups to censor and limit the historic freedoms associated with academic rights on the campus. While we are currently focusing attention on campus protests, this rightful concern should not blind us to the other side of the same coin; namely, encroachments on academic freedom.

Until recent times, there was an unspoken axiom of American politics that academic life and political life were incompatible. Few professors were in the political arena. It was political suicide for a candidate for public office to be suspected of professorial traits. Even as late as the end of World War II, most of the college campuses seemed to reflect their acquiescence in this concept.

Even the students were strangely quiet on public questions. Whether this was due to lethargy or indifference or a sense of making up for the time the postwar generation had already lost in military service is irrelevant at the moment. Regardless of cause, the Halls of Ivy after World War II seemed blissfully isolated, either by design or by accident, from the hard realities of the world.

What produced the change to ferment and even turbulence may be many overlapping forces. A single issue, however, seems to have galvanized the impact. That issue is Vietnam.

This is not to say that it took the shock of war to bring academia back to earth. One does not have to be partisan to suggest that the arrival on the political scene of the late John F. Kennedy did have the effect of evoking a new and more acute interest in public affairs among the student generation. The young President's arrival also seemed to inspire a new political awareness among the academics themselves.

In its initial resurgence, this "renaissance" was triggered by such new ideas and programs as the Peace Corps. Politically, moreover, the Russians had already played a significant role in accounting for the revival of political awareness. With the launching of Sputnik in October, 1957, many Americans were stunned by the realization that they had no monopoly on scientific genius or wisdom. Since that memorable event, the physical scientists have plunged more deeply into the political fountains dotting the nation's landscape. In fact, it has even become respectable for academics to venture more boldly into the public arena.

Thus, the combination of idealism and personal inspiration on the one hand, and the harsh realities of Russian scientific exploits on the other, thrust the academic community into the center of the Nation's political stage. It is not unfair to say that noble inspiration and sheer fright combined to implicate the intellectual society in the politics of the 1960's.

What might have been an orderly transition from indifference to involvement was converted into a near violent plunge into the cauldron of world affairs by a single issue—Vietnam. What the violence of Vietnam has evoked in the way of dissent is perhaps less important than what it has threatened in the way of traditional campus freedoms. But one of its fringe benefits has been the joining of the interests and concerns of the Halls of Ivy with those of the Halls of Government. In campus teach-ins and in Senate hearings the dominant uniting force has been dissent.

However, this new union of "interests" is a mixed blessing. Different freedoms and different degrees of responsibility attend the academic and the political areas. It is important that we separate and examine carefully the consequences of Vietnam dissent for each. On the campus the right at stake is the right to think otherwise, or even the right to be wrong. But in the political arena what is under attack is the right to be responsible or, more bluntly, the right to be right.

The right to disagree is a firm tradition of the academic world; but there is more to it than that. It is the *obligation* of the campus to provoke dissent. Currently, the extremes of some of the demonstrations and dialogues from our universities have obscured the importance of "dissent as dissent" in that setting. This is not to apologize for the more flagrant displays of intolerance also coming from the campus today. Few would defend the stability or the dignity of the dissenter who describes public policies as being projected by "power-mad militarists," "war-mongers," "blood lechers," or "murderers of our youth." Among the campus critics, there surely are those who like to think they are taking orders from Moscow or Peking. Some of them may be professional revolutionaries. There are those, too, who even lack the credentials of campus residents. But none of these attributes should be permitted to intrude upon the right "to think otherwise," a concept historically embedded in the academic traditions. In no case should they be used as an excuse to extinguish the obligation to inspire ferment on the campus and in the classroom.

The sometimes frightening noises coming from Berkeley, Cambridge, or Madison tend to be lifted out of context. Their volume often belies their meager numbers. Newswise, protest invariably claims more attention than support. What may be more alarming, if less conspicuous, is that the extremes of campus activities have begun to panic those groups of individuals in our land who have historically preempted the role of keeper of patriotism and Americanism as well as the role of morality and academic freedom.

Largely because of Vietnam we are about to be caught up in a series of new witchhunts and predatory raids against traditional academic rights—almost always, of course, in the name of the Constitution or the Founding Fathers, but really aimed at stifling the other point of view. Already these impulses threaten to shut the doors on free inquiry and to inhibit free expression. In recent years, this trend has experienced a sort of resurgence even without the crisis in Asia, aided and abetted as it has been by numerous extremist groups who skillfully promote a lucrative trade in suspicion, fear, smear, and hate.

The classroom, long a handy target in the lexicon of the extremists, has suddenly become an even better mark because of the emotions unleashed by the campus antics in protest to Vietnam. It would be serious indeed if current attacks on academia get out of hand, but the record is already replete with warning signals.

On one state university campus in the West, a professor of English—identified at one time with Student Non-Violent Coordinating Committee—has come under attack from certain self-appointed censors of his conduct. His job remains in jeopardy. On another campus, a law against leftist speakers has been revived. This statute, enacted by the North Carolina Legislature in 1963, prohibits Communists and pleaders of the Fifth Amendment from speaking at any state educational institution.

Dr. Frank Graham, speaking about the Carolina law, has said, "The free market of ideas in the historic American view is a basic part of the American tradition of free enterprise. 'Gag laws' repressing the freedom of assembly and speech are expressions of the totalitarian way and are contrary to the American way."

The North Carolina case is by no means the end of the line. The Virginia department of one of the larger veterans' organizations has adopted a resolution urging the State Assembly to ban communist speakers from the campus. Similar proposals are pending in other states.

These bring squarely into focus the right of a school's faculty and student representatitves to invite speakers of all persuasions, including the extremes of the right and the left, to the campus. Once leftist speakers have been banned, little defense remains even for the extreme right-wingers. And with both of the extremes out of the way, what remains of the rights of the "center?" As John Donne put it, " . . . and therefore never send to know for whom the bell tolls; it tolls for thee."

A teach-in at the University of Miami prompted the use of one of the newer weapons of the extremists—the recorded telephone message. Invented by a Florida physician, W. C. Douglass of Sarasota, this device plays back messages previously recorded under the patriotic name "Let Freedom Ring." It can be connected into any telephone exchange in the country. Over 100 devices are now known to be in existence. It is a convenient tool for extremists because of its particular advantage that it has not been the subject of regulation by the Federal Communications Commission, and the voices and sponsors of its often extreme accusatory messages remain anonymous.

After the Miami teach-in, residents in the area were telephoned by unidentified callers and asked if they knew what was taking place on the campus of their very own university. If they wanted to know, they were told to dial 221-6767. In response to that number a woman's voice said in part, "This is 'Let Freedom Ring.' Last Tuesday night at Miami's own little, red schoolhouse, there was a strange assortment of pinks, punks, beatniks, and left-wing educators assembled for the purpose of pleading for a Soviet line against the Communists." An extended diatribe then proceeded to link anyone who had attended the teach-in with individuals who were accused of being Socialists, Communists, Pacifists, and oddballs. A United States Senator who had participated was described as being "shoulder to shoulder with a Marxist who advocates selective assassination."

It was not surprising that such irresponsible and reckless assaults on character and on people in general excited the fears of otherwise well-meaning citizens. The storm which threatened to engulf the campus jeopardized much more than the rights of the participants themselves.

It would be inaccurate, however, to leave the impression that such outbursts and assaults are the private property of extremist groups or of self-designated patriotic societies. The quest for "conspirators" and "plotters" behind our many complex public problems has readily found sponsors in the Halls of Congress itself. Tensions over Vietnam have aggravated the abuse still further. A former member of the United States Senate has gone "Let Freedom Ring" one better. From a western campus, he sought to warn the world that "the little, red schoolhouse is redder than you think." He asserted that on the modern campus Communistic beatniks and foreign-born, fuzzy professors are destroying true Americanism.

Equally alarming was the outburst of a Member of the House of Representatives who has questioned whether a professor who had participated in a teach-in and was critical of Vietnam policy should be allowed to receive funds from the Federal Government. The Congressman charged that for the professor to be granted those funds was a "shocking inconsistency."

What is even more "shocking" is that a Member of the Congress should raise such a question in the first place. Colleges and universities have always had to contend with those who wish to proscribe teaching and research with limits reflecting the political and cultural convictions of the time. But I agree with the thought embodied in a decision of the United States Supreme Court which declares, "If there is any fixed star in our constitutional constellation, it is that no official, high or petty, can order what shall be orthodox in politics, nationalism, religion, or other matters of opinion or force citizens to confess by words or act their faith therein."

The task of retaining a national equilibrium about protest and erratic protestors is made more difficult because of the curious attributes of the better publicized among the dissenters. The bearded and the unwashed have too often taken over the headlines from the genuine and the sincere. For example, in autumn, 1967, several hundred young people demonstrated at the Department of Justice against the war in Asia and proclaimed they were turning in nearly a thousand draft cards. The Department proceeded to open the bag of cards for a more careful analysis. In it they found a miscellany of genuine and phony registrations, a mishmash of statements, xerox copies and letters of asserted official status. Legal certification could be established for only about 60 persons out of the several hundred represented. The rest of the "draft cards" were a mass of doubtful material. Among the 200 or so actually identifiable, nearly two dozen indicated a history of mental disorders including suicidal tendencies. Among the protestors, likewise, were at least four college professors who had been classified 4-F for mental reasons. The purpose of mentioning this breakdown is not to attach a stigma to any individual person but rather to show the kind of riffraff which is also surfaced by the efforts of the more sincere and rational war objectors involved in the protest against Vietnam.

Riffraff is a term not only applicable to persons, however. It can be applied to language as well. Professors and other academic intellectuals for whom one can assume status and sense of responsibility seem to have contributed a riffraffish language to the realm of criticism on Vietnam. A distinguished professor of political science categorically asserted that the President of the United

States lies for "kicks." Others refer to the President of the United States and the Secretary of State as "war-mongers" and "mass murderers." I have heard professors, while haranguing an audience of students, ask, "How many babies have you burned today, Mr. President?"

These are hardly the phrases or terms over which a reasonable critic should take issue with the President of the United States on questions involving the overseas commitments of our country. Yet, it is precisely accusations of this wild kind that inflame passions on the campus and which more and more seem to characterize the "peace movement."

Perhaps the subsequent march on the Pentagon was the ultimate in protest irresponsibility. What started out to be a high-level and even high-minded demonstration against war in Asia rapidly deteriorated into a public orgy of excesses and obscenities perpetrated by only a few hundred of the several thousand for whom the march represented a deep, personal commitment. In hindsight, some of the dissenters themselves have pointed to the Pentagon assault as the eye-opening experience which showed the recklessness of some of the groups which—like so many leeches—fixed themselves to the peace movements. The extremes of this revealing march make it easy to remember the observation of British essayist Charles Montague who wrote, after the First World War, "War hath no fury like a noncombatant."

Their numbers are multiplied by those who are deliberate draft-dodgers or those running away from the responsibilities of growing up. These, in turn, in their own reckless conduct, have discredited the genuine pacifists who in their protests sought to find a place in the pursuit of conscientious-objector status.

And more recently, even as high-minded and conscientious an objector as Eugene McCarthy has found one of his most nagging problems to be that of the extremist left-wing zealots who were striving to use his movement for their own petty ends. It is this pseudo-intellectual riff-raff which has done much to downgrade the respectability of honorable and constructive dissent.

In their extreme tactics of barring military recruiters and representatives of Dow Chemical from the campus, or stopping inductees from reporting to selective service stations, they have preempted for themselves the right to judge right from wrong, good from bad, denying that right at the same time to any who disagree with them. Others among them have destroyed both the right of free speech and the right to listen when in chorus they have tried to shout down the Vice President of the United States or the Secretary of State. In this action they deny to others the identical freedoms they are advocating for themselves. The old adage that two wrongs do not make a right certainly is applicable here. And all of the partisans from both sides would do well to read again the warning words of Tom Paine, who wrote in 1795, "He that would make his own liberty secure must guard even his enemy from oppression."

To those who are upset with what one editorial writer described as "the cockeyed professors and pacifists and anarchists" on the campus, I would remind them that to enforce thought control upon our institutions of higher learning would do far more damage to our civilization and our Nation than can the fulminations of the most radical of students and the most irresponsible of professors.

Nor dare we take comfort in the lame hope that the current attacks are mere nitpicking assaults that will soon fade away. As our past history long since should have reminded us, such small beginnings can readily explode into dangerous attacks on everyone's freedom. From Vietnam to the suspension of all unpopular dissent, it is but a short distance.

Even now the issue of academic freedom is assuming major proportions on the national, political scene. It appeared in a New Jersey gubernatorial contest where the question at issue was retaining on the payroll of a state school a professor who embraced the Viet Cong. It also was present in the Governor's race in California.

The temptations for politicians to plunge into predatory missions on the campuses of our state universities are great; but they must be discouraged. Supreme Court Justice Frankfurter, who had academic experience at Harvard, once noted the importance of defending the four essential freedoms of a university—to determine for itself on academic grounds who may teach, what may be taught, how it shall be taught, and who may be admitted to study.

To this note should be added a statement of Chief Justice Earl Warren who cautioned, "to impose any straightjacket upon the intellectual would imperil the future of our Nation . . . Scholarship cannot flourish in an atmosphere of suspicion and distrust. Teachers and students must always remain free to inquire, to study and to evaluate, to gain new maturity and understanding; otherwise our civilization will stagnate and die."

Freedom is a precious possession. And we should periodically take inventory of its blessings and its ramifications. To destroy freedom in the name of protecting it betrays, rather than preserves, our national traditions. Yet, there have always been those persons who would, in the name of liberty, seek to deny it to their opponents.

To pass laws against ideas is futile. No matter how unpopular and unwanted, ideas cannot be legislated out of existence. Neither can they be silenced by a resolution from a veterans' convention. The only way to defeat an idea is with a better one. Patriotism cannot be invoked by legislative edict, nor decreed by administrative order, nor achieved by loyalty oaths. To endure, true patriotism must be inspired, not commanded.

It is imperative that we not sacrifice freedom of dissent on the altars of censorship, bigotry, or intolerance. To the professors, this is the heartbeat of academic freedom. It is also one of the sustaining pillars of all human freedom.

But even as it is essential that we guard against restrictions on academic freedom, the academic community itself must remember that this is a two-way street.

While it is indispensible to preserve the right to think otherwise, it is equally indispensible to preserve the right to be right. This means that, as we protect the right of dissent by respecting the dissenter and his point of view, we are compelled at the same time to protect the right of the decision-maker not only to decide but to explain and to defend the basis for that decision.

It does as much violence to the right of dissent for students and professors to parade out of a church in the middle of the Vice President's speech (as they did at American University) or to jeer and hoot and howl in protest against the speaking efforts of the Secretary of Defense (as they did at Harvard) or to attempt to drown out the remarks of the Secretary of State through synchronized chanting (as they did at the University of Indiana) as it does for a government to curb the liberties of students on the campus. The unwillingness to listen by "tuning-out" reflects a closed mind.

Nor are the violent efforts to prevent a speaker from being heard or to deny to others the right to hear any less a violation of the principle of free speech than the more direct abrogation of that right by legislation or decree. None of these square with the inherent obligation of a university to question or to doubt.

Academic freedom must be balanced with academic responsibility. How best to strike that wise balance must ever remain within the province of good judgment. It cannot be legislated through formula. Neither can it be forfeited to the emotions set loose by Vietnam. Freedom on the campus must be calculated consciously and achieved deliberately.

CHAPTER XIV

Executive Power and Foreign Policy

The war in Vietnam has brought into sharp focus a contest between the President and the Senate (some Senators) over the relationship of their respective responsibilities in shaping foreign policy. This has always been so. In fact, the American ship of state was launched in 1776 upon waves of discontent with executive authority. The image of George III has been known to every American school boy as arbitrary authority, and the colonial governors epitomized unbridled power to many of the provinces.

The Thirteen Colonies embarked upon their newly independend careers without an executive. And it was only after the near debacle of the colonial period that a need for centralized control of the national government came to be recognized. Nowhere was the requirement for executive power more clearly in evidence than in the realm of foreign relations.

Our Founding Fathers recognized this fact of public life by creating under the Constitution a strong Chief Executive. The President was assigned treaty-making powers and was made Commander-in-Chief in time of war.

Deeply rooted in the hearts and souls of the leaders of the new republic, however, was an ingrained distrust of the powers of the President. This has continued down to the present day.

The issue of executive power in foreign policy tended to rear its head during the administrations of strong Presidents and to languish through inattention during the administrations of weak Presidents. While on occasion the Judicial Branch of the government asserted its powers, the other two branches of the government have been the principal contenders.

What the President's role should be in a nuclear age, whether the division of responsibility between the President and the Senate can survive in a nuclear age are questions at stake in the present dispute.

The Presidential power in foreign affairs derives mainly from Sections 2 and 3 of Article II of the Constitution. Section 2 states that " . . . He shall have power, by and with the advice and consent of the Senate, to make treaties, provided two-thirds of the Senators present concur; and he shall nominate, and by and with the advice and consent of the Senate, shall appoint Ambassadors, other public Ministers and Consuls . . . " Section 3 of the article states that " . . . He shall receive Ambassadors and other Public Ministers . . . "

The treaty-making power of the President received a great deal of attention from the framers of the Constitution. Writing in *Federalist No. 75* Hamilton stated that "Though this provision has been assailed, on different grounds, with no degree of vehemence, I scruple not to declare my firm persuasion, that it is one of the best digested and most unexceptionable parts of the (Constitution)." One of the main objections to the clause was that the making of treaties, which have the force of law, was taken out of the hands of Congress which had been granted the power to make all other laws. Hamilton discussed this problem at length in the *Federalist* and noted finally that the treaty power " . . . seems to form a distinct department, and to belong, properly, neither to the legislative nor to the executive . . . the executive (is) indispensible in the management of foreign negotiations . . . while the vast importance of the trust, and the operation of treaties as laws, please strongly for the participation of the . . . legislative body in the office of making them."

With the exception of the clauses mentioned above, the Constitution contains few details about how foreign policy is to be made or carried out. In practice, the President has usually been responsible for the outlines of our foreign policy with Congress exercising varying degrees of direct and indirect influence. From the founding of the United States to the end of the 19th Century, Congressional influence was considerable. A good example of this was the expansion in the late 19th Century of American interests in East Asia. Congressional pressure for a vigorous policy in Eastern Asia came mainly from the industrial New England states where manufacturers were looking for markets for their goods. To put a shirt on the back of every man in China was the dream of every textile mill owner in the northeast.

With the birth of the 20th Century, responsibility for American foreign policy became more and more the province of the President. Theodore Roosevelt, William Howard Taft, and Woodrow Wilson freely used United States forces to protect American lives and property in the Caribbean and Central America without obtaining Congressional consent. In 1914 prior to committing Congress, President Wilson ordered United States forces to seize the Mexican port of Vera Cruz in order to "enforce respect" for the American government. This contrasts widely with the 1824 action of John Quincy Adams who said, when queried by the Columbian government as to what action the United States would take should a European state intervene in one of the new Latin American states, "The ultimate decision of this question belongs to the Legislative Department of the Government . . . "

By far the most significant changes in the role of the President and foreign policy have come about since the beginning of World War II. The trend begun by Theodore Roosevelt, William Howard Taft, and Woodrow Wilson accelerated rapidly under Franklin Roosevelt through the use of executive agreements. One of the most important of these was the agreement with Britain to exchange overage destroyers for British bases. As in the case of many other executive agreements, the destroyers-for-bases deal was based on the President's power as Commander-in-Chief of the Armed Forces. However, other Presidents in the past quarter century have turned to executive agreements to effect a myriad of commitments and agreements ranging from military assistance to cultural exchange. Thus programs for the training of foreign military officers and for sponsoring tours of visiting artists are negotiated and agreed to without either the advice or the consent of Congress.

Obviously, the most significant reason for the increased power of the President in the era since the second World War has been the advent of the nuclear age. We live in a time when fifteen minutes may spell the difference between life and death for hundreds of millions of people. In the past 25 years there have been times when the only sure thing that could be said about the next 24 hours was that no one really knew if we would live through them.

Concomitant with the onslaught of the nuclear age has been the growth of the American role as the most powerful nation on earth. The framers of the Constitution showed more bravado than truth when they adopted the eagle as the symbol of their fledgling nation. The Thirteen Colonies, weak, economically depressed, and ridden with petty jealousies, had little or no influence in world affairs. Their main asset was their distance from the great powers of Europe. They were hard put to defend their shipping from even the coastal pirates of North Africa.

Today, the symbolism of the eagle has come to fruition. America is a great power. Her actions cause reverberations throughout the world and must, therefore, be carefully considered and delicately executed. Yet, these actions must be executed swiftly. The decision-making process may be reduced to a matter of minutes. The time allotted by events to decision makers is all too often less than the time it takes to assemble a quorum in Congress. More than ever, the authority to make decisions and take action must be located in one place. Hence, the foreign-policy role of the President has grown like a snowball rolling down a long, steep hill. From rather meager beginnings broadly shared with Congress we have come to an age when the press of time scarcely allows Congress more than a passing glance at some of the most important decisions in the history of mankind.

We would do well to consider here the role of Congress, and more particularly the Senate, in foreign affairs. What is its role and what ought it to be?

As President Kennedy once noted, "Success has many fathers; failure is an orphan." This comes close to the nub of pinning responsibility for American policy.

The Congress of the United States, President Woodrow Wilson once observed, is a "disintegrated ministry," a jealous power center with a built-in suspicion of, if not outright antagonism toward, the President.

The role of Congress today is essentially negative. Appropriations can be withheld or cut, as is so often the case, with foreign aid bills. The Senate can refuse to act on treaties or ambassadorial appointments. Congress as a whole can pass legislation that will greatly affect foreign relations (witness the recent spate of tariff bills). But these are all negative actions—positive action with regard to foreign relations must come from the President. The President can negotiate a treaty for a new Panama Canal—Congress cannot. The President can order troops to Lebanon—Congress cannot. The President can announce a new program to combat the ills of underdevelopment—Congress cannot. What Congress can do in each of these cases is to react. The only way it can make its reaction felt is to react negatively, to deny funds, to vote against the treaty, or to pass a resolution calling for the President to "bring the boys home."

It goes without saying that Congress does not exert the influence that it did during the 19th Century. John Quincy Adams' reply to the Columbian government would not get past the first drafting officer in the State Department today. It would be foolish to try to ascribe the decline of Congressional influence to any one particular reason or set of reasons, for the real causes are manifold.

Two reasons do stand out, though. One is the nature of the times we live in, and the other, which may or may not be part and parcel of the first, is the failure of the Congress, particularly the Senate, to meet the demands of these times. The United States has diplomatic relations with more than 110 countries. There are another dozen or so with which we do not have relations for one reason or another. It goes without saying, that most Senators, even those who are members of the Foreign Relations Committee, just do not have the time to follow closely the affairs of a given foreign state. Vietnam, the Middle East, and the Common Market can be counted on to receive a smattering of attention from a given Senator. But who in the Senate today can present an informed opinion on the relationship, if any, between a civil war in Nigeria, a coup in Dahomey, and mercenary rebellion in the Congo? Who on the Senate floor can offer one whit of solid advice as to whether we should recognize Outer Mongolia? What would we gain from such recognition? What would be its effect on our relations with the other countries of Asia, particularly Japan, China, and South Korea? What would it mean in terms of our relations with the Soviet Union? Would it give us a window into China? There are any number of reasons why some members of the Senate should be well informed on these topics; but, alas, too many Senators view their subject in "political" black and white, i.e., Communism is bad; therefore, we should not recognize Communist states.

The fact of the matter is that it comes all too naturally to a Senator to play the foreign relations game according to how many votes he thinks it will win him in the next election than to play it on its merits. Thus, we find Senatorial globe-trotters expounding their segregationist views in Africa. The Senate floor itself makes a great pulpit for attacks against aid to Arab countries by members with large Jewish constituencies. A prime example of this occurred during debates on food assistance to Egypt. Nasser was damned as the predator of Israeli interests even though knowledgeable persons in the Israeli Government really preferred American food aid to him to continue as the lesser of the evil alternatives that were available. They reasoned that this might be one force of restraint or at least a contact to hold in check Nasser's ambitions toward driving Israel into the sea.

Food assistance to two other countries—Poland and Yugoslavia—cleared in 1967 following debate based on much the same rationale used for Egypt. The Executive branch of our government had based assistance to both countries on the theory that it would help wean them away from the Soviets and eventually result in more independent policies on their part. Additionally, the programs afforded a point of mutual interest between our governments and served as a very tangible point of contact. Yet, Senators from states where sizable blocks of voters are of Slavic or Eastern European ethnic background felt compelled to lash out blindly at the programs.

That individual Senators feel that they can engage in this sort of action reflects a lack of knowledge on their part about the extent of their influence. How can they expect to make an impression on the man in the street "back home" without also making an impression on the chief of state and the foreign minister of the country they are attacking? Their words for the residents of Podunk Junction may well be carried by any of a dozen news services to all of Africa, Asia, and Latin America.

If the floor of the Senate provides a pulpit for its members, then televised hearings of committees, particularly those of the Foreign Relations Committee, can only be characterized as the center ring of a circus. The Secretaries of State and Defense have sometimes been made to appear as no less than foreign agents, or even common crooks fighting for their lives. The indignities that have been practiced upon them by Senatorial inquisitors have tended to downgrade the highly responsible roles they fill.

The appearance of Secretary of State Rusk before the Foreign Relations Committee in March, 1968 revealed a great deal about the mechanism of televised hearings on foreign policy. Called under the pretense of hearing about foreign aid, the hearings concentrated instead on the war in Vietnam. They continued for 10½ hours in two sessions during which the Secretary of State was under constant attack and sometimes questioning—all of it under the stark glare of television lights.

Nearly all of the Senators on the Foreign Relations Committee showed up at one time or another, which stands in contrast to the attendance of committee members during non-televised hearings.

At the end of the first day of hearings, the charge was levied against the Chairman that he did not permit the Secretary of State to finish that same evening because there was no available television time for the "Dean Rusk Show." Rusk was forced to come back the following morning for another 4 hours of interrogation.

Many of the Senatorial inquiries were in the form of long speeches. The Senators seemed to have difficulty in placing question marks in their texts. What was also conspicuous was the number of Senators who, immediately upon finishing their own speeches, left the hearings—obviously too busy to hear what the Secretary might have to say in reply.

While the Chairman was careful to admonish the Secretary about keeping his answers brief (five times he was told by the Chairman to shorten his responses), the Committee members seemingly went on without end (and without admonition). In fact, the record reveals that there were 55 cases in which Committee members made statements 200 words or longer. Others of the Committee were at times reluctant to permit the Secretary the opportunity to finish a statement once he had started—interrupting his responses with new bombardments and/or questions. The record reveals that Rusk was interrupted no less than 56 times without being permitted to finish.

The point of it all is that there was less evidence of dignity in searching inquiries into the problems of American policy in Asia, less sincerity and intensity in pursuing the right to know, than some of us might have wished. And when it was all over, Secretary Rusk seemed to have endured the ordeal very well indeed. He had abided his patience and kept his "cool."

It was a little surprising at times that some of the Committee members deemed it necessary to ask the kind of questions they did, for they were obviously questions about which even the casual newspaper reader would already have been informed.

The brilliance of the Secretary's conduct has tended to obscure what seems to be an emerging fault in the senatorial structure in this day of television. To begin with, the Secretary was under intensive pressure in the glare of lights for an unconscionable length of time. Lesser men would have "cracked" under the strain. It would seem to me to be beneath the dignity of the high office of Secretary of State to expose it to the kind of public spectacle this show became.

A second complication of the televised hearings was the continual temptation for individual Senators to pitch for television exposure rather than to probe for information. The danger, as I see it, is not only one of downgrading the dignity of government, but also that of forfeiting a meaningful role of the Senate in the processes of foreign policy.

With all of the concern being expressed these days about the power of the Executive vis-a-vis the Congress, I would submit that in this instance it is the Congress itself that may be frittering away its chance for a continuing responsible role.

One alternative is to abolish television. This may be unrealistic, though. Television seems to be here to stay even in the Committee room.

Therefore, the most reasonable other alternative which our times permit us is for Senators to work harder at upgrading their own role—their individual performances—during the televised proceedings. In any case, it is open to serious question whether the whole proceeding can really be in the national interest. In these modern times of America's new world position when nearly every breath we take is recorded around the globe, a slip of the tongue or an intemperate response from a Secretary could easily complicate international questions and perhaps jeopardize the nation's security.

What the Senators *really* need to know is developed in executive session—or at least off camera.

In still another way have the emotions vented by Vietnam affected Congressional procedures in foreign policy.

It is difficult to avoid the impression that the Senate Foreign Relations Committee preferred to hear witnesses whose views were diametrically opposite to those of the Administration. In 1967 on the question of Asian policy, the Committee conducted a "seminar" series on China. In its course the seminar gave the impression of arraying academia against Secretaries Rusk and McNamara. When I questioned the Chairman on this point, his response was that Rusk and McNamara had been invited to testify, but both had refused.* My point to him, however, was, if we are going to take testimony on Asia from Henry Commager, let's match him with an equally astute academician on the other side of the question—like Oscar Handlin from Harvard. If we are going to listen to Harrison Salisbury from the *New York Times*, let's also hear Joseph Alsop or John Steinbeck. If we're going to listen to George Kennan, let's also hear Dean Acheson. And if General Gavin can be given time before the Committee, why can't Maxwell Taylor be called? In sum, it was a one-sided seminar. When I voiced my complaint in a public way before a group of my colleagues, one of the Senators said, "Well, why don't you guys bring in Arleigh Burke and Curtis LeMay?"

The point is that the emotions unleashed by the Vietnam dialogue were taking a severe toll of the objectivity of those seeking to probe the inner recesses of theory and fact in the Far East. Much of what is now being said about the role of the President and the Congress in foreign policy is colored by the tensions of the present crisis.

By way of recasting the issue of executive authority in a calmer atmosphere, we can turn outside to a scholarly monograph on the question which appeared in 1961. The time was the beginning of the

*February 22, 1967.

new JFK Administration; the journal, the *Cornell University Law Quarterly*. And the writer was J. William Fulbright, Senator from Arkansas, Chairman of the Senate Foreign Relations Committee.

In those quieter days the Chairman made the following points:

1. That the executive must be given more power in the conduct of foreign affairs.

   "Has not the time arrived . . . when we must give the executive a measure of power in the conduct of their foreign affairs that we have hitherto jealously withheld?"[1]

2. Presidential decision-making in foreign policy provides a quality of leadership superior to the alternatives available under our system.

   "The source of an effective foreign policy under our system is Presidential power. This proposition, valid in our own time, is certain to become more, rather than less, compelling in the decades ahead. The pre-eminence of Presidential leadership overrides the most logical and ingenious administrative and organizational schemes."[2]

3. The principal weakness in foreign policy leadership at the present time derives from the system of checks and balances where Congressional ·authority intrudes upon that of the President. These intrusions manifest themselves in several ways:

   (a) The Secretary of State is required to devote a disproportionate amount of his time in personal appearance before Congressional committees.

   "The Secretary of State and other high officials are obliged to expend prodigious amounts of time and energy in shepherding their programs through the glacial legislative process."[3]

   (b) Policy has to survive the often-times uninformed assaults from individual Senators. A local constituency may supersede the national interest.

   "The typically successful politician (in the Senate) [does not] find it imperative to school himself in the requirements and problems of foreign policy."[4]

4. In a nuclear age it would be difficult to pin down decision-making responsibilities if left in the hands of independent-minded and parochial Congressmen.

"It is highly unlikely that we can successfully execute a long-range program for the taming, or containing, of today's aggressive and revolutionary forces by continuing to leave vast and vital decision-making powers in the hands of a decentralized, independent-minded, and largely parochial-minded body of legislators."[5]

5. Increased Presidential power is necessary in foreign affairs even though the prospect of it may be disagreeable or even dangerous.

"The enhancement of Presidential power is a disagreeable and dangerous prospect. It is . . . a compelling necessity, however, when set against the alternative of immobility, which can only lead to consequences immeasurably more disagreeable and dangerous."[6]

The wisdom of the foregoing assessment, I venture to predict, will better withstand the tests of history than will some of the utterances currently making the rounds in the Senate on this same question. They all simply point up what has happened to the foreign policy-making process in a world of instant communications. The machinery of policy decisions assembled nearly two centuries ago simply has not been able to keep pace with the changing requirements of modern realities. If the democratic process is to be salvaged, we must be prepared to move toward more clean-cut Presidential authority in foreign policy.

The key to this process is that of pinning responsibility and clearly defining authority. This is not meant to demean the role of the Congress but only to sharpen the process in conformity with the changing of times. The extent to which it would impinge upon the checks-and-balance system would be offset by the greater gain in affixing responsibility. In giving up a measure of the old system of checks and balances, the limited loss is overcome by a greater gain. A clearer recognition of responsibility for decisions and action is achieved.

Is there, then, a useful role for the Senate in the foreign policy field? The question is more easily posed than answered. Yes, the Senate can play a very useful role in foreign affairs. But to do so it must update its procedures in the foreign relations field as well as upgrade the sense of responsibility among its members to focus on the big questions rather than the more sensational or passing small questions. The Senate ought to address itself in advance to the broad outlines and direction of American policy. If it were to do this and agree to spend more and more time in dialogue on foreign policy issues, it could recover a more meaningful role in the direction of policy. It will not be able to perform a meaningful role if it persists in putting domestic constituent interest first and national interest second. If the Jewish or Slovak or segregationist vote is placed ahead of well-founded policy for the Middle East, Eastern Europe, or Africa, then the Senate will continue to lose ground to the Executive in the shaping of American foreign policy.

Not only must individual Senators rise to a higher sense of responsibility, but the chairmen of important committees—Foreign Relations, Appropriations, and Armed Services—must be willing to live up to the obligations and responsibilities that a chairmanship entails. They should accept the fact that as chairmen they have given up some of their freedom to express their views indiscriminately. They gave up some of that freedom to become Senators and must recognize that more must be given up when one becomes the chairman of a committee.

The Senate might also want to consider the possibility of devising an orderly way to deny its chairmanships to members who are totally at odds with the foreign policy of the government. These men would then be in better positions to speak out against the policy without the damaging repercussions that result from the pronouncements of committee chairmen.

Finally, we only delude ourselves if we believe that the Senate will ever be able to redress the imbalance that has come about between Congress and the Executive in foreign policy matters. The times in which we live require a stronger and stronger Executive in the field of foreign affairs. The realistic options for the Senate are to decide whether to yield the entire field to the President or to reestablish the Senate's role in a constructive way. In my judgment, the latter alternative is not only promising but indispensible. It will not be realized by looking upon the President as a rival or with a sense of "getting even," or approaching the question out of a sense of pique or jealousy with regard to who has more power. It will only come about when the Senate looks critically at itself and determines to mobilize its efforts on a higher plain.

In sum, the role of the Senate in foreign relations must be recast in the context of today's requirements.

1. This will require that the Senate committees should focus increasingly on the broad outlines of policy rather than on the minutia and the incidentals of specific cases or problems.

2. This will mean that the individual Senator must be prepared to devote a larger proportion of his time to foreign policy questions than to local questions. It means that he will have to place the national interest even above his constituency. More importantly, his constituents will have to demand it of him.

CHAPTER XV

God and War in Vietnam*

War at any time tortures the God-fearing man or woman—causes him to search his soul again and again in terms of his religious ethic and his moral principles. In a time of crisis the weakest among us are often quick to drag the Lord in on "our side." None of us have forgotten the classic of Pearl Harbor when, after years of tortured hesitation over our moral obligations in the Hitler crisis, we were suddenly singing in chorus, "Praise the Lord and pass the ammunition."

Not the least of our countrymen to have been beseiged by those who knew which side God was on was President Abraham Lincoln. He once responded to a group of emotional petitioners of his time who sought to assure the President that their deity was on his side, by saying to them: "Who are we to tell the Lord which side to choose. I only pray that I might be on God's side."

*This chapter has been drawn from the reporter's transcribed notes of an address by the author for the National Staff luncheon of the National Presbyterian Church held in Washington, D.C., on September 11, 1967.

For those who want a thoughtful and penetrating analysis of the role of the church in the current dialogue on Vietnam, the volume prepared by the Office of the General Assembly of the United Presbyterian Church in the United States of America entitled *Vietnam: The Christian—the Gospel—the Church* would be worthwhile.

Wishing to be on the "right side"—or better—the side of right is one thing; but determining which that is becomes quite something else again. No conflict in modern history has posed more contradictory or complex moral questions to believers than the struggle in Vietnam. None have been fraught with so much frustration, emotion, and despair. For the first time in human experience, families are witnessing a war that is waged in the living room night after night on television. More than that, by invading the privacy of the home, it also affects the inner-most privacy of one's moral and religious ethic.

As a consequence, honorable men whose moral principles are unquestionably high and whose religious faith remains equally dedicated often find themselves at opposite ends of the issue of Vietnam. That some "Christians" write off those of us who support American policy in Asia as warmongers and barbarians is a judgment which does violence to the basics of the Christian ethic.

Who dares to justify the loss of a son, a husband, or a father? Whether such a loss occurred in Vietnam, in Flanders Field, on a highway, or as a result of the cruel and indiscriminate ravages of disease, the net effect is quite as monstrous in any case. Who can justify either the death of a loved one or the remorse of those who loved him? Job asked such a tortured question of God. Many are asking it of mankind now. God did not make excuses to Job; nor, I dare say, will mankind make simple and loud excuses to those families bereaved by personal losses in Southeast Asia.

Certainly a United States Senator, who supports our policy in Vietnam, cannot and should not presume the unseemly role of explaining the irretrievable loss of a loved one. But neither can a Senator avoid comment when his conduct has been part of the chain of events that led to the deaths of so many sons.

Even if there was a response available which sought to justify the death of a man, it would be a massive offense. No man can say in a world where at times there seems but little sanity, "You must die, while you on the other hand may live." Presidents, generals, scientists, Senators are no more and no less mad than those who disagree with them. They, too, agonize and ask out of deep grief the question "Why?" of a sometimes outrageous world.

Senators no less than ministers of the gospel walk at night along silent streets—tormented and torn over the consequences of their decisions. In those lonely and late hours one is tempted to conclude that the world in fact is deranged and that we, too, are slipping the moorings of sanity. But not for long, for that path leads us to retreat, despair, and more madness.

Having confessed this, however, one then comes face to face with the reality of the moment. A man's remorse over the death of a son or a woman's tears over the personal loss still does not make the world go away. It behooves us, then, as people of good works and abiding faith to come to terms with the world that is. It is in this context that I propose to assess the role of our country in Asia as it affects a man of God.

The key to understanding the world that is, is recognizing the international community as a jungle world where there is no law. The human race has made almost no progress in the science of living together in a community of nations. Waging peace, thus, becomes a matter of coming to terms with the world as it is rather than a world which might have been or should have been or, hopefully, some day may yet be.

If we are to advance the cause of peace, therefore, it is necessary to begin where we are and wage it as we must—often in terms dictated by the circumstances of the moment rather than by the idealism of one's hopes and dreams.

Jesus did not say, "Blessed are the pacifists." Rather he said, "Blessed are the peacemakers." Those are two entirely different mandates. Waging peace is far more difficult than waging war. As someone once observed, unless or until we learn to wage peace as vigorously as we always manage to wage war, we will never achieve peace in our time.

Waging peace can even involve waging war in the name of peace. This is what is happening now in the Far East. That this seems at once frightening and contradictory to both moral and ethical principles is understandable, but it is not hopeless. The late Adlai Stevenson reminded his colleagues in the United Nations on one occasion that the best chance for strengthening the world organization, for achieving a larger measure of economic development, and for agreeing upon a measurable nuclear disarmament pact is first to reestablish stability and a balance of force and power in the wake of the last world war.

It is well to remark on Mr. Stevenson's observation that he was advocating a new balance in the world not as the end which we seek but as the beginning at which we start. This is an important distinction. For him this would become a starting point, not a stopping point. And so it should be for the rest of us as well. If we are to advance the cause of the "goodness" of man, we have to start with what we have where we are.

At the end of World War II, the United States found itself in a strange, new role. No longer were we protected by a ring of friendly nations from the naked confrontations of power in a lawless world. No longer could we scan the rival power camps to select our favorites or those with whom we might choose to stand. For the first time we found ourselves at once on the front line of the world and one of the two sides which emerged from the ruins of World War II. Even so, the first impulse of the American people was to try for a new post-war world of ideals and broad principles. We shared our enormous economic treasures, for example, not only with our wartime allies but also with the vanquished nations and ultimately even with the newly suspect Russians. The Americans, moreover, offered to share with the Soviets what was momentarily a monopoly on atomic power.

All too soon, however, these American dreams had to be joined with the brutal realities of surviving in an old world—*even an immoral world*—in which surviving means a willingness to *risk* the use of force in order to prevent its use by others. It was in such a setting as this that the succession of Soviet-American crises in Iran, Greece, Turkey, Berlin, Cuba, and Korea occurred. That narrative is sometimes capsulized in the phrase "the Cold War."

In accommodating ourselves to the world that is, we Americans have pursued for the more than twenty years since the end of World War II a fundamental concept related to international events— namely, that no one nation should be permitted again to dominate either Europe or Asia. The consequences of having ignored or neglected that concept in the 1930's produced both a Hitlerized Europe and a Japanese Asia. Each development involved the United States quickly and irretrievably in not one war but two world conflicts waged simultaneously.

It must remain understandable, therefore, when today we ponder the consequences of pretending not to see small acts of aggression in such vast areas of Asia, that some of us are haunted by the specter of other mistakes from our recent past. The history buffs here in this audience perhaps must surely sometimes have wondered what might have happened if Japan had been stopped in Manchuria in 1931, or if Hitler had been stopped at the Rhineland in 1936. Or the man sensitive to "moral judgments" must be willing to ask himself: "Where stood I when those acts of aggression in the 1930's occurred?" Or, "To what degree am I responsible as a 'moral' individual for the massacre of six million Jews because Hitler wasn't stopped sooner?" Or still, "How many millions of other lives might have been saved if . . . ?"

The policy adopted at the end of World War II of preventing any one nation from dominating Europe is one whose success is no longer open to question. Historians, moreover, would probably agree that the high-water mark in the development of that policy was attained during the Berlin Airlift in 1947 and 1948. Of that crisis, the late Winston Churchill once observed that, "If you Americans had acted this time as you did after the First World War, Russia would be on the Atlantic Coast of Europe today." This is a dramatic observation, but nonetheless true.

Who is there among us to deny that the whole climate of Europe has changed in these last years? Who would deny that the prospects of peace in Europe are much improved today? These fortuitous developments directly reflect the successes of American policy. Harsh as some of those policies may seem when cast in a strictly religious context, one has to ask: What suffering was spared because of them?

Be it noted, however, that the achievement of a new balance in Europe was not enough; for the more populous half of the globe was left out. After twenty years, the balance of Asia remains in flux, still open to question and currently to challenge.

It is at this point that the man of God is entitled to ask: What right have we in America to seek a new balance in Asia? Asia, after all, he might say, belongs to the Asians—not to Yankee imperialists! The question is a proper one. The innuendo is irrelevant. When we remember that the imbalance of Asia in 1941 involved us in a great world war in the Pacific (in fact, it was this war which triggered our declaration of war against Hitler), we ought to have learned from the experience of our time that what happened in Asia to Asians makes a difference to the United States.

I would be the first to hesitate to assign our country a role there for moral reasons simply because morality is so many different things at once to so many people. Let me put it this way: That our obligations in Asia derive from a sort of moral responsibility of history to live up to the consequences of our rather large military victory in that part of the world in 1945. It would have been the easiest of all alternatives to pack up and go home after the signing of the Japanese Surrender aboard the battleship *Missouri*.

Consider, however, what the United States did to Asia as a result of World War II.

Japan was shattered, crumbled, and in ruins. China was in the throes of the convulsions of change, the dimensions of which still are not certain even now. The traditional, if long outdated and even morally questionable, colonial structures maintained by the British, French, and Dutch collapsed—most of them under pressure from us. Nearly the entire East became a vast and tempting political vacuum into which all kinds of forces sought to flow—some for good, some for evil. Unfortunately, where a political vacuum exists, the advantage lies with the predators who more aggressively will move quickly to get there "firstest with the mostest."

The forces of good, on the other hand, are slow to mobilize and commendably reluctant to impose their institutions or concepts on new areas.

Given these hard facts of 1945, the United States—it seems to me—bore a very heavy responsibility as the only powerful nation emerging from the devastation and chaos of the Far East with sufficiently great capabilities for putting the meaningful pieces of the ruins back together again as a new starting point for a more stable Asia. It not only was in our own national interest to seek a stabilized East, but it was also a responsibility to Asians themselves as human beings. This was the "Why" of the war in Korea, of the presence of the Seventh Fleet in the Straits of Formosa, of the thrust of American planes and military equipment to India during her border crisis with China in 1961 and 1962, of the landing of Marines in

Thailand also in 1962 to discourage the aggressors who sought to absorb the tiny kingdom of Laos. As Berlin was the turning point in Europe, I dare say historians will now judge that Korea was the turning point in Asia.

It is from this cloth that Vietnam is cut. This is the "Why" of our presence in Southeast Asia.

For the religious person with his revulsions against war and violence, it is necessary to ask what would have been the consequence had the United States not checked the act of aggression across the 38th Parallel in Korea or stifled the thrust from the Mainland of China toward Taiwan or toward India. How many more thousands or even millions of people would have been destroyed?

Likewise in Southeast Asia. Even as Ho Chi Minh's National Liberation Front was moving across the 17th Parallel separating the two Vietnams, they were simultaneously occupying, in violation of the 1962 "truce," the eastern plains of Laos. Others of them were, at the same time, setting up "beachheads" in the five Northeastern provinces of Thailand, the northern provinces of Burma, and, as we are now learning belatedly from Prince Sihanouk himself, even in the border provinces of Cambodia.

The countries of Southeast Asia today are convinced that the American intervention in Vietnam spared them blood baths at the hands of militant guerrilla groups. Most of them are quick to say that they themselves lacked the resources, the military capabilities, and the political stability to rally an effective resistance. Nor were they unmindful of the fact that Mao Tse-tung was already proclaiming that these moves were the "wave of the future." At that very moment Mao had reason to believe that China was on the verge of a major breakthrough by means of the PKI Party in Indonesia. Whatever American critics may think they know about the intentions of Mainland China or the goals of the guerrilla cadres of the NLF, the small Asian countries themselves remain convinced that they would have come under the domination of China and that their countries would have been ravaged by bloodshed and terror had not the Americans stood firmly in Vietnam.

But that is the big picture. What about the little picture? The Christian (or Jew, Buddhist, Mohammedan) who abhors the loss of even one life must ask himself, how could you salve your conscience if we had forfeited the decision in Vietnam itself to the forces of Ho Chi Minh, dedicated as they were by self-declaration to exterminating the several hundred thousand refugees who had fled from Mr. Ho's benevolent dictatorship? The prospects of that blood stain should make even the most compassionate moralist shrink in horror.

Finally, the man of God must ask himself, how do we come closer to one world or to a world under law or to a climate of brotherly love? By abandoning Eastern Asia to the turmoil of blood and strife? Or by seeking to condemn and restrain and minimize the spread of terrorism and violence? In the light of the record of events during the past twenty years in Asia, I believe the burden of proof lies with those who would abandon Asia to chance. Those, in my judgment, blithely forget the history of our time.

In Asia we have come so far along the road toward orderliness and toward peaceful change that we dare not falter now even as the end may be dimly seen. Prime Minister Lee Kuan Yew, of the tiniest and newest government in Southeast Asia—Singapore—put it best when he said that, because of the American presence in Vietnam, Eastern Asia is closer to stability than at any time in this century.

How, then, do we measure the role of the United States in these troublesome times? What will be the judgment when we some day are hailed before the bar of history to stand trial for our deeds? No one can know for certain, but we are entitled to make an educated guess. I believe we shall stand tall and acquitted—that our policy around the world has been at once unselfish and that it has moved the conglomerate of nations much closer to the chance for building a better international order. For after all, it's the chance that is at stake. War never wins peace, but it can win a chance to do something about peace. It is that chance which the smaller nations in Asia believe we are winning for them.

But even as we do, we win a chance for ourselves as well. The price we've already paid for that chance ought to haunt us every night. What we do with that chance will determine the course of history for our time.

This brings us back, then, to where we started—namely, how a person with a deep sense of moral responsibility can rationalize the deeds of violence and the loss of life which, at times, seem to overwhelm us. What this Senator has come to on those lonely confrontations with his conscience and his principles is not only the tragic recognition that death ever remains senseless and that lament and remorse might purge for the moment, but they never can become a substitute for confrontation and the faith that men can and will be more humane, more generous. That caprice thrives on failure to act is a lesson that not only life teaches us but that history painfully will not let us forget. The chief characteristic of madness is caprice, and the failure to come to grips with reality, with what IS rather than what should have been.

This is why our position of strength in Eastern Asia must be coupled with a sense of compassion and understanding, locked in by a sophisticated sense of restraint. The course ahead must be neither the wanton destruction of everyone that gets in our way, as the big-bomb advocates would have it, nor the timidity of the doves who would seek security by hiding from reality. In moments like these we can derive both wisdom and guidance from one of the prayers of the late Reverend Peter Marshall when he served as Chaplain of the United States Senate. Confronted as those of his time were by similar kinds of frustrations and emotions and impatience, he beseeched the Lord,

> "Oh God, save us from hot heads that
> may lead us to act foolishly;
>
> And, God, save us from cold feet
> that may keep us from acting at all."

CHAPTER XVI

VIETNAM: Setting the Record Straight

Underlying the doubts and misgivings about American policy in Southeast Asia is the assumption that something went wrong with carefully laid plans in Vietnam. What *did* go wrong? Did something happen in the critical period between 1963 and 1964 which caught the Administration off guard? After the Presidential race of 1964, why did American policy suddenly escalate? How could the United States become so deeply implicated with escalated manpower needs so soon after the November political campaign was ended?

Or was it the consequence of what happened at Geneva as far back as 1954 which had already set the course of events in the two Vietnams? It is the answer to these questions which this chapter seeks to resolve.

Was the American involvement a succession of "inadvertencies," as some critics contend? Was it a series of improvised responses to ad hoc crises? It makes a difference in the validity of the public uneasiness as to the accuracy of this assertion. In answering these questions it is important to distinguish between the basic policy of our being in Southeast Asia and the policies of trying to adjust to the changing events in that part of the world. The first is the strategic concept; the second involves tactical adjustments to protect the first.

No assertion has contributed more to the confusion about the American presence in Southeast Asia than that which contends that

President Johnson found himself trapped there by circumstances unwittingly agreed to by President Kennedy who had been trapped in turn by President Eisenhower's commitments in Vietnam. To put it the other way around, the Critical Establishment has tried to believe that the American presence was the result of a succession of accidents and inadvertencies stumbled into by at least three American Presidents who had no freedom of decision to avoid them.

If the charge is true, a case can be made to show that the United States should honor its commitments there but should find a way to got out as gracefully as possible. If the assertion is false, then it is high time the mischief done by it be corrected.

In researching the pertinent materials through five administrations, beginning with President Franklin D. Roosevelt at the end of World War II, I have found a series of statements by each President, by his Secretary of State, and by a succession of participants in policy-making—all of which add up to the simple fact that the United States was consciously committed to withholding Southeast Asia from the grasp of either China or such other aggressive forces as might prey upon it. The charge that our presence there was the result of an unintended series of accidents is certainly mistaken to say the least. In a harsher sense, it is both phony and cruel at the same time because of the doubts to which it has given rise in the minds of many of our people. A close study of the record will bear this out.

Since 1941, five Presidents have faced a task completely new in American history: The necessity of directing the involvement of the nation in world politics. Each of those Presidents in turn has been required to address himself to the size of the country's commitment—a measure regulated by the intensity of the crisis at that time. From Franklin Roosevelt through Lyndon Johnson, the Chief Executives have consistently stressed the impossibility of the United States withdrawing from the world. They have gone further, moreover, by insisting that the security of our nation depends upon a tolerably stable balance of power not only in the West but in the Far East as well.

President Roosevelt in his eighth State of the Union message said,

" . . . the future and the safety of our country and of our democracy are overwhelmingly involved in events far beyond our borders. . . . We are committed to full support of all those resolute peoples, everywhere, who are resisting aggression and are thereby keeping war away from our hemisphere. . . . We know that enduring peace cannot be bought at the cost of other people's freedom."[1]

United States policies in Asia in the aftermath of this commitment have been a testament to the sincerity of this government in fulfilling its pledges.

As President Truman went on to point out in his third State of the Union message January 7, 1948,

"Twice within our generation, world wars have taught us that we cannot isolate ourselves from the rest of the world. We have learned that the loss of freedom in any area of the world means a loss of freedom to ourselves."

Three years later President Truman (January 8, 1951) said in another State of the Union address,

"Our country has always stood for freedom for the people of Asia. Our history shows this. We demonstrated it in the Philippines."

As far back as May 9, 1950, Secretary of State Dean Acheson issued a statement following an exchange of views with the Foreign Minister of France in which he said,

"The United States recognized that the solution of the Indochina [Vietnam] problem depends both upon the restoration of security and upon the development of genuine nationalism and that the United States' assistance can and should contribute to these major objectives."

On September 23, 1951, a joint communique issued following discussions between the commander-in-chief of the French forces in

Indochina and officials of the Departments of State and Defense stated,

> "The participants were in complete agreement that the successful defense of Indochina is of great importance to the defense of all Southeast Asia."

On July 1, 1952, John M. Allison, Assistant Secretary of State for Far Eastern Affairs, said in an address at the University of Washington, Seattle,

> "Indochina has been said to be the key to all of Southeast Asia. . . . The United States has recognized that the struggle in Indochina . . . is an integral part of the worldwide resistance to . . . attempts at quest and subversion."

On April 16, 1953, President Eisenhower referred to the threats of aggression in Korea and in Southeast Asia as,

> " . . . threats to the whole free world community to be met by united action."

He called for,

> "an end to the direct and indirect attacks from the security of Indochina and Malaya."

The President then made it clear that he believed Korea and Southeast Asia were cut from the same cloth as he warned,

> "For any armistice in Korea that merely released aggressive armies to attack elsewhere would be a fraud."

Secretary of State John Foster Dulles echoed a similar thesis to that of the President when he spoke of the common threat of China which stretched all the way from Korea to Southeast Asia:

> "In Indochina the outcome affects our own vital interest in the Western Pacific. . . . There is risk that as in Korea, Red China might send its own army into Indochina. The Chinese . . . regime should realize that such a ˙ second aggression could not occur without grave consequences which might not be confined to Indochina."[2]

It is obvious Secretary Dulles was warning Peking that continued aggression on its part could mean war with the United States.

Almost from the outset of postwar diplomacy, the United States regarded Japan and Southeast Asia as the two great prizes in the Pacific. For them to fall into the hands of an aggressive power, it was argued, would be to jeopardize not only the chances for restoring Asia to balance, but it would obviously endanger the national interest of the United States.

Assistant Secretary of State for Far Eastern Affairs, Walter S. Robertson, put this bluntly in late 1953 as follows:

"In Indochina, as in Korea, our fundamental objective is in the creation of real strength on the side of the Nationalist Forces and confidence among them that the future belongs to them. . . . It is not necessary for me to enlarge upon the consequences that would follow for the whole free world if the Communists broke through Korea or Viet Nam in their drive to add the industrial power of Japan and the resources of Southeast Asia to the manpower of China that they already control."[3]

This can be said, then, to be the main structure supporting the concept of American policy in Eastern Asia following World War II; namely, to protect the industrial power of Japan by erecting a shield across Korea and by raising a defensive umbrella over the small, independent countries of Southeast Asia.

As early as 1953 the tactical innovation of guerrilla infiltration employed as the chief instrument of the new aggressors in Southeast Asia was pin-pointed by those making policy in Washington. In October of 1953, Under Secretary of State Walter Bedell Smith, speaking at the University of South Carolina said,

"In Indochina the Communist apparatus, working through local elements, has . . . resorted to force to gain control. The . . . guerrilla movement marches under a banner as fraudulent as any ever devised. It purports to represent the forces of nationalism and independence, although clearly an arm of aggression receiving direction, supplies, and equipment from the Red masters of China.

"If it [Indochina] should fall to the Communists, it might well open the door to all Southeast Asia. And once having grasped this vital area, the Communists would be in a position to exert overwhelming pressure on neighboring areas."[4]

The Secretary of State reiterated the same point at the conclusion of the Geneva negotiations when he said,

"We should bear in mind that the problem is not merely one of deterring open, armed aggression but of preventing Communist subversion which, taking advantage of economic dislocations and social injustice, might weaken and finally overthrow the non-Communist governments."[5]

What Secretary Dulles was stressing was that it was the fragile, almost delicate, nature of the new governments in Southeast Asia which left them especially vulnerable to internal terrorism. Acts of violence which more mature governments could put down as a matter of course could be fatal to the prospects of a brand new country just beginning to experience independence. It was this more subtle and covert form of subversion which the American Government feared the most in Southeast Asia. The fact that the new tactic would avoid major open confrontations, as it happened in Korea— for example, made it more difficult to detect, to cope with, and to mobilize public opinion to thwart then the conventional, frontal assaults of the North Koreans across the 38th Parallel.

The Secretary of State had already implicated the Hanoi Government of Ho Chi Minh in these devious tactics as tracing the line of overall direction to Peking. He pointed out that an estimated 2,000 military and tactical experts were largely trained and equipped in China. He emphasized:

"If the Communist forces won uncontested control of Indochina or any substantial part thereof, they would surely resume the same pattern of aggression against other free peoples in the area. . . . This would be a grave threat to the whole free community [in Southeast Asia]. The United States feels that that possibility should not be passively accepted but should be met by united action. This might involve serious risks."[6]

The accuracy of the Dulles warning can be clearly seen from the vantage point of hindsight. His fear that if forces of aggression got even a part of Indochina they would resume the same pattern of force against others of their neighbors is borne out by the attacks from Hanoi on Laos, Cambodia, and South Vietnam—in some cases by direct assault, in others by infiltration. That the United States would regard such a development as "grave" and that to challenge it would involve "serious risks" are conspicuously borne out by today's events.

Why Indochina made a difference to the United States was a question to which the Under Secretary of State Bedell Smith addressed himself in particular. During a television interview, he was asked the question, "Why is Indochina important to Americans?" In response Smith said,

> " . . . the vital basic question is: Shall we, or can the free world, allow its position anywhere and particularly in Asia to be eroded piece by piece? Can we allow . . . expansion of Communist Chinese control further into Asia? Propagandists of the Soviet Union and of Communist China have made it clear that their purpose is to dominate all of Southeast Asia. Remember that this region helps to feed an immense population. . . . It is a region that is rich in raw materials. . . . Communist control of Southeast Asia would threaten the Philippines, Australia, and New Zealand directly, would threaten Malaya; it would have a very profound effect upon the economy of other countries in the area, even as far as Japan. . . . So what's at stake in Indochina?   It is the human freedom of the masses of people for all that enormous area of the world."[7]

In this declaration, the American Government was saying that the natural and human resources of Southeast Asia made a difference to the balance of the world and that to withhold the area from an aggressor power would contribute to the chances of peace in the Far East.

From Paris Secretary of State John Foster Dulles and the French Foreign Minister George Bidault issued a joint statement which said,

"We recognize that the prolongation of the war in Indochina, which endangers the security of the countries immediately affected, also threatens the entire area of Southeast Asia and of the Western Pacific."[8]

The two Ministers pledged their countries to a joint effort to secure the area against aggression. The shape and form of that effort was to be spelled out at approximately the same time that the Geneva discussions were underway in the summer of 1954. Their efforts bore fruit in the Southeast Asia Treaty Organization (SEATO) signed on September 8, 1954. Rather than becoming a joint effort, however, the major buildup of the new pact fell upon the United States Government.

As a forerunner to the pact, Under Secretary of State Bedell Smith had declared at Geneva,

"The significance of Korea and Indochina is worldwide. Powerful forces are behind the complex influences that make these two areas the focus of potential war for all of us, East and West. . . .

"We stand prepared to pledge our resources to the constructive purposes of peace. We shall be compelled to build more alliances for defensive security only if it is a continuing menace to our national safety and to the safety of all nations whose interests are bound together with ours. . . . "[9]

Bedel Smith's explanation was constantly reemphasized by other spokesmen for the American government in the late 1950's. For example, in 1956, the Secretary of State linked all of the frontiers of Eastern Asia to the same chain of national interest of the United States when he said,

"We have by treaties solemnly recognized that an armed attack against Korea, Taiwan, and Viet Nam would be dangerous to our own peace and security."[10]

President Eisenhower in a nation-wide radio and television appearance explained to the American people our role in Southeast Asia. He said,

"We gave military and economic assistance to the Republic of Vietnam. We entered into a treaty; the

Southeast Asia Security Treaty—which plainly warned
that an armed attack against this area would endanger
our own peace and safety, and that we would act
accordingly."[11]

And at Gettysburg College the President further explained
American policy in Asia,

"Strategically, South Viet Nam's capture by the Communists would bring their power several hundred miles
into a hitherto free region. The remaining countries [in
Southeast Asia] would be menaced by a great flanking
movement. . . .

"The loss of South Viet Nam would set in motion a
crumbling process that could have grave consequences
for us. . . .

"Our own national interests demand some help from
us in sustaining in Viet Nam the morale, the economic
progress, and the military strength necessary to its
continued existence. . . . "[12]

It can be seen, thus, that throughout the eight years of the
Eisenhower Administration, American policy in Southeast Asia was
repeatedly reaffirmed in unambiguous terms. It rested upon the
belief that American security was directly affected by events in
Southeast Asia and that the national interest of the United States
regarded the struggle in Korea and the struggle in Indochina as the
extreme points of a long arch which encompassed an identical
concern in the defense perimeter of our country.

When President Kennedy came to office, the crisis in Laos
temporarily overshadowed the developments inside Vietnam. By late
1961, however, the new President felt compelled to increase U.S.
military and economic aid to South Vietnam. The emphasis in the
official statements of the Kennedy Administration was on staying in
Vietnam " . . . until we win." In fact, the concern over Vietnam to
Kennedy was only a manifestation of the larger question of security
in Asia.

Shortly after assuming office, Kennedy had said,

"In Asia the relentless pressures of the Chinese Communists menace the security of the entire area—from the

borders of India and South Vietnam to the jungles of
Laos struggling to protect its newly won independence.
We seek in Laos what we seek in all Asia and indeed in
all of the world—freedom for the people and independence for the government. And this nation shall
persevere in our pursuit of these objectives."[13]

In a conversation in Washington, President Kennedy told the
visiting Vice President from Nationalist China, Chen Cheng,

" . . . the United States is determined that the Republic
of Vietnam shall not be lost to the Communists for lack
of any support which the United States Government can
render."[14]

In a major address before the United Nations General Assembly,
President Kennedy made it clear that, in his view, the wars of
liberation were merely fronts for subverting the legitimate governments in all of Southeast Asia. He said,

"The first threat on which I wish to report is widely
misunderstood: The smoldering coals of war in Southeast Asia. South Vietnam is already under attack—
sometimes by a single assassin, sometimes by a band of
guerrillas, recently by full battalions. The peaceful
borders of Burma, Cambodia, and India have been
repeatedly violated. And the peaceful people of Laos are
in danger of losing the independence they gained not so
long ago.
"No one can call these 'wars of liberation.' For these
are countries living under their own governments. . . . The very simple question confronting the
world community is whether measures can be devised to
protect the small and weak from such tactics. For if they
are successful in Laos and South Vietnam the gates will
be open wide."[15]

Soon thereafter, the President announced in a news conference,

"The systematic aggression now bleeding that country
[Vietnam] is not a 'war of liberation' for Vietnam is
already free. It is a war of attempted subjugation—and it
will be resisted."[16]

The President's brother as Attorney General joined his voice in the same chorus of appraisal of the American goals in Vietnam when he said,

> "We are going to win in Vietnam. We will remain here until we do win. . . . In a flagrant violation of its signed pledge at Geneva in 1954 the North Vietnamese regime has launched on a course to destroy the Republic of Vietnam."[17]

President Kennedy's Secretary of State Dean Rusk reaffirmed the dimensions of American national interests in Southeast Asia. Speaking at Davidson College in North Carolina, he said,

> "The stakes are greater than South Vietnam itself. All Southeast Asia—the independence of its people and their right to develop in their own way—is at stake. And beyond this region the international community confronts a question that affects the lives of men and women—and of nations—on every continent: Shall this form of external aggression be allowed to succeed?"[18]

A year later in an address before the Economic Club of New York, Secretary Rusk stated,

> "The strategic importance of South Vietnam is plain. It controls the mouth of the Mekong River, the main artery of Southeast Asia. The loss of South Vietnam would put the remaining states of Southeast Asia in mortal danger.
>
> "But there are larger reasons why the defense of South Vietnam is vital to us and to the whole free world. We cannot be indifferent to the fate of 14 million people who have fought hard against communism—including nearly 1 million who fled their former homes to avoid living under Communist tyranny. Since we went to the aid of Greece and Turkey years ago, it has been the attitude of the United States to assist peoples who resist . . . aggression."[19]

Secretary of State Dean Rusk from the very first had viewed the American interest in Eastern Asia in the larger context of all of that part of the world. His critics would do well to review his many declarations on American policy in the Far East. It would assist them in recovering their own perspective of at least the Secretary's grasp of the problems of American policy in the Orient.

President John F. Kennedy reinforced the views of his Secretary of State in regard to the Far East policy of the United States. In a news conference he said that his government was not going to withdraw from Vietnam.

> "In my opinion, for us to withdraw from that effort [Vietnam] would mean a collapse not only of Vietnam but Southeast Asia. So we are going to stay there."[20]

During a television interview with Walter Cronkite, President Kennedy addressed himself to a question about the United States being committed on the far fronts of the world. He said,

> "We . . . made this effort to defend Europe. Now Europe is quite secure. We also have to participate—though we may not like it—in the defense of Asia."[21]

In another televised interview with Huntley-Brinkley, the President expressed concern lest the American people get so impatient with the course of events in Southeast Asia and so upset about the things that were going on inside the government in Saigon that they would want to give up in despair and go home.[22]

The President's determination to stay and not to be confused by bad events in Saigon make interesting reading, particularly when laid alongside the recent views of his brother, Senator Edward M. Kennedy. The latter, it will be recalled, upon returning from an extended study of the refugee problem in Vietnam reported in a February 4, 1968, *New York Times* interview that "there also is a question of how long the American people will support our efforts in that country if the corruption continues."

It was the President's view obviously that Vietnam was incidental to the problem of American policy in Southeast Asia. Like President Eisenhower before him, Kennedy thought that the central question was the security of all of Southeast Asia with its vast treasure of both people and resources. Obviously, he regarded Vietnam as the key to unlocking that treasure. And he further believed it important to the containment of China that the region be kept beyond the reach of the Peking Government.

At a news conference, President Kennedy sought to explain more particularly what the United States policy was toward the government in Saigon.

> "What helps to win the war, we support; what interferes with the war effort, we oppose. . . . In some ways I think the Vietnamese people and ourselves agree; we want the war to be won, the Communists to be contained, and the Americans to go home. . . . We are not there to see a war lost and we will follow the policy . . . of advancing those causes and issues which help win the war."[23]

This, then is a part of the body of evidence sustaining the conclusion that the United States has had a constant policy of containing China in the large sense and stopping aggression in the more specific cases in order to achieve stability in Eastern Asia. Five Presidents, beginning with FDR and without deviation, regarded the outcome of events in Southeast Asia to be of the gravest concern to the United States. Every Secretary of State and their supporting aides and assistants reaffirmed in straight-forward language this continuing dimension of American policy in Eastern Asia. The record itself should lay to rest the insinuation, the innuendoes, and the misrepresentations which have sought to cast a shadow of doubt over the commitment of the United States in that part of the world.

Whatever kind of a case the Critical Establishment may contrive at from here on out, let it at least not perpetuate the old falsehoods about accidents and inadvertencies.

It is crystal clear that, at the end of the war against Japan in 1945, American policy immediately proceeded on the assumption that Eastern Asia would become the focal point of a cold war contest for the balance of power in the Far East. The stresses and strains would stretch all the way from Korea around through Southeast Asia to the subcontinent of India. It was destined to achieve its most explosive dimensions along the 38th Parallel in the north and along the 17th Parallel in the south. But there was no hesitancy at any time about the importance of the United States holding these anchor positions.

The American judgment that all of Southeast Asia was important to the new balance is what produced the particular efforts at strengthening the economy and shoring-up the security structures of the entire region.

Thus, the SEATO pact and the heavy economic commitments to the countries bordering the China Sea did not in themselves commit the United States to stand in Vietnam. Rather, it was exactly the reverse. The decision to contain Mainland China and to prevent the fall of Southeast Asia to aggression in any form required implementing such a strategic concept with tactical programs—both military and economic in their nature.

Boiled down to its basic fundamentals, our policy in Eastern Asia is one of defending the area by whatever measures subsequent crises might demand.

This becomes the key to understanding the policy of the United States in that part of the world.

This assumption was behind the first steps undertaken by the Truman Administration and subsequently continued during the two Eisenhower Administrations. Nowhere in the official papers, among the memoirs of those who participated in shaping the policies, nor even in the hindsight declarations of some of the principals, is there anything which suggests that during the 1950's there was a basic disagreement on the importance of keeping Southeast Asia from falling into the hands of "the other side." It seemed to be a strong consensus that policies aiding and abetting the independence of the small countries would be important in preventing the dominance of the Chinese in all of the area. To this extent, therefore, it is wrong to ascribe our current position in Vietnam to a series of "accidents" which overtook succeeding Administrations.

American policy started, therefore, with the containment of aggression in Asia, just as it had in Europe. In no sense was this an inadvertent commitment. It was a policy well understood by the Congress, as the Senate debates on the SEATO Treaty disclosed, and the basic position received strong bipartisan support.

What did happen was that nobody initially could foretell the enemy's tactics, his timing, or his responses. It is in this phase of the events in Vietnam where one can find more firmly lodged the arguments questioning specific decisions of precise actions (or lack of them).

Sometimes we forget that a democratic society like ours has no tightly drawn master plan for the world—no *Tanaka Plan;* or *Mein Kampf.* Since the role of the United States was largely a defensive one at the beginning—we were not interested in building an empire or controlling Indochina—it could be argued that our innocence was our weakness. Inevitably, we were at the mercy of those in Hanoi (or Peking) who were constantly probing for weakness in the region and attempting to create a totalitarian successor-state to the old French Empire in Indochina. No one (not even in a free society!) could know precisely what responses the events of the future might require or what force levels might be needed because of the American presence.

Whatever went wrong in Vietnam went wrong only in the sense that the speed of changing events or the second-guessing of an enemy's intentions were misjudged or ill-timed by some of the American officials on the spot.

It is impossible to separate this phase of the story from the Geneva Conference itself. We have already seen that the discussions at Geneva in 1954 were vague and indecisive. It is pertinent to recall that the Geneva Conference convened in the aftermath of the Korean War. The experiences in that conflict and the lessons from it, likely had a lot to do with the coloring of our judgments at Geneva and in Vietnam in particular. Parallels from the Korean experience influenced the way in which we viewed the problems abandoned by the French in Indochina.

Out of Geneva also came the conviction that no settlement of the bitter rivalries within Vietnam was possible, that there was no real chance for meaningful elections on a nationwide scale, and that each side was bitterly determined to destroy the other. Therefore, it seemed wise to gamble on a divided Vietnam at the 17th Parallel and hold such a line for the purpose of winning time for other factors to erode the militant tensions between the two portions of the country.

In winning that time, the American judgment was that a government in Saigon with a conventionally equipped army to serve as a "trip-wire" warning of an overland invasion, just as had happened in Korea, would be the effective way to hold the line. (The International Control Commission—ICC—in 1956 had already condemned North Vietnam for increasing the size of its conventional army.)

The emphasis of the American assistance to Vietnam was to train regular, large military units of battalion and regimental strength to fight in open engagements on large fields of battle. (Again, like Korea.) This judgment was not a mistake quite so much as it was just not enough. In retrospect, while it turned out to be the wrong decision, it was couched in the strategic theory of the diplomacy of John Foster Dulles and was in fact quite explicable and consistent with our posture elsewhere around the world. As it turned out, the South Vietnamese Army was trained for the wrong type of war in the wrong kind of place. It was wrong, however, only because North Vietnam chose to respond with a *different* kind of warfare—the guerrilla cadre units.

When Ho shifted to guerrilla warfare, the Americans were not prepared for it. But we did try to shift the Diem Government's defensive posture over to the Strategic Hamlet model, used successfully in Malaya. We introduced the special forces techniques (American military advisers) and counter-insurgency. One can argue that our response to Ho's new tactic was clumsy, but it certainly was not inadvertent.

Meanwhile, as we now know in hindsight, Hanoi had already determined that its best chance to destroy the South lay not in the direct confrontation of regular forces, but rather by infiltrating the local level with carefully trained revolutionary teams.

Even so, the hopes were high for the new government in Saigon under Ngo Diem between 1954-1957. And 1957 was probably the high point, at least to outward appearances for some of the encouraging developments lacked depth. The fragile surface structure of achievements under the new regime apparently escaped the fullest appreciation of many of the American officials on the scene—at least until that veneer began to crack in 1959-1960.

From 1959 on, the picture has, in tactical terms, been quite symmetrical. Every time Hanoi has raised the ante, the United States has covered the bet. There have been delays and disputes but not hesitations about the basic concepts. (It is even conceivable that the Hanoi Politburo has been torn by dissension over "inadvertencies" as well. While we did not think the North would throw in their main force units by 1964-65, Hanoi surely did not dream that within two years the American ground commitment would jump from 25,000 to half a million.)

Likewise, the status of the two Vietnams as envisaged at Geneva has come in for much misrepresentation. The misunderstandings of what Geneva did or didn't say in this regard give rise to most of the arguments about a Vietnamese "civil war." If this is true, then indeed there is strong reason for the dissenters to deplore internal meddling by the Americans. However, the facts do not bear out this assumption.

According to the critics, the Geneva Accords of 1954 are alleged to have created two "temporary zones" in Vietnam, not two "states." This interpretation strains the facts.

The only signed Accords at Geneva were specific military agreements by the French and the Democratic Republic of Vietnam (North Vietnam). There was a political pronouncement at Geneva which referred loosely to elections in two years but which *nobody signed.* This is a key to understanding the wrongness of the allegations of those who argue that somebody broke a sacred agreement to hold free elections in two years. *There was no such formal agreement at Geneva.*

The United States Government and the new South Vietnamese Republic, moreover, rejected the entire Geneva package.

The most that even the optimists among the neutral observers could expect was that the military armistice which settled on the 17th Parallel might win enough time and avoid enough violence between the competing groups in Vietnam to progress toward countrywide free elections.

The pessimists, on the other hand, were worried about the designs of Ho Chi Minh and his Hanoi regime which declared its intention to seize the South by elections, forfeiture, or violence.

It should be noted, however, that the critics of American policy in Vietnam have tended to overdraw severely what was agreed upon at Geneva and what was expected to follow in the wake of the conference.

Not long after Geneva, Ngo Diem took over and began the job of building a stronger non-Communist Vietnamese state south of the 17th Parallel. Diem—far from being an American stooge—was a long-time Nationalist whom Ho Chi Minh had once tried to involve in his "popular front" government.

Between 1954 and 1958 the Republic of Vietnam (South Vietnam)—far from being considered a temporary zone—achieved the status of a sovereign state in international law. Indeed, in 1957, the Soviet Union actually proposed that both North and South Vietnam be admitted as separate nations to the United Nations.

The United Nations General Assembly on February 28, 1957, (with the support of France, Great Britain, and the United States) adopted 40-8 a Resolution finding South Vietnam qualified for membership in the United Nations. The Security Council at the United Nations followed through with a similar endorsement September 9, 1957, by a vote of 10-1. The dissenting vote was the Soviet Union's veto which killed the measure.

The point is that both in international law and in the view of the United Nations, South Vietnam had become an independent nation; and the conflict in Indochina was—and is—between two nations, one of which has utilized insurgency techniques in combination with conventional invasion to disguise its aggression as "civil war."

As indicated elsewhere, it is rational to argue that the United States made an error in judgment in ever getting mixed up in Asia in the first place (as the isolationists contend). But our intervention was in support of a *legitimate state* to which we had treaty commitments under the SEATO protocol and which lay athwart an area which had already been defined by two Presidents (by 1957) as in the American national interest.

That the United States got into a situation with unanticipated dimensions cannot be denied. Yet, the roots of our policy were wholly in accord with the absolute will of the United States Senate in approving SEATO (the Manila Pact) and the decisions of the President. Our logical progression cannot be faulted—the quantitative aspects of it were simply unforeseen.

It is fair to ask, as the critics do, what would have happened had we aligned ourselves from the beginning with Ho Chi Minh. This, of course, was the other major option open to the American policy-makers when the French left. Could Ho have been built up as an Asian "Tito" and a buffer against Chinese expansion? No one can say for certain.

But we are entitled to second-guess history. For many people, history begins the day they discover a problem. That problem was "discovered" in the early 1960's. It had already been forgotten, for instance, that in his famous "Defense Perimeter" speech of January 12, 1950, Secretary of State Dean Acheson explained our policy of containing China by expressing the hope that in the process such containment might spur Mao Tse-tung to become another Tito. (British commentators in particular became enamored of Mao Tse-tito.)

The fact is that in terms of world Communist organization, he did become a "Tito;" that is, he eventually set up a national Communist regime not only independent of Soviet domination but actually hostile to it. The fact that Mao became a "Tito," however, did not elect him to the international order of "good guys." The difference is that Chinese capabilities and their disproportionate size to their small neighbors makes Mao's regime a special problem for the security of the Asian mainland.

Similar observations are valid regarding Ho Chi Minh. It is all right to have a Tito in Yugoslavia who, so far at least, has no overt territorial schemes against his neighbors. It is quite another thing to regard Ho as a "Tito" in the light of his terrorist-state concept when applied to his neighbors (who include not only South Vietnam, but Laos, Cambodia, and northeast Thailand). The very pattern of Ho's policies and the record of his deeds both inside his own country and across the borders of his neighbors' ruled him unacceptable as an Asian Tito.

Meanwhile, back in Saigon, there emerged the question of "the American puppet," President Ngo Diem. At the very beginning, the Americans were less than enthusiastic about Diem. He was, in a sense, a creature of the earlier French regime. Whatever else, Diem was a fact of life in South Vietnam by the late 1950's. Whereas it was predicted at the outset that he could not last six months, his government did survive for more than six years.

Far from being a puppet, Diem was a strong-willed Vietnamese Nationalist who vigorously resisted American efforts to reshape his policies. Here again the critics have tried it both ways: (1) They kick the Administration around for not dictating to its "puppets" in Saigon, and (2) They attack the Administration for running a "corrupt neo-colonialist" government in South Vietnam. This is a typical illustration of the unwillingness of those in dissent to take their stand on one policy position or the other, rather than slip between and among the many alternatives.

American policy toward Diem did in fact vacillate. There were many uncertainties about how far to go and how fast to move. Few, if any, parallel experiences were available for guidance. By the time of their demise in 1963, Diem and his brother Nhu had become increasingly suspicious of the United States' intentions. Rightly or wrongly, they were convinced that the CIA had been involved in the abortive coups of November, 1960, and February, 1962.

But the important things to recall are:

(1) That by all the standard readings which could be taken, Diem did surprisingly well. Even Hans J. Morgenthau went on record in support of Diem's "miracle." Wilfred Burchett, the Australian Communist journalist in Hanoi, referred to 1962 as "Diem's year."

(2) That in overall strategic terms, the character of the regime in Saigon (dictatorial, military, Mandarin) was as irrelevant to the fundamental controversy as was the character of the Polish regime in 1939. Once the decision to contain aggression in Asia had been made, we could hardly then expect the enemy to pick a battlefield of our preference.

(3) The measured successes of Diem's regime probably triggered the Hanoi decision to launch "wars of liberation" against the South because Ho Chi Minh's hopes that the southern republic would collapse had been frustrated.

In hindsight, the shortcomings of the Diem regime become more stark than the realities of the time would justify. The extent to which Diem and the American advisers were to blame for the shortcomings remains impossible to determine. Suffice it to note that the Americans in Vietnam did not enjoy the absolute power which the British colonial lords exercised in Malaya. The very worst that could be said of the American posture in Vietnam is summarized in the critical phrase "client-state." It is this difference in the power of command that colors the assignment of responsibilities for mistakes.

Few would quarrel with one obvious blind spot in Diem's Government, however, that of its too-narrow political base. Even while the Hanoi-trained cadres were digging in at the village level, the government in Saigon was making no serious efforts to establish a broad, political base of its own. Those who knew him best say that Diem thought too much in terms of the old Mandarin rulers looking after the people rather than putting down communication lines with which to establish communications with the people. Brother Nhu was even worse.

A third brother, however, Ngo Dinh Can did grasp the fundamentals of a political machine and had a semblance of one operating in a few places. He was never permitted, however, to carry his political mechanism through to the ultimate measure of control which the village system required. (In this context we should not jump to the conclusion that the Communist-organized rural areas were established out of love and dedication. They were ruthlessly run with an iron fist which combined terror with control.)

Diem can be faulted in another area: The neglect of local security. Large military units were not designed to protect local village areas. And even his police units reflected the French colonial tradition in which police were to protect the administration and the administrators—not the people. In the mind of the average Vietnamese peasant, this is the real meaning of the word "police." This is critically important in understanding the breakdown in the Diem security complex.

Why Diem would accept this approach to security with so little concern can only be understood if one remembers that this is the way it had always been done, under the French and under the Vietnamese Mandarins themselves. Thus, to count up the numbers of policemen and then conclude that the government was in command of local security is to miss the point.

A third area in which Diem is commonly faulted is land reform. The record suggests that the government made more progress in the redistribution of land than most critics have realized. That it was not enough progress and that it was too late also miss the point. The success of some of the resettlement programs was sufficient to hasten the Hanoi decision to intervene by violent means in order to head off further progress toward economic stability. It was always my personal assessment, after two lengthy visits with President Diem, that at both times—in 1959 and in 1962—he was, particularly during the earlier visit, genuinely convinced of the importance of land reform and was personally involved in achieving it. By the latter date, however, (1962) disillusionment, political distortions, and local bitterness had obviously intruded upon his efforts and his hopes.

Against this backdrop of at least partial failures, one must place the American administrators responsible for some of the events which unfolded in 1963.

In charge of the American programs in Vietnam was the head of the country team, Ambassador Frederick Nolting; and in charge of the military phase, General Paul D. Harkins. Among the critics, these two are the most available "fall guys" upon whom to place the blame for the succession of crises and near disasters. Once again, hindsight and the popularity of singling out scapegoats both have a habit of wrenching events out of the perspective of their time.

In terms of the old yardsticks used to measure progress, both the Ambassador and the General rightfully saw hopeful gains in South Vietnam. Neither of them, moreover, had the clear-cut power of a proconsul or a military dictator as, for example, Sir Gerald Templer had enjoyed for the British in Malaya. Together, they were only official representatives of the United States Government in somebody else's country. Vietnam was not a colony. What an American Ambassador or a military commander might do was severely limited by this circumstance.

Nor is this to ignore the conscious warnings being made by assistants further down the administrative ladder. One of the prices in the administrative game is for the administrator at the top of the hierarchy to exude optimism even at the moment when serious uncertainties may exist. This is the name of the game, whether it be in Saigon or Washington, D.C. Stemming as it does from the kind of optimism that says Americans can do anything (and usually succeed!) the instances of failure invariably catch up with those who happen to be caught at the top at that moment.

Keeping this in mind, one can fault both men in hindsight for misreading Hanoi's innovation of guerrilla infiltration. This is what went wrong with our estimates. The seriousness of the new tactic from the north apparently was never fully grasped until it was too late. That is not to overlook the desperate efforts undertaken by Diem and his American advisers to change his concept of internal security and shift to the strategic hamlet plan. Popular as it has become to condemn the strategic hamlet approach, that effort came closer to success than its sudden demise suggests.

It worked rather well in the central highlands of Vietnam, for example, where the very structure of the village system lent itself to the idea; six or eight small hamlets, clustered together in a related area, could quickly regroup in the center of their complex behind strategic fortifications, barbed wire, bamboo stakes, trenches, and tunnels. The trouble was that in the South, in the delta area, the peasants were strung out in long thin lines of settlement along the banks of canals and could not easily be regrouped within a central strategic complex. The system, therefore, offered little chance of success in that part of the country.

In still other areas Diem's neglect of local security prompted "quickie" efforts to string barbed wire around ill-prepared assortments of villages in order to symbolize the new security policy. The fact that no one bothered to concern himself with the deeply entrenched Viet Cong within the barbed wire enclosures turned out to be its undoing.

Another miscalculation was the under-estimation of how completely the Viet Cong had built up their political apparatus in large sections of rural Vietnam. This mistaken judgment continued until late in 1963.

To be sure, some of the Americans on the scene were thrown off guard by the temporary setback to the Viet Cong in 1962. In that year several thousand additional American military advisers had been moved into the country accompanied by large numbers of helicopters. This introduction of men, military "experts," and a new weapon of mobility prompted the VC to pull back from their build-up. There was a tendency, therefore, for the American administrators to issue optimistic estimates of the future prospects in Vietnam—an optimism that characterized the briefings to which I was exposed both in Saigon and in the outlying villages in December of 1962.

If there was a turning point in the fortunes of the South Vietnamese, it might well be the national holiday period of Tet in 1963. It was then, apparently, that the Viet Cong decided the time was near when they would have to move quickly to divide

South Vietnam and to immobilize the government in Saigon if their own chance of seizing control was to be preserved. It took the remainder of 1963 to complete the staging for the final takeover of the South.

Looking backward, it is now possible to see the unfolding of the fateful events leading up to 1963. The stage had already been constructed by Hanoi as far back as 1957. In that year the North Vietnamese evidently gave up on the government of South Vietnam collapsing of its own weight. If the Hanoi Vietnamese were to succeed in their defined goal of taking over all of the South, they had to plot a course that would bring down the government in Saigon.

Events in Laos in 1961-62 had already foreshadowed the approaching crisis. In Laos, Hanoi succeeded in diverting attention from their true objective which lay south of the 17th Parallel. For it was in Laos that Ho Chi Minh knowingly prepared to violate a "negotiated truce" in 1962 by deliberately keeping North Vietnamese troops in Eastern Laos. The obvious purpose was to permit the seizure and the control of that long corridor of land running down along the eastern borders of Laos called the Ho Chi Minh Trail. This was to become the main highway for men and supplies into South Vietnam.

However, the North Vietnamese scheming in Laos produced some adverse fallout. Souvanna Phouma, the nearest to a national leader which the many factions in Laos could agree upon, began as a collaborator with the communists in the North. He was critical and distrustful of the Americans. But by late 1962, Souvanna Phouma was shocked by the flagrant violations of the truce practiced by the North Vietnamese. His shock was sufficient to swing him not only away from his posture of neutralism, but actually very far over to our side. As he discussed it during my visit with him in Vientiane in late December of 1962, he already saw more clearly than most leaders in that part of the world that the real intent of the Hanoi Government had been to use Laos to aid and abet its designs in South Vietnam.

By January, 1963, therefore, both the Viet Cong and Hanoi believed themselves on the way to a total takeover of South Vietnam. Their contrived program of sharpening their political apparatus and tightening their control at the village level was stepped-up. This was to remain the dominant note for the year 1963.

Nineteen sixty-four became the year of action, the time when the careful preparations finally permitted the North Vietnamese, through the NLF, to show their hand. An American Presidential election was held in that same year and, though only a coincidence, had the effect of playing tricks on the public's grasp of what was happening in Southeast Asia. Even while Hanoi was launching its first line of troops in large numbers across the 17th Parallel, a process which began probably in early 1964,[24] both major candidates in the American election were still talking about the Vietnam which preceded this major turn of events.

There are those who argue that the Presidential campaign trail was littered with false arguments and outright lies, particularly by the incumbent. Such criticism misses the point. As of October, 1964, when both candidates were making their final plea to the voters, the most that was then known to either candidate was that South Vietnam was still the theater for guerrilla activities, social unrest, and factional rivalries in Saigon, but nothing that would require any major shift in the American commitment there.

Candidate Johnson's declarations that American boys would not be sent to a far land where the people themselves didn't defend themselves, simply reflected the best that was known—that the 25,000 American advisers there were sufficient, along with the Vietnamese army, to hold the line. In no sense did it mean that American policy was shifting away from whatever commitment was necessary to hold Southeast Asia. It only reflected the judgment that the price had not gone up and the hope that it wouldn't be raised.

Candidate Goldwater was operating in the same context. His more extreme proposals of defoliation and of going on to a more substantial military offensive were proposals aimed at liquidating the same limited problems to which candidate Johnson had addressed himself. Goldwater had no special insights nor secret intelligence about the upcoming new dimensions of the war even then being escalated on orders from Hanoi.

This is worth stressing because of the hindsight reactions—especially among the critics who argue that President Johnson ran as a peacemaker and Senator Goldwater as a warmonger and that the victorious candidate, now President in his own right, stole the

Goldwater theme. Those who feel that they were "betrayed" by Lyndon Johnson are guilty of wrenching the facts out of context. The Johnson statements not only were those of a candidate but also those of the President of the United States whose best information at that moment suggested less flamboyant risk-taking than candidate Goldwater did in his less responsible way. Neither man yet knew of the Hanoi decision to escalate the war.

While Ho Chi Minh, as we have seen, probably moved his first frontline units south in the spring of 1964, they did not show up in captured cadres or through other forms of intelligence until after the November election.[25]

The year 1964 becomes the hinge year upon which the violent escalation of the hot war in Vietnam, as we now know it, hangs. In Hanoi, two new steps were taken, both of which sharply escalated the conflict in South Vietnam.

One was the systematic infiltration into the South by Southerners who had previously been taken north to Hanoi for training and indoctrination. These cadres numbered around 40,000 in 1964. The American advisers had been increased to about 25,000. The International Control Commission (ICC) meanwhile, had verified the extent of the new infiltrations. It did not require an American intelligence estimate to confirm the figures.

The second step was to send south a new family of weapons. This latter factor was extremely significant. The importance of the new weapons need reemphasis at this point, too. What this meant was that the Viet Cong for the first time could outshoot its equal or greater numbers of South Vietnamese regulars in any confrontation. The South Vietnamese were still equipped with conventional American weapons, such as the M-1. The introduction among the VC of the new AK-47 rifle and the new 7.62 class of weapons made it possible for guerrilla groups to outgun the ARVN units.[26]

In recapping, then, "What Went Wrong?," the shift of tactics by Hanoi in 1963 and 1964 escalated in a very large way the dimensions of the military problem in the South. Neither the United States nor Saigon reacted quickly enough to this new escalation.

This failure to react is not without parallel. It suggests the American experience in response to the Wehrmacht and the blitzkrieg in the 1940's.

In World War II, for example, Hitler seized the continent with a new military concept which caught the old soldiers of the traditional European military off guard. The Americans learned from that period, restructured their whole strategy for recapturing Europe, and thus mobilized their great advantage in resources to strike down the Hitler threat.

Now in the Far East, the lessons learned from World War II in marshalling overwhelming strike power dominated the concepts of how to cope with the determined threat from Hanoi. When Hanoi in turn changed the rules of the game by reverting to the guerrilla cadre approach, it took the allies, particularly the Americans, some time to restructure their own concepts of how to cope with it. Once this was done, however, the mobilization of American resource capabilities ultimately was brought to bear on the aggressions into the South.

Any recap of "What Went Wrong?" would have to include the failure by the Americans to recognize the importance of local security forces when Diem had asked for aid in that area. As far back as 1960 the United States either denied such aid or deferred it as an "expendable priority." The Americans finally came around to it when they tried to assist in mounting the counter-insurgency tactic epitomized by the "strategic hamlet" approach. This effort failed because it turned out to be too late and inapplicable to some areas.

By 1964 what was coming to a critical head was the full impact of Hanoi's decision apparently reached in 1957—seven years earlier. It was in that year when Hanoi was surprised to discover that South Vietnam was actually erecting the infrastructure of a state or nation. Were this to succeed, Hanoi would be forever denied the chance to take it over. Therefore, they had to thwart the efforts of the Saigon Government to achieve it.

By 1964 Hanoi apparently reached the decision that the guerrilla phase of the assault by means of the village platoon cadres could safely be escalated to the next phase. That phase involved moving line regiments into the South for direct confrontation with large military units. The sequence was something like this. After Hanoi triggered the new build-up which began early in 1964 with new weapons and Hanoi-trained troops, American intelligence verified this stepped-up dimension in November of 1964 shortly after the American election. From that point onward events were crowding the government of the United States into *a searching reassessment of the adequacy of its commitment in Vietnam.*

It was late in December, 1964, nearly two months after the American Presidential race, that elements of the North Vietnamese 95th Regiment were discovered in the South. When that regiment took to the field, it triggered the critical decisions made in Washington in January and early February of 1965.[27]

Even with that escalation, however, there was still one more surprise six months later. In June and July of 1965 it was discovered that the regular military units of South Vietnam were far less ready for the stepped-up new offensive from the North than had been the long-standing expectations. It was by that time that Hanoi tipped its hand toward its intentions to launch a massive military thrust across the narrow waist of the northern part of South Vietnam via Pleiku, thus, proposing to cut the South in two. The deterioration of conditions inside South Vietnam was not only hastened by this direct and open military confrontation sought by the North in the spring and early summer of 1965, but simultaneously the Buddhists in the South delivered their own political body blows behind the lines. There is no evidence to suggest that this internal turmoil was coordinated in any way by influences from Hanoi but only represented the coincidence of disasters with which the Saigon Government was suddenly confronted.

It was at this point—and not until this point—that the American Government took a hard look at how many troops might be needed in Vietnam. The question that was put to the Americans was this, How many troops will it take *not to lose in the south*? No one asked at this point, How many troops *will be needed to win*? (We're talking about July, 1965.) This is an important difference.

The estimate in answer to the first question was relatively small—perhaps a quarter of a million men. Between this date (July, 1965) and the following spring, the next question was raised, How many troops will it take to win? In making this latter estimate, American military leaders found it difficult to apply a formula that would allow for the complexities of hit-and-run guerrilla tactics. It was easier to provide an estimate to the first question about how to stop Hanoi in main force actions. Once the main forces were stopped, however, the advantages quickly shifted to the North.

Under whichever strategy, the North never has had to defend any center of population or any center of government—not even a provincial capital. All the North had to do to win was to frustrate the defenders—to hit-and-run—to prevent law, order, and stability from taking hold. Thus, built-in to the new estimates had to be educated guesses on how many men it would take to clear and hold VC areas. What constantly fouled-up the American estimates were the viability and the initiative which reposed in the village platoon cadres of the Viet Cong.

The contrasting responsibilities of the two sides in Vietnam—the guerrillas, on the one hand, and the Saigon Government, on the other—was the difference between tearing down and building up. It is obviously much simpler to destroy, to reek havoc, than it is to build or to establish order.

How stark the difference was borne home to me in an incident I encountered north of DaNang during a visit there several months ago. In a foray into the rural area we came upon a small river across which there had once been a bridge. The structure had since been blown up, and its ruins lay partially submerged in the stream. The Vietnamese officer who was my guide pointed to the bridge and explained that here was the burdensome difference in the problems facing the two sides. He said, "It takes four or five years to train a man to build a bridge like that, but it takes only about that many minutes to train a man to blow it up."

Finally, in summing up the story of this interval in Vietnam, two other points need to be made. One is in regard to the Tonkin Gulf Incident which occurred on August 4, 1964.

It is imperative that we note that the North Vietnamese had already made the decision to take the South by main force action several months before Tonkin Gulf. (March to August, 1964.) What this says is that Tonkin Gulf *was not*, in fact, the definitive incident—however one chooses to interpret it. It means that, *Tonkin or no Tonkin, the Americans would have had to make a decision to stop the main force thrust by the North Vietnamese.*

The second is that at no time had the Americans drawn a clear line in which they said to the North, If you cross this line it means war. This is another way of saying that the North Vietnamese probably misjudged American intentions. They may have believed the stories coming out of Washington about how American participation was limited to "advisers" or how Vietnam had to be saved by the Vietnamese themselves.

Was this not the same kind of mistake the United States had made previously in Korea? There is much reason to believe that the North Koreans never thought the Americans would stand and fight along the 38th Parallel. Likewise, the same could be said about the Japanese decision to strike at Pearl Harbor. Nobody had made it clear that the national interest of the United States lay as far away as the Philippines or Eastern Asia. But then if one chooses to pursue this line of historical parallels, he would also have to include Hitler's misreading of American intentions as well as the miscalculations of Kaiser Wilhelm in the First World War.

Therefore, as one strives to reassess the sequence of events related to "What Went Wrong?," it is necessary for him to conclude that there was never a basic decision made to abandon Southeast Asia or to rule it outside the bounds of American national interest. The miscalculations along the way, on the other hand, (mistakes, if you prefer) were errors in timing or in shifting tactics rather than substantive changes in the strategic importance to the United States of the new balance of forces in East Asia.

The principal factors which need to be included in the formula of "What Went Wrong?," are the basic North Vietnamese decision (as far back as 1957) to take specific steps to topple the Diem Government, and their determination to dislocate the non-military programs in the South that edged toward ultimate stability. For the Americans, the problem was made difficult not only because of the strains coming out of the Diem Government, but particularly after the fall of Diem in November, 1963, the United States in Vietnam was dealing with a succession of weak governments. This was a major liability.

While critics are prone to contend that the Americans had set up a "police state" in Saigon, the exact contrary was the case. So much so in fact that while striving to cope with an effectively structured "police state" in Hanoi which employed an efficient "terror" machine to implement its policies, it was necessary to drag along an ineffective and cumbersome series of administrations in the South.

The ultimate American build-up to larger and larger numbers of troops was always in response to preceding escalations by Hanoi.

It would be no exaggeration to say that the Americans hoped that the first contingent of 327 military advisers in 1960 would be all that the crisis in Vietnam would require. The American goal, simply put, was that the two Vietnams would leave each other alone—that the 17th Parallel would be respected and that a bare handful of Americans would be capable of assisting the South Vietnamese in their quest for security.

Such was not to be the case, however. As the National Liberation Front steadily increased the tempo of its interference in the South, it then became necessary for the United States to equate the new escalation.

First, there had been the reinfiltration of the old Viet Minh cadres (80,000-100,000) around 1957, who had earlier regrouped in the north after the Geneva Conference in 1954 and who were subsequently to be led by LeDaun, a southern member of the Lao Dong Politburo.

This was followed by the second major escalating step from Hanoi, launched in the spring of 1964, with the introduction of the regular army units from the North. Their base camps were first discovered in November of that same year. In other words, the 325th PAVN Division got its marching orders down the trail to Koatum and the central highlands long before the United States began the bombing of North Vietnam (February 7, 1965) and which was not discovered until after the American Presidential election of November 3, 1964.

A third escalation was the decision from Hanoi to reequip the Viet Cong main force units with the 7.62 family of automatic weapons. These guerrilla forces were so equipped by the early spring of 1965.

If we put these three factors into the equation and then add the political and administrative chaos in Saigon which followed the collapse of the Diem Government, we have the factual background for the United States' decisions in 1965 to (1) bomb the sanctuary and (2) introduce ground forces and logistical support designed to keep the armies of South Vietnam from being overrun.

The earlier feeling of optimism about Vietnam characterized by the pronouncements from American officials in 1962 and 1963 was now replaced by the sobering realization that Hanoi was "going for broke."

In retrospect it is not only clear that the American optimism was ill-founded, but that optimism in itself conditioned the American public to expect success in Vietnam rather quickly and at a very low price. It is on this circumstance that most of the public unhappiness with American policy and much of the popular belief about credibility hangs.

The answer to the question "What Went Wrong?" thus looms more clearly.

First, the enemy raised the stakes by increasing his own efforts. Had he not done so, the real progress that was taking place in the early 1960's might have continued and a stable independent South Vietnam—invulnerable to the more subtle forms of aggression—would probably have been created without any deeper American involvement.

Second, the enemy's sharp escalation of the war met with great and dramatic success. In the short period of a year the situation in South Vietnam plunged from one of promise to one of such deterioration that the Communist assault could be stopped only by rushing in hundreds of thousands of American combat troops. The deterioration reflected both the inadequacies of the ARVN for this type of conflict, but it also reflected the consequences of the stresses of the Diem Government and the United States Mission in Saigon on economic and social benefits. The failure under Diem for either his government or the Americans who were with him to build a broader political foundation was a costly one.

To be sure, the people of South Vietnam were the beneficiaries of the Diem Administration and the American assistance programs. But they were not participants in any real political sense in the decisions that were being made and the progress that was being achieved. They were not inspired to become a practicing part of the new life.

Thus a political vacuum existed. It was precisely the type of political vacuum which the Communists needed to mount a "people's war." In a situation where the broad mass of the population neither exercised nor felt any responsibility for its government, it was not difficult for the Communists to create their own political substructure among the population. Through the widespread use of calculated terror, it was not hard for a relatively small number of committed men to establish control over the large number who were merely passive.

In essence, the Diem Government and its American advisers left too much of the rural political field to the Communists. Our failure to recognize the seriousness of this vulnerability is, it seems to me, a major criticism that can be made of American policy prior to the period of our massive involvement.

Out of this error flowed another mistake—that of assuring ourselves too often and too publicly that a heavier involvement would not be necessary. I do not question the sincerity of the optimists. Considerable progress was, in fact, taking place. There were grounds for believing that we had an effective formula. But in a situation in which our strategic commitment was so right, we should not have been so quick to assure ourselves and the enemy that what we were doing was all that was necessary and, implicitly, all that we would do. It led our own people to underrate the importance of our commitment. It may have led the enemy to do the same. We were tempting him through the creation of a rural political vacuum. We were doubling the temptation by public statements that implied that if he took advantage of the vulnerability we were not prepared to meet the challenge.

A review of "What Went Wrong?" is incomplete if it is limited to the misjudgments made in the changing dimensions of the struggle in Vietnam. Unless the assessment is confined to the tactical mistakes, it distorts the whole issue of "Why Vietnam" by lifting it out of context.

What is more, it is now clear in hindsight that there was no conspiracy at any level to conceal developments in Vietnam. Such things as were taking place that were not reported were usually not known or genuinely judged unimportant. That some of those judgments turned out to be wrong reflects human frailties rather than the connivings of a conspiratorial sort. At no time, that I have been able to discover, did any dialogue at the policy level or debate behind the scenes give reason to doubt the need for a determined American stance in Southeast Asia.

We *were* right, and we *are* right in believing that it is in our national interest to withhold the area from the domination of any other Asian power. We were and are right in filling a moral obligation to assist a small and independent nation from having its national life snuffed out by aggression from beyond its borders. We were and are right in insisting that the temporary military armistice line drawn along the 17th Parallel at the Geneva Conference be respected by both sides. We were right and are right in believing that two Vietnams offer a better chance for long-range peaceful change and stability. We were right, and we are right in formalizing these commitments in a treaty pact (SEATO) and striving to live up to them. We were and are right in believing that the United States cannot afford a world in which aggressors are permitted to impose their will by force on their victim.

CHAPTER XVII

Where Do We Go From Here?

The question of "Where do we go from here?" is one whose answer depends more upon the other side than upon ourselves. If our reasons for being in Vietnam are the right reasons—and I believe them to be so—it is necessary to examine those options that would seem to give us the chance to get out, at least before the limited objectives of this conflict are realized.

No withdrawal would be consistent with our goal of stopping aggression by force or of containing Mao Tse-tung's "wave of the future." Until the immediate aggressor stops his invasion and until the "wave of the future" is successfully contained, there can be no room for considering any measure of withdrawal from Vietnam.

The achievement of the first eventuality would permit a sharp de-escalation of the commitment. But the determination of the second of those prerequisites may take a very long time, as it already has in Korea and in Western Europe.

In the light of the consequences of the Tet offensive of last winter, it may be necessary to measure the need for a more formidable American mobilization in South Vietnam itself. For the purposes of stepping-up the prosecution of the war, this could include economic and social personnel as well as military.

If one can fault the course of the United States policy until now, it is that—by a step at a time—it has sought to achieve its limited objectives at the lowest possible cost. This has left the initiative and the ultimate decision on the intensity of the conflict to the other side.

It may be that we ought to take a hard look at a strenuous and closely knit mobilization of all of the resources available in and around Vietnam to speed-up the tempo of the events there as well as to recapture some of the initiative.

While this would raise the understandable fear of still larger casualty lists, it could in fact reduce them. Even doubling the present manpower available in the area would permit the assignment of larger numbers of personnel to the necessary security operations at all levels and even to a good many temporary nonmilitary responsibilities.

In any case, it is time that we get away from our fixation on some magical numbers' ceiling which we think may hold the solution to the problem. We only kid ourselves if we determine first what manpower we will accept and then ask later how many are necessary to achieve our goal.

This brings us to the hard core of the problem of ending the conflict. So much debate has centered around the conditions for negotiations that we have tended to lose sight of why we were there in the first place. Critics of our policy in Vietnam have put the cart before the horse. It is necessary to remind ourselves that we didn't stand in Southeast Asia in the beginning just for the fun of negotiating. We went in there to prevent somebody else from taking over the region.

In short, *two Vietnams become the hard base of American policy in Southeast Asia. How we return to the 17th Parallel and the fostering of independent governments on opposite sides of that line remains the crux of our problem.* Can a return to the results of the Geneva Conference of 1954 be negotiated? It is difficult to see how. Neither side has much it can negotiate in that realm.

What about a coalition government? It depends upon who would be coalesced. The more common suggestion from such leaders of the dissent as Senators Fulbright, Kennedy, and McCarthy is to include the National Liberation Front in the Saigon Government.

Not only would this be unrealistic, it would be fatal to the basic concept which American policy seeks to carry out; namely, to prevent the seizure of South Vietnam by force.

Whatever illusions may have prevailed among the critics for the past two or three years about the National Liberation Front, the time seems to have passed when even the most friendly assessment of the NLF is no longer valid. No one can seriously question now that North Vietnam is running the National Liberation Front and that, at the very least, it is only that—a front.

A few weeks ago, Hanoi's top diplomatic spokesman in Europe, Mai Van Bo, made clear to the Swiss Government that any peace settlement in South Vietnam can be achieved only through Hanoi. No dissident groups in the South, he said, were free to negotiate separately.

It is also clear today that, in important political matters, Hanoi prefers to bypass the local NLF chain of command. It deals instead with the Communist Party's central office in the South. The key political leader in South Vietnam with whom Hanoi has chosen to deal, Nguyen Van Muoh, who has been in the South only since 1960, operates as a member of the North Vietnam Politburo.

Finally, the tight strings of political control are matched in the military operations as well. In the headquarters of every Viet Cong military district is a 15-watt radio receiver which transmits all major orders from Hanoi. Top officers from the North Vietnamese regular army, moreover, constantly inspect and direct NLF units in the South. The NLF's senior military commander, Tran Van Tra, carries the rank of Lieutenant General in the North Vietnamese Army.

In the event of possible negotiations or a compromise attempt to structure a coalition government, Hanoi has made it crystal clear that the NLF would remain only as a front for, or a junior partner to, the North.

It is the foregoing circumstances which narrow the range of possible options available to the United States in Southeast Asia. That is why the chances of formal negotiations remain remote.

Given the basis of American policy in Southeast Asia, it is impossible to imagine the Allies negotiating any conditions short of withdrawal of North Vietnam from the South. Likewise, it rules out most of the proposals for coalition governments.

By the same token, North Vietnam can hardly afford *politically* to *negotiate* its own withdrawal from the South. The government in Hanoi is too irrevocably committed to taking all of Vietnam. Its propaganda purposes, its party line, its prestige, its diplomatic and political "face" have all been tied to that end.

The Americans, on the other hand, dare not negotiate less than the *status quo ante bellum.* This means contending for the validity of South Vietnamese independence and recognizing its status as a national state in the international community. The United States has no negotiating option but to return to the 17th Parallel at which point it all started.

What does all of this mean in relation to the talks currently going on in Paris? It means that very little in the way of substantive agreements is likely to come out of those conversations. Popular expectations in the United States are already far outrunning probable realities. Not only are the Paris discussions likely to be long and nerve-racking, they are not likely to produce a neatly packaged, brightly wrapped, negotiated settlement in Asia.

What is more apt to happen is that at some quiet moment during a lull in the truce the two sides may secretly meet in a back room away from the press and out of range of the cameras and there work out a formula for military disengagement.

For example, in return for Hanoi's agreement to pull the Ninth Regiment Regular Forces back across the 17th Parallel, the United States might agree to withdraw the particular military units currently located with the Ninth Regiment. Or, the elements of the North Vietnamese 226th Division in the northeast could be pulled back across the Demilitarized Zone in exchange for a withdrawal from the area of the related American units. In this way could the intensity of the combat be gradually scaled downward.

It is most unlikely, however, that an arrangement such as this could be negotiated publicly if for no other reason than the fact that Hanoi denies there are any of its regular troops in South Vietnam. To proceed publicly to a withdrawal of those units would pose internal political questions for the North Vietnamese Government which it would be reluctant to assume.

If or when the military intensity should decline, it may be possible to open other questions. The possibilities in that case still remain severely limited. To remain true to our often-expressed purpose of isolating the violence of the war in Vietnam; of limiting it to as restricted an area as possible; of holding in check the risks of a larger conflict, requires that we accept less glamorous˟ solutions to the war.

This is to suggest that the intensity of the fighting in Vietnam is not likely to decline by negotiations nor by escalation of its dimensions. A subsidence of hostilities, however it takes place, will enable the two sides simply to break contact, each retaining its own area of national identification set apart by an unnegotiated but mutually observed demilitarized zone along the 17th Parallel.

My specifics for the steps to be taken toward a more peaceful and stable order in Eastern Asia follow:

1. The United States should renew its pledge to guarantee the peace and stability of all Southeast Asia.

Beginning in 1946 the new emerging nations of Southeast Asia pinned their plans and took their risks on the assumption that the United States would guarantee the peace in that area if necessary. This means that a whole generation of governments, political leaders, and social-economic changes have been undertaken by these individual countries in the confidence that they would be shielded in their efforts from takeovers launched from outside their territorial boundaries. These expectations account in large measure for the political evolution and the economic advancements characteristic of most of the small nations in Southeast Asia and certainly of those that lie along the perimeter of Eastern Asia—like the Philippines, Taiwan, and South Korea.

Just now their doubts about American intentions are rising again. The intensity of dissent here at home has fostered these new apprehensions, accentuated more recently by President Johnson's withdrawal from the Presidential race. It is imperative, therefore, that the government of the United States reaffirm in unequivocal terms its intention to stay the course in Southeast Asia. Only in this way can the gains of twenty years' policy be firmly held.

Not to hold them would place in jeopardy much more than just Southeast Asia. Upon the firm declaration of the United States "to see it through" hangs the future of Korea and, thereby, of Japan itself. For if Southeast Asia is forfeited, a Korean settlement comes unhinged. This development in itself would unleash new and powerful military and political pressures on Japan. What it would do to the guarantee of an American nuclear umbrella over both Japan and India in return for the pledges of each of those nations not to divert their economic endeavors into the production of nuclear weapons is shattering to contemplate.

Like the ripples which result from dropping a pebble in a pond and multiply outward, to central Asia and to Europe it would mean that the intricate fabric of political balances around the world woven so carefully during twenty years of Cold War diplomacy would come unraveled.

2. *We must start with two Vietnams.*

The complications of an artificial boundary line creating two Vietnams are well understood. The basic elements of nationalism, language, and culture cannot be ignored. But for the moment they are overshadowed by the larger question of the territorial ambitions of Hanoi and the disruptive capabilities of guerrilla tactics in relation to all of the other governments in the area.

Even as this is being written, the news headlines record the steady advances being made by both the Hanoi brand of Communist as well as that from Peking. More than 30,000 North Vietnamese troops are now reported in Laos. Others are operating in the northwest and southeast of Cambodia. They have stepped-up their activity in Thailand. The Laotians, moreover, are now reporting the presence of Chinese troops in Northern Laos. Other guerrilla activity has recently surfaced in Northern Burma as well as in Northern India. In all of these latter instances, the evidence suggests that the units were trained in Red China.

This message should come through loud and clear to those who try to believe that an American withdrawal from Vietnam is a rational option. There is not much question about Hanoi's intentions. The North Vietnamese plan to seize as much of the surrounding territory as they can get away with. If past experience is any indication, the more they are able to seize, the more they will try for. The chances of the governments of the countries in Southeast Asia successfully to withstand these new aggressions would be severely weakened by any retrenchment on the part of the United States.

For these reasons a divided Vietnam represents the more promising of the alternatives available. Its historical precedence, going back many centuries, allows for the rivalries and the differences which two Vietnams symbolize. Furthermore, the 17th Parallel negotiated and compromised at Geneva in 1954 probably comes as close to a realistic demarcation as can be achieved amid these trying times; *at least it is a place to begin.*

3. *A massive mobilization of all capabilities inside South Vietnam.*

Some headway has already been made in this direction. The manpower draft laws have been tightened up. Contrary to what at least one Presidential contender has asserted, the Saigon Government began on March 1 to draft 19-year-olds; and more recently, it started to take its 18-year-olds. (The extent of South Vietnamese manpower mobilization may be better kept in perspective if one compares it in proportionate terms to our own. The numbers of South Vietnamese now serving in their military forces, if matched in proportion to population, would equal more than 12 million troops in the United States.)

There has been a measurable tightening up of the administrative machinery within the government. Province chiefs have been replaced. Politicians suspected of loose administration or corrupt practices have been dismissed. More recently in an effort to broaden the political base within the government, a new prime minister has been designated and a more representative cabinet has been appointed. It is too early to judge the effectiveness of these recent actions.

At best, however, this is only a small beginning. What is required is a general mobilization of all resources—military, economic, and material. Sufficient military manpower should be put in the field to contain the military activities of the North. Additional manpower should be assigned a top priority for securing the pacification areas in "the other war." Unless and until the countryside behind the line has been secured and its human and natural resources are no longer available to the enemy, the erosive threats of hit-and-run activities by guerrilla bands will remain constant.

Meanwhile, similar priorities should be accorded the selection and training of qualified technicians and administrators at all levels. If necessary, substantial increases in American manpower should be made in order to link Americans and Vietnamese together to speed up "know how" and perfecting techniques (such as the tightening of customs controls, tax collections, and budgeting procedures).

Tactically, this means launching this new offensive in the less difficult areas and then spreading it as steadily as possible in every direction. At all times the military security operations must be carefully integrated and synchronized with the economic and administrative mobilization. Its central task should be to prevent the enemy's main force units from interfering in the processes of stabilization behind the lines. Only as this positive approach succeeds will the enemy be denied his options which, until now, have left him with the initiative.

This formula offers little to comfort the impatient politicians racing toward November, 1968. But in the words of one of its chief advocates, Sir Robert Thompson,

> "If we plan for a long haul, we may get quick results.
> But if we go for quick results, we may at best get a long haul."[1]

4. Collective efforts for Southeast Asian development programs.

Outside of Vietnam itself the time won by thwarting the ambitions of Hanoi should also enable Saigon's neighbors in Southeast Asia to join together in collective efforts to strengthen their own regional fabric. The beginnings are already under way.

The Asians are busily trying to get new programs off the ground that they themselves will be responsible for—all aimed at making Eastern Asia more stable. These programs include the following:

a. Asian Development Bank—which was launched at the initiative of a Burmese by the name of U Nyun,

b. The Mekong Basin Commission—with blueprints for power development as vast as the Tennessee Valley Authority,

c. Asian Pacific Council—formed almost two years ago,

d. Association of Southeast Asia—has been reactivated,

e. The Southeast Asian Ministers of Education—are now organized,

f. Conference on Asian Economic Development.

These and other groups like them include cooperative efforts on hydroelectric power, transportation, resource development, scientific and technical research, trade and finance. They have been launched by Asians, with Asians, and for Asians. Without the American presence in Vietnam in the first place, it is doubtful that they would have, or could have, been undertaken at this time.

5. New Southeast Asian security forces.

Hopefully, the economic, social, and resource development schemes already launched will ultimately pave the way for stronger security structures in the Far East. Both in diplomatic and military terms, the East Asians should prepare to take over increasing responsibilities for the balance of power and the security requirements of their part of the world. Whether they are willing to do so hinges upon the confidence they can develop in the American willingness to backstop their security. More than guns, or even a balance of power, these new nations in Asia need a long period of time for replacing the dominion of fear about China which has disturbed their calculations for so many centuries.

On this matter, I think it is safe to assume that the East Asians themselves are far more philosophical than are we. Whereas we tend to worry about occidentals in an oriental world, the new nationalist leaders of the Far East find themselves wedged between the predominant power of the United States in the Pacific and China on the mainland. They are also realistic enough to know that their own future can be largely conditioned by one or both of these powers. The conduct of the Asian governments at the present time, as revealed in statement after statement from the leaders themselves, makes it clear that they prefer the United States in a limited role of counterweight—perhaps even as the lesser of the evils—but more probably as a dependable, respected, and generous friend. In sum, non-Chinese Asians seem to be identifying more readily with a judicious exercise of American diplomacy and power in Asia than they do with their fellow Asians in China.

As the Asians themselves restructure their own security system, the United States would—in similar proportion—be able to recede from its present posture. This is not to suggest an American retreat from Asia but only a reapportioning of the relative roles between East and West. Over a long course, a carefully managed retraction of direction of American power to be replaced by a new emerging

Asian power structure would, at the same time as it avoids the creation of new political vacuums, also correct the current American over-presence.

6. *The containment of China remains an imperative of American policy.*

As the Tunku of Malaysia has declared, "China is the number one threat to the security of Asia."

All other developments in the Far East in recent years flow from this central concern. For some, the harmless intentions of Peking remain uppermost in their hopes. It often triggers polemics about "dominoes." The hard fact of the moment is that the theory of dominoes is irrelevant when we are already confronted by domino facts.

ITEM. Peking supplied hundreds of thousands of weapons, leadership, and direction to the PKI in Indonesia and only narrowly missed seizing the control of the Republic of Indonesia.

ITEM. Peking instigated the near total disruption of the government of Laos.

ITEM. Peking deliberately infiltrated and structured the forces of revolt in northern Burma.

ITEM. In the wake of Peking's aggressiveness, Hanoi has kept several thousands of its own troops in Laos in total violation of the so-called "negotiated truce."

ITEM. Hanoi not only infiltrated South Vietnam, but dispatched its own trained cadres into Northeast Thailand and the border provinces of Cambodia. By means of national liberation fronts, Hanoi 'has sought to synchronize the pulling down of established governments among its neighbors.

As President Marcos of the Philippines said, " . . . For you to renounce your position of leadership in Asia, is to allow the Red Chinese to gobble up all of Asia."

7. *China must be reinvolved in the politics of the world.*

This cannot be a "first one, then the other" proposition. *The efforts to draw China back into the mainstream of international affairs should proceed simultaneously with the efforts to contain her.* Both facets of policy should be concurrently pursued. To strive for one without the other would only delay—and perhaps even jeopardize—the realization of both.

While there is no ready prospect for the Chinese accepting reinvolvement, we must bend every effort to induce them to do so. This must ultimately lead to recognition and participation in the United Nations; to strong economic ties as well as other types of intercourse common among sovereign states. It would seem to be totally unrealistic to talk about settling the great problems of the world at the same time that we pretend a third of the people of the world do not exist.

From a psychological point of view, it is doubly important that, whatever isolation of China occurs, that decision should best be reached in Peking rather than in Washington. Let it be crystal clear, however, that this proposal would not involve abandoning the Chinese Nationalist Government on Taiwan. Basic to the proposal is the concept of two Chinas.

8. A Marshall Plan for Asia.

By winning the time which holding a firm line around Mainland China makes possible, we reach a relative state of stability which best of all affords us the opportunity to take long and positive strides toward a more prosperous and peaceful Asia. This means that we will have won the chance to put into practice in the Far East those constructive lessons we learned from the Marshall Plan program in Western Europe.

To be sure, the level at which such a program can be launched in East Asia will be much different; but the goals should be the same.

North Vietnam should be included in the programs. North Korea should be included. And certainly Mainland China. River development schemes, for example, should not be limited to the Mekong Valley. Both flood control and hydroelectric projects should be expanded to include the Yangtze and Yellow Rivers and others.

Not only should a program of this breadth be undertaken because it is right and fair, but also because it is wise. It would proceed from the simple thesis that any program which narrows the disparity between the economic development of the very rich nations and the very poor nations creates a better atmosphere for peaceful change.

To undertake a program of this magnitude involving nearly two billion people, as it must, will entail great risks and great costs at the outset. The gains, however, that it would make possible would far outweigh the liabilities. The sooner that we understand that tomorrow's world is centered in Asia—just as yesterday's was centered in Europe—the sooner we will prepare our minds for the realities ahead.

In reflecting upon this eight-point program, one can readily see that it makes no pretenses at being specific or rigid in its broad outlines. But it does supply a tone, and it does point in a direction which would be consistent with the momentum of our times and the expectations of people.

At the same time it would couple with these factors a greater sense of guidance and orderly change than one would expect from some of the much looser platitudes being bandied about.

Is there any assurance that in undertaking this approach to peace in the Far East we would have any guarantees that there would be no more "Vietnams" or "Koreas?"

The answer is obviously "No." One would be foolish to pretend to believe them impossible. Too many forces at loose in the world are subject to the whims of too many other governments to be absolute in the realm of predictions. But it would seem fair to conclude that the chances of new explosions in Eastern Asia will be less rather than greater if we "stay the course" in Southeast Asia.

The above policy suggestions convey in their context a subtle assurance to the rest of the world that the United States—with all of its great power—intends to employ that force with the greatest of restraint and with the gravest sense of responsibility.

No better evidence of this new sophistication in American policy need be cited than the Pueblo Incident of last January. The Pueblo affair served to remind all of us that the 38th Parallel separating North and South Korea remains a tenuous truce at best. It reminded us further that the reasons which required the involvement of the United States in the Korean War in the first place are still very much present. Should the truce line be flagrantly violated, for example, the stabilizing effect of the two-Korea concept would have to be reestablished once again.

The Pueblo Incident, while it reflected a deep sense of caution and national "cool" on the part of the United States, served also to remind both Koreas that the Americans intend to honor their commitment to preserve the integrity of the 38th Parallel as a national boundary between the two. The spate of criticisms from the capital in Seoul in the wake of the incident should not obscure the importance of the firmness of this American commitment.

Other limited wars are not out of the question. Thanat Khoman, the Foreign Minister of Thailand, has said, "If the United States holds in Vietnam, there will be no second Vietnams, no third Vietnams." One cannot be quite so certain that he is right.

It is easy to worry about the frontier of Burma, for example, or the weak links in the boundary chain along the Himalayan frontier between India and China. It is safest to observe—especially in international politics—that one should cross only one bridge at a time.

This brings us back again to the probable events if, instead of seeing it through in Vietnam, we yield to the other option of a gradual withdrawal. What happens then when Thailand says we need help to hold our provinces in the northeast along the Mekong River, and the United States replies she will back them? The government in Bangkok would be foolish to believe that the Americans meant what they said. Their accommodation instead would have to be made with a competing source of power and guarantees—say, Peking.

Or what happens when Laos and Cambodia both call for help because of the invasions of these tiny countries by the armies of Hanoi? Would they believe a new American commitment to aid them in resisting aggression, or would they have to place their bets elsewhere in the light of our withdrawal from Vietnam? Then, what of Burma? Malaysia? Indonesia? The Philippines?

When viewed from this angle, Vietnam becomes the hinge of all Southeast Asia. It does not take a wild imagination to envisage the next stage beyond that: The uncertainties and the doubts which would be triggered in Taiwan, Korea, and Japan.

Hanging in the balance in Vietnam, therefore, is the chance for a favorable equilibrium in Asia. Whether that is to be an Asia dominated against its will by a militant new China or whether it is to become an Asia in which the non-Chinese Asiatics strike their own balance with China remains undecided until the test of the American will in Southeast Asia has run its course. The rising capabilities of the smaller nations of the Far East to contribute their own weight to the maintenance of peace in the area remains a real possibility if the United States persists in holding a firm line behind which these small countries are safe to develop and to consolidate and to work together.

The realization of this goal will begin to reflect a sort of working coexistence among the competing forces in the Orient and permit a gradual retraction of American power to be replaced in turn by non-Chinese Asian power which will then compensate for the current American predominance.

All of this will take time. The key words for American policy remain "time" and "patience." "Staying the course" becomes the key to the chance for long-range success.

But more important is the measure which the times of crisis are now taking of the patience and sophistication of the American people themselves. Imperative as the containment of China or the reestablishment of stability may be in Southeast Asia, perhaps even more significant is whether the people of the United States pass the test. The test goes beyond our "staying the course" in Asia. It is whether we, as a preeminent power in the world, can meet successive crises with sophistication, restraint, and a national perseverance.

In sum, can the United States live up to *all* of the responsibilities of world leadership? We can—if we will.

REFERENCES

Chapter I—Good News From Foggy Bottom

[1] Walter Lippmann, *The Cold War:* A Study in U. S. Foreign Policy (New York, 1947), p. 27.
[2] Lippmann, p. 29.

Chapter IV—The Far East Policy of the United States Since 1945

[1] *The New York Times,* Oct. 9, 1951, p. 2.
[2] *Public Papers of the Presidents: Dwight D. Eisenhower, 1954,* "The President's News Conference of April 7, 1954," p. 383.

Chapter V—The Geneva Conference—1954

[1] Sir Anthony Eden, *The Memoirs of Sir Anthony Eden: Full Circle* (London, 1960), p. 141.

Chapter VII—Vietnam: Right Place, Right Time

[1] Dean Acheson, "Acheson on Our Vietnam Policy: An Asian Greece," *The Sunday Star* (North American Newspaper Alliance), Jan. 16, 1966.

[2] *The New York Times*, "Letters to the Editor," June 6, 1965.

[3] *Congressional Record*, Sept. 15, 1966, p. 22744.

[4] *Congressional Record*, Sept. 15, 1966, p. 22744.

[5] Lin Piao, "Long Live the Victory of the People's War" (written in commemoration of the 20th anniversary of victory in the Chinese people's war of resistance against Japan, which falls on 3 September), *Peking New China News Agency International Service*, transmitted in English on Sept. 2, 1965.

[6] General Omar Bradley, "My Visit to Vietnam," *Look*, Nov. 14, 1967, p. 34.

[7] Kenneth T. Young, "The Stakes in Vietnam," *Current History*, Jan. 1968, pp. 22, 24.

[8] Bradley, p. 31.

Chapter VIII—Dissent in Perspective

[1] *Congressional Record*, Febr. 1, 1968, p. S761.

[2] *Congressional Record*, Febr. 5, 1941, p. 577.

[3] *Congressional Record*, July 9, 1941, p. A3300.

[4] *Congressional Record*, July 9, 1941, p. A3300.

[5] *Congressional Record*, Jan. 21, 1941, pp. A178-9.

[6] *Congressional Record*, Febr. 5, 1941, p. 600.

Chapter X—The Incredibility Gap

[1] Walter Lippmann, *New York Post*, Oct. 21, 1967.

[2] *Congressional Record*, Aug. 18, 1967, p. S11808.

[3] *Congressional Record*, Aug. 18, 1967, p. S11809.

[4] *Congressional Record*, Aug. 11, 1967, p. S11373.

[5] *Congressional Record*, Aug. 11, 1967, pp. S11374-5.

[6] *Congressional Record*, Aug. 11, 1967, p. S11376.

[7] *Congressional Record*, Aug. 11, 1967, p. S11380.

[8] *Congressional Record*, Oct. 2, 1967, p. S14007.

[9] *Public Papers of the Presidents: John F. Kennedy, 1963*, "The President's News Conference of August 1, 1963," p. 616.

[10] *Public Papers of the Presidents: John F. Kennedy, 1963,* "Transcript of Broadcast on NBC's 'Huntley-Brinkley Report',", Sept. 9, 1963, p. 659.

[11] *Congressional Record,* Jan. 19, 1968, p. S158.

[12] *Congressional Record* (text of speech reprinted), Jan. 29, 1968, p. S529.

[13] *The Washington Post,* Jan. 26, 1968.

[14] *The Washington Post,* Febr. 5, 1968, p. A8.

[15] *Parade,* Febr. 18, 1968, p. 2.

[16] *The Sunday Star,* Febr. 25, 1968.

[17] *The Sunday Star,* Febr. 18, 1968.

[18] *The New York Times,* Febr. 19, 1962.

[19] *The New York Times,* Febr. 9, 1968.

[20] Arthur M. Schlesinger, *A Thousand Days* (Boston, 1965), pp. 321, 324.

[21] Franz Schurmann et al, with Forward by Arthur Schlesinger, Jr., *The Politics of Escalation in Vietnam* (New York, 1966), p. 11.

Chapter XII—Brickbats from the Campus

[1] Hearings before the Preparedness Investigating Subcommittee of Senate Armed Services Committee, Aug. 25 and 30, 1966, pp. 30-1.

[2] *Public Papers of the Presidents: John F. Kennedy, 1963,* "The President's News Conference of March 6, 1963," pp. 243-4.

Chapter XIV—Executive Power and Foreign Policy

[1] J. William Fulbright, "American Foreign Policy in the 20th Century under an 18th-Century Constitution," *Cornell Law Quarterly,* Fall 1961, p. 2.

[2] Fulbright, p. 2.

[3] Fulbright, p. 5.

[4] Fulbright, p. 6.

[5]Fulbright, p. 7.
[6]Fulbright, pp. 12-13.

Chapter XVI—Vietnam: Setting the Record Straight

[1]Franklin D. Roosevelt, "Eighth Annual Message," Jan. 6, 1941.

[2]Address to the American Legion, St. Louis, Missouri, Sept. 2, 1953.

[3]Address to the Chamber of Commerce, Louisville, Kentucky, Oct. 14, 1953.

[4]Oct. 20, 1953.

[5]July 23, 1954.

[6]Speech at the Overseas Press Club, New York, Mar. 24, 1959.

[7]Interview Columbia Broadcasting System Television, *The American Week,* April 11, 1954.

[8]April 14, 1954.

[9]May 9, 1954.

[10]Address at Iowa State College, Ames, Iowa, June 9, 1956.

[11]May 21, 1957.

[12]April 4, 1959.

[13]State of the Union Message, Jan. 30, 1961.

[14]August 2, 1961.

[15]Sept. 25, 1961.

[16]Jan. 11, 1962.

[17]Statement at Saigon Airport, Febr. 18, 1962.

[18]Febr. 22, 1962.

[19]April 22, 1963.

[20]July 17, 1963.

[21]Columbia Broadcasting System interview, Sept. 2, 1963.

[22]National Broadcasting Company interview, Sept. 9, 1963.

[23]Sept. 12, 1963.

[24]Hanoi may have made the decision to commit regular units of the NVA to the South as early as December, 1963. In any case, regular units were infiltrated by the spring of 1964, according to interrogation of a captured North Vietnamese officer of a support regiment who was responsible for the transportation of supplies

from Cambodia through Laos to Route 96. Furthermore, interrogation in 1965 of four North Vietnamese army soldiers of the 325th NVA Division corroborates the same date period.

[25] See published intelligence table of regular NVA regiments moving across 17th Parallel (September, 1964 onward), *Congressional Record,* May 9, 1968, Page H3610, Table III. It indicates the presence of the 95th North Vietnamese Regiment was verified in the South in December, 1964.

[26] Defense Intelligence Agency report, July, 1967. See table published in *Congressional Record,* May 9, 1968, Table V, Page H3610.

[27] See footnotes 24, 25 and 26 above.

Chapter XVII—Where Do We Go From Here?

[1] Sir Robert Thompson, "Squaring the Error," *Foreign Affairs,* April, 1968, p. 453.